The Old Man and Me

RC Larlham

RC Larlham

Black Rose Writing

www.blackrosewriting.com

ISBN: 978-1-61296-251-1

PUBLISHED BY BLACK ROSE WRITING

www.blackrosewriting.com

Printed in the United States of America

The Old Man and Me is printed in Palatino Linotype

ACKNOWLEDGMENTS

To Dick Larlham, The Old Man, without whom there would have been no stories, and no book, and to Hattie Larlham, Mother, who supported us all in the best and worst of times, I offer thanks and gratitude I never rightly expressed while they were here to hear it. To my sister Lyndella, who put up with me from earliest days, and to my own children Matthew and Elizabeth who endured the best and worst of my parenting… my thanks and my love. To my brother Giles, the best doggone storyteller I ever met, thanks for teaching me that background makes a story a tale Bro.

To my Gather.com fellow writers and the readers of stories and tales, I offer a heartfelt "Thank you!" From the very first Old Man and Me story, they asked for more, and then again more, thereby keeping me writing, and in the process discovering (much to my astonishment) a joyful past I was sure had been the most terrible time in my life. Out of that group I want to acknowledge Kathryn Esplin-Oleski, the best friend I've never met, and the first and most constant to tell me I had to make a book of this. There were many others who said the same, but David K., Kevin E. and Char H. were especially constant in pushing me to turn the stories into a book.

And finally, I must thank with overwhelming gratitude, one Len Maxwell. Without Len, you would not be reading this book. Len is a retired editor, and when I asked for a recommendation, he recommended himself without hesitation. Five chapters at a time, Len turned my best efforts from just a bunch of stories into a manuscript worthy of submission for publication.

DEDICATION

To my beloved Luvly Laura. Darlin', this one's for you. You always loved me, even in the worst of it, and you always believed in me and in my eventual and ultimate success in everything I tried to do. I'd give anything to have you here to share this.

The Old Man and Me

INTRODUCTION

I Remember – Earliest Memories

I am riding in something, maybe a stroller, maybe a wagon or a pushcart, on a wooden sidewalk. All the houses are sitting up above us on "telephone poles." I am less than two years old. This is my earliest memory.

I watch the iceman stab the ice over and over, very fast, and finally break a great brick of it away from the giant piece in the wagon. I watch him grab the ice one-handed with the tongs and sling it up on the leather over his shoulder. I follow the iceman up the wooden stairs on the side of the house. He goes into the kitchen and opens the small top door on the wooden icebox and swings the ice into the little space. I am three years old.

I hold my mother's hand as we walk to the park to swing on the steel-pipe swing set. She pushes my little brother's stroller one-handed down the uneven sidewalk. I swing a while. Then we go down to the train station to watch the big steam engine trains come through. The weather is cold. I am three and a half years old.

I wake up to the sound of a man's voice, and my mother's. I get out of bed to see. My father picks me up and sits me on his lap. He is home from South America in the middle of the night. He pulls sandals out of his suitcase and puts them on me. The next day I learn a new word, a Spanish word – *huarache* (sandals). I am still three and a half years old.

I stand at the window with my grandmother and little brother and watch the tornado come toward the house. It turns before it gets there. I am five years old.

I sit by the window, looking at the snow. I want my Mommy and Daddy to come home and bring my new little sister. I am five and a half years old. I will remember almost everything from this time forward.

CHAPTER 1

The Old Man and I Meet

Early Childhood – Happy in a Little Red House

The Old Man was a young man of 31 then. The date was July 28, 1942. He didn't know it, but his wife was headed to the hospital, facing an all-night labor to give birth to... me. The Old Man was basking in the election that had unionized the company building the high-steel water tower on which he was working... and made him a Shop Steward.

Not everyone was happy about the election outcome or the new safety rules that came with it. The basking ended as a spanner bounced off his aluminum hardhat. It was, according to the rivet-bucker who dropped it, "A real good test of that doggone ting!" The bucker was not known as a fan of hardhats, union stewards... or unions, for that matter. There was some question about whether the skillful rivet-bucker, who caught badly thrown red-hot rivets in a narrow, funnel-shaped "horn" for a living, had actually dropped the spanner. In the interests of protecting their newly won gains, the union declined to investigate the incident.

The Old Man found himself in the same hospital as his wife but neither knew the other had been admitted. Hardhat or no, the Old Man had a beaut of a concussion (he could count ten fingers... on either hand), a jammed neck and a couple of sprained tendons that kept his head at a funny angle for a month. For the night, however, he had a bed in the orthopedic wing of a hospital in Rahway, New Jersey.

His wife, my soon-to-be mother, was ensconced in the maternity wing and drugged to a fare-thee-well, as they were wont to do in the '40s and '50s. She kept asking for the Old Man. "Where's Dick? I asked you to call him! Why isn't he here?" No one wanted to tell her that he *was* there... out of the Emergency Room and now admitted, or that the doctors were worried about closed-head injury, a much less treatable condition then than now.

By the time I squalled with my first hit of oxygen, the Old Man had been told I was on the way. Wrapped in a too-often washed robe and wearing slippers two sizes too big, he stormed to the elevator and headed for Maternity, arriving too late to see Mother before she was taken to the delivery room. Fortunately, final labor and delivery went rapidly, and Mother and I were presented to him in short order (July 29, 1942, 6:02 am, to be exact).

Having satisfied himself that I wasn't truly twins (he *knew* there was only one of Mother although he could see two) and having determined that a concussion headache is nothing to try to ignore, the Old Man allowed himself to be persuaded back to his room.

Once she discovered what had happened to the Old Man, Mother, a registered nurse with hospital experience, was furious that he'd been able to get all the way to Maternity on his own. She was fully aware of the possible complications for a man with a head injury. Hattie Gadd Larlham, RN, was the daughter of an iron-willed West Virginia mountain preacher with a five-church circuit. She was also the wife of a high-steel welder, and she had learned to take a head-on approach to problem solving. Five feet ten inches tall, with a steady gait and spine straight as a steel rod, she strode to the nurse's station, found a phone and held a short, unpleasant discussion with the charge nurse on the Old Man's floor. He did not return to visit us until he'd been discharged.

From 1946, when I was four, through the spring and early summer of 1950, we lived in a little square two-story house, with red asphalt shingle panels that looked like bricks. They didn't, really – but they were cheaper than real siding.

The house sat at the back of a deep front yard, on the north side of a county road called Infirmary Road. The house and yard were surrounded by the wheat fields of the farmer to the east of us, a nice enough man named Henry (The Old Man called him Hank), with a daughter my age. Henry did have one fault... he wanted to buy the house in which we lived (as I learned *much* later). Unfortunately, so did the Old Man. The woman who owned it made a deal with Farmer Hank. Whatever the Old Man said was his final offer, she would allow Hank a final raise. And so it eventually was... but that was far in my future. In 1946, I was happy in the Little Red House.

A creek marked the west side and rear (north) property lines and a scraggly tree line marked the east boundary. The property might have been an acre and a half. After we'd been there a year or so, my mother built a chicken-wire fence across the creek, and up into the back yard, into which she ensconced a gray gander and his harem.

The Old Man was trying to find a way to earn a living that didn't involve travelling from state to state with Chicago Bridge and Iron, and his immediate enterprise was selling Army Surplus out of the basement of the house between road trips. Eventually, he set up a real Army-Navy Surplus store, but so did everybody else, and the Old Man's, being on a side street in a town of ten thousand people, didn't last long. My mother was working across the road from the house as a nurse at the County Infirmary, after which Infirmary Road was named (neat how those things work out, eh?).

CHAPTER 2

Nina and the Tornado

We called The Old Man's mother Nina instead of Grandma, or Gramma, or Gran, or – well, you get the idea. Nina was *her* choice, and she insisted on it. We never knew why, unless she'd misunderstood the European *Nana*, which is possible, because her husband (long dead before I was born) was an English immigrant.

Nina lived in a town named Greenwood Lake, New York. It was a "summer town," and she and her father ran a "hotel" (we'd call it a bed-and-breakfast today) for summer residents and actors on the Appalachian vaudeville circuit. In winter, it was a hunting lodge. After her children were all grown and married, she sold the hotel, and bought a "Sears house." Really, she bought a house from the Sears, Roebuck and Co. Catalogue, and made her sons and sons-in-law build it for her.

But, she was alone and, from time to time, she went to live with one of her children. This time was our turn. When I was about five, Nina and my little brother and I were in the house alone one early summer evening. The Old Man, my mother and my baby sister were out.

It was a dark and stormy night. Well, it *was*! The wind blew branches off the willow by the front yard creek and the sky turned from light gray to charcoal to black and then to green. None of us, including Nina, knew that when the black clouds turned pea-green, it meant they're full of hailstones refracting the light and really bad trouble was on the way.

We stood there, watching out the window with all the fascination of moviegoers entranced by the murderer creeping up on the house-full of innocents. As the leading edge of the super-cell (a term exactly no one had *ever* heard in those days) passed over us, the rain came. Huge drops fell in a mass so dense it was not possible to see the grass from the side window. The downpour lasted but moments and was replaced by lighter rain and hail. Golf ball-sized chunks of ice pounded the roof until I wondered if it would break and turned the lawn to a sea of mud in seconds. What it actually did to the roof doesn't bear thinking about – which I didn't at the age of five. As soon as the noise stopped, I forgot about it, because...

About a half-mile up the road, a black, whipping, undulating snake dropped from the rear of the cloud. As it touched down, limbs and boards began to fly. The tornado widened and approached the Peterson's house and engulfed it. Later, as we drove by, I realized that the Peterson's house had been turned ninety degrees – the front door was now the side door – otherwise, the house looked intact. At the age of five, I had no idea of the terrible damage done inside that house, so I didn't understand why they tore it down.

The tornado seemed to pull itself toward the cloud and shrink... but as it continued toward us, it re-extended as the narrow snake it had been. It approached the house, throwing trees and "stuff" in all directions until it was less than a hundred yards away and we just stood at that window and watched. About a hundred yards before it reached us, it started to move to the right of its original path.

The tornado crossed the road, and moved away up a farm track lined with cherry trees. As it moved up the track, the trees uprooted and fell toward the tornado, creating an "X-pattern" like the track of a giant tractor tire across the track. Moments after it reached the end of the track, the tornado rapidly became very skinny, and dissipated.

The sky lightened rapidly, and the thunderhead passed off to the southeast, leaving us in bright sunshine. The glare from the hailstones that covered the yard inches deep was too much to look at. We left the window.

Nina made dinner and then read us stories. Eventually, the Old Man and my mother came home. I told them all about the big snake in the sky. I couldn't understand why the Old Man was crying. My mother was too, but mothers are allowed to.

CHAPTER 3

Random Memories from the Little Red House

To Catch a Cricket:

My Aunt Ella, Mother's oldest sister, *loved* to fish for bluegills. She lived across a dirt road from a city reservoir where fishing was permitted. Aunt Ella fished with any bait she could scrape up: worms, bits of meat that were "off," hardened bread balls – and crickets. According to her, crickets were the best bait God ever invented for bluegills. But she was old, she said. Her poor back and arthritis in her hands made it too hard to catch something as fast as a cricket. I kept asking if I could catch 'em, and finally, when I was about five, she showed me how and promised me a nickel for every five I could catch. So, for at least that summer, every time we saw Aunt Ella, I gave her a coffee can filled with crumpled newspaper and crickets. But the money wasn't the real attraction... catching crickets was.

Each evening, the Old Man and I would take to the pasture and fields across the road, newspaper in hand. I would take a half-sheet and crumple it loosely. The Old Man would lift the end of an old long-dead log or pick up a small rock or board. We looked for anything that had lain on the ground for some time. I'd shove the crumpled paper under it, and the Old Man would replace the object, resting it as lightly as possible on the paper. There were cattle, including a bull, in the pasture, and Farmer Black who owned *that* farm wasn't nearly as friendly as

Farmer Hank. But the Old Man talked Farmer Black into letting us catch crickets... so long as we were out of the pasture before the cows were let out for the evening, and we had to wait for them to come in for morning milking to go back out.

Each morning, the Old Man would wake me and we'd go cricket-catching before he went to open his store. We could never be sure when milking would be over, so we'd try to hurry. It wasn't all that hard really. The Old Man would lift up whatever was resting on the newspaper. I'd pick up the paper and stuff it into the coffee can and shake it. Crickets would fall out, slow and stupid in the chilly morning, into the can, and I'd put the chewed paper back. About once a week, we'd have to change the paper because the crickets would have chewed most of it. Each location usually yielded as many as a half-dozen crickets, and I'd wind up with a silver half-dollar and sometimes more, every weekend.

There were days the lifted logs revealed garter snakes, much to my great fear, and much to the Old Man's amusement. He always carried a stick and he'd lift the snakes away. And there were days the milking herd came out before we were ready, bull and all. The Old Man would say, "Grab the can, Charles," and pick me up and jog to the fence. The bull never chased us, but the Old Man was taking no chances.

Eventually, the Old Man's store failed. He found a job as a welder in a Cleveland suburb, but it was a night job. He worked from eleven at night until seven in the morning, far too late in the day for crickets still to be chilled and slow. The cricket hunting was over.

The Great Guildersleeve:

The gander in the back yard pen was a grey goose although every goose in his harem was pure white. He had no name at first, but he was an escape artist. After several escapes, my mother named him "The Great Guildersleeve" after a magician and escape artist of the day. I'd be out in the yard playing and he and his harem would suddenly be out of the pen. Most of the time, they'd head for the wheat field, until the wheat grew too tall for them to find weeds (they ignored the wheat). Occasionally they'd come into the yard and wander around, swim in the creek, and eat the watercress, which would upset the Old Man mightily. He loved fresh watercress (he called it peppergrass, although it looked very little like grass) on his ham sandwiches.

Mother would call and we'd herd the geese back to the pen, waving dish towels and yelling, laughing at their determined running waddle... until the day I learned that ganders weren't to be trifled with by little boys.

On that day, Guildersleeve followed his harem into the pen and then, as I rushed to close the gate, he attacked. Hissing and flapping, he ran at me, beak open wide. I was terrified and couldn't move, so he grabbed my stomach in his beak, pulled me close and began to beat me with his wings. Mother, laughing so hard she could hardly get to me, finally pulled him off and tossed him into his pen. I never went near the geese again, and eventually they no longer populated the back yard.

Steam Thresher Exhibition:

Farmer Black hooked onto every new idea put forth by the Farm Bureau and the local Department of Agriculture Conservation Office Extension Agent. He carefully plowed his planted fields in contour strips, alternating corn, soy beans, alfalfa hay and wheat. He annually rotated the crops as well. He fed his dairy cattle the usual mash and turned them out to pasture, but he had another feed source that he claimed increased milk production. Perhaps it did but, at the same time, it decreased the enjoyment by his neighbors of the local fresh air environment significantly. Farmer Black's wonderful milk production enhancer was beer mash from a Cleveland brewery.

Every Saturday, a large dump truck would pull into his yard. I watched in fascination as the bed of the truck slo-o-o-owly lifted. Suddenly, the rear gate would swing open, and the contents of the truck would slide out... filling the air with the odor of sour beer. The bed would drop, and the gate would slam home with a bang (heard a full second or more after it closed).

None of this endeared him to his neighbors, especially Farmer Hank, who thought that his cross-street neighbor was a show-off and inconsiderate to boot. The Old Man hated the smell but he liked Farmer Black, who allowed him to hunt his property, unlike Farmer Hank, so he complained about the odor, but in a joshing way.

One late summer Saturday, the Old Man called us all outside. Down at Farmer Black's barnyard stood what looked like part of one of the train engines I used to see in Ravenna... and it was puffing steam. The giant flywheel on the side spun at great speed and the piston made an awful racket. Men were standing around and, every once in a while, someone would open a door at the rear of the engine and toss in a chunk or two of firewood. I was thunderstruck.

The Old Man looked down at me and grinned. "Want to go see it?" I couldn't answer and the Old Man laughed. "C'mon, let's go see it work."

We walked down the road and crossed at the farm. The odor of sour beer was overpowering. The Old Man walked up to the group around the strange machine and a conversation I don't remember, in fact probably didn't really hear, ensued. There was a lot of excitement and, at some point, the men all headed for the field of wheat nearby. The men swung scythes (an instrument of torture with which I later became all too familiar) into the wheat, some with practiced ease, some with great effort and little result. The Old Man picked up a cradle scythe.

Wheat soon began to fall in sweeping rows with older boys and girls picking up armfuls, pulling out a few stalks and wrapping them around the larger bundles, called sheaves. They stacked the sheaves together into shocks. Later the men stopped scything and went and got wagons pulled by horses and tractors. As they drove slowly along the rows of shocks, two men with pitchforks would attack each shock, lifting individual sheaves off it and tossing each sheaf up into the wagon where another man would carefully place it. Sheaves were criss-crossed to tie the load together.

During all this, there were men feeding wood into the steam engine. The wagons were pulled up and the sheaves were tossed into a great funnel in the thresher. The thresher itself was chocked and blocked and attached to the steam engine by a fabric and rubber belt wrapped around a spinning hub on the steam engine and one on the thresher. It was given a half turn where the ends connected to make a "Möbius strip." By doing that, the belt constantly changed sides, wearing evenly on both sides and avoiding "cupping." The thresher that the belt drove was a great noisy machine in its own right. From inside it came the sound of flails driven by the spinning hub pounding the wheat to separate the grains from the heads atop the straw. A stream of grain and dust poured from a narrow chute into a wagon with stake-and-slat sides. A fountain of wheat straw, and even *more* dust, erupted from a wider chute into an open-sided wagon on the other.

I didn't know it at the time, of course, but it had been a heavily-advertised old-timers show. An exhibition of farming "as it used to be" sponsored by the County Extension Agent from the local Conservation Service office. There were probably old tractors (I seem to remember a steel-wheeled version or two), other threshers, small versions of the nine-bottom plows then in vogue, and many other pieces of "old-time" farm equipment. I remember only the thresher.

By the time all was done, the women had set up tables in

the yard and a traditional farmers' meal was the order of mid-day. It was surely a day of wonder.

Swimming Pool :

We had, of course, no swimming pool but my mother improvised. We had a huge galvanized washtub and my brother and sister and I would sit in it while the summer sun tried to stew us. The water was cool and the hose was handy to keep it from over-warming. It was as good as a pool any day for two little boys and their sister in the country summer sun.

CHAPTER 4

Salted Cod, Night Crawlers and Dandelion Wine

The County Infirmary was a large, forbidding, red-brick institution, comprising three floors and a basement. The living quarters housed, in dormitory rooms, the indigent elderly and infirm of Portage County. It was always overcrowded, understaffed and lacking all but the most basic necessities of life (and sometimes those). My mother worked there as the nightshift Charge Nurse.

The infirmary or "County Home," as most folks called it, was across the road and about a quarter mile north of us. It included a working farm so pastures and crop fields swept past our house to a barbed wire fence, its wires grown into the flesh of scrubby chokecherry and Osage-orange, that separated them from the fields and pastures of Farmer Black... he of brewery mash cattle feed infamy. In good weather, those who were able were expected to help with farm work. It's doubtful they accomplished a lot, but those who could were put to driving tractors for baling hay, pulling manure spreaders and such.

Others found themselves milking the dairy herd, which comprised a dozen or so Holstein milkers and a few heifers (young cows that had yet to bear calves and so did not yet give milk). Most of what was produced from the farm was consumed on site. The residents at least had fresh milk and fresh fruit and vegetables during late summer and fall. There were also apple and pie-cherry trees, but I don't know whether they saw any real use.

One morning, my mother arrived home, bringing with her a stranger... an elderly man with a shock of unruly white hair whom she addressed as "Uncle Ike." I actually have a vague memory of the Old Man, my mother and "Uncle Ike" sitting at the table trying to figure out exactly how he was related to her. He was a Workman and the Workman family was kin to both the Gadd (Mother's maiden name) family and the Higgins (*her* mother's maiden name) family. Isaac was a popular name in the Workman family. I believe he was likely more a second or third cousin to her than uncle, but we all came to call him Uncle Ike.

Before long, Uncle Ike had moved in. Mother couldn't leave "family" in the hellhole that was the Infirmary and Ike drew a miner's pension, and had some other income of small amount. He could, in other words, pay room and board. And so, Uncle Ike joined us in the little red house. So long as he lived with us, neither the Old Man, Mother or my brother and I knew what was likely to happen next. Ike had "interesting" habits (bathing regularly being *not* one of them).

At some point early in his stay, Ike ordered a dozen wooden half-kegs of salted cod delivered to the house. Unfortunately, he told no one of this impending largess ("'Fraid you'd tarn it daown," said Ike when pressed on his lack of sharing skills) so when the Forney's Meat Market truck showed up and the driver began carrying wooden half-kegs into the basement, Mother hadn't the faintest idea what was going on.

"Jes' a coupla butts o' fish, Hat," said Uncle Ike. "Ah lahk t'gnaw on a chunka cod naow an' agin'."

"Dick, come out here quick!" bawled "Hat." The *only* person I *ever* heard call Hattie Larlham "Hat" and get away with it was Uncle Ike and it was a sore point between them so long as he lived with us. Because people had called her "Hat" earlier in life, and she hated it, she had invented the name "Pat" for herself. She insisted everybody use it. And everybody did, even the Old Man... everybody except Uncle Ike Workman.

My brother and I were, naturally and inevitably, in the way of everybody in the conversation... *and* we tried to be *part of* the conversation. "Fish butts," said Giles (all of four and a half). "Unca Ike's gots fish butts." And he took off running and laughing as Mother reached for him, saying, "Giles; that will be enough." I took off with him.

"Fish butts... fish butts. Uncle Ike gots fish butts," we sang as we ran and dodged.

"Charles! Giles! Come here!" The Old Man missed entirely the humor in Uncle Ike's "fish butts." We came. "Sit!" He pointed to the porch swing. We sat.

"Ike, you can *not* keep that much fish in the basement. It'll rot and stink up the whole house." The Old Man was not in a conversational mood. "I can already smell 'em."

"Hat, Ah *needs* m' cod," pleaded Ike, ignoring the Old Man entirely. "Ah needs protein – *lots* of protein. Muh doctor said so. You heard 'im."

Mother looked at The Old Man. "The doctor *did* say he needed more protein. And you don't really smell them, yet." She turned to Ike. "If I smell fish upstairs just *once...*"

And so... we had fish in the basement. I don't remember whether the house smelled of fish, but I *do* remember that the basement did. As it turned out, the butts were for more than fish. As they emptied, Ike built slanted shelves in the basement, and hinged the lids of the butts. Then he visited a diner or two and made arrangements to collect their used coffee grounds.

Now, we lived, as I've said, on a country road, and the

diners were at least a mile or more away. Ike walked to and from, carrying a rubber-lined sack of coffee grounds on the return trip. It had to have been a startling sight... a rail-thin old man, white hair going in all directions (Ike never wore a hat, summer or winter), striding along that empty country road like Ichabod Crane, carrying a sack slung over his shoulder.

The butts were set upon the slanted shelves and coffee grounds were emptied into the butts.

"Ike, *what* are you doing?" the Old Man asked.

"Just pickin' up a little money," and Ike would say no more. Throughout fall and winter, he made his daily trek for coffee grounds, ate an *amazing* amount of uncooked salted cod, cleaned and placed the butts on the slanted shelves and filled the butts with coffee grounds.

Came spring, and a new curiosity arrived – a large crock, glazed on the outer surface but not the inner. It sat in the basement, empty for a little while, and then my brother and I and Farmer Moore's daughter were put to work collecting dandelion blossoms. As we brought in peck baskets full of blossoms, Ike would inspect them, removing every speck of stem or leaf. "Makes it bitter," he'd say. "You have to be more careful." But we were children and careful wasn't in our nature.

"Makes *what* bitter?" asked the Old Man. Ike just grinned and carried the cleaned dandelions to the basement and dumped them into the crock. Eventually the Old Man figured it out.

"You have my children helping you make wine!" He was outraged.

"Naw. They're just pickin' flowers."

"Yeah, we're just pickin' flowers, Daddy."

"Dick," Mother was in a conciliatory mood, "there's no harm. I used to pick blackberries my mother made into wine."

The Old Man threw up his hands.

Ike filled his crock, poured in water, sugar and whatever else goes into making wine (Hey, I was six years old; I didn't memorize the recipe.) and covered the crock. Then he began carrying home narrow-necked, screw-cap, one-gallon glass jugs. When the wine was ready, he filled the jugs and set them in a row on shelves in a cooler part of the basement.

Soon after, men from the Infirmary began showing up. They would hand Ike a quarter or two, and he would give them a waxed-paper lined, brown paper lunch bag partially filled with coffee grounds from the cod-butts. It didn't take long to discover that the bags also contained night crawlers. Ike had been farming night crawlers in the butts all winter, and now he was selling them to the denizens of the Infirmary (and others as word spread).

There were fishing lakes and creeks around (one separated our yard from Farmer Moore's wheat field), and the bluegill and catfish loved night crawlers. For much of the summer, Giles and I would hold the bags open while Uncle Ike counted out twelve night crawlers into them, and tossed in a handful of damp coffee grounds. He gave us a penny a bag, so I counted carefully. But Ike didn't cheat. We each wound up with dozens of pennies in our banks.

Then people began showing up in cars, and giving Ike dollar bills in exchange for gallon jugs of dandelion wine. But that didn't last long. Ike hadn't "finished" the wine before he bottled it. He screwed down the caps, and started selling it. A day or so after the first couple sales, there was a loud "POP!"

from the basement... then another. Over a period of only a couple days, at least a dozen bottles blew up. Ike's days as a wine merchant were over.

Ike ate raw salted cod and raised night crawlers at our house for the next couple years. When we bought a house and moved, he did not come with us.

Epilogue:

About six years later, my mother was cooking, and she ran out of vinegar. "Charles," she said, "go down in the basement and get that gallon of vinegar sitting on one of the fruit shelves."

I went down and brought the only gallon jug I could find. "It doesn't have a label, but it looks right."

Mother was busy, and just pointed to the counter. "Put it down there and open it, Charles."

I put it on the shelf and uncapped it. She reached for it and started to pour. Within a second she uprighted the jug and passed it under her nose. She began to laugh. "It isn't vinegar... it's wine! It's Uncle Ike's dandelion wine!"

CHAPTER 5

First School, First Grade, First Day

The year I turned six was a momentous year. I started school (no Kindergarten for us – bung 'em straight into a full school day in first grade) and promptly got my hands whacked with a ruler. I had read completely through *Dick and Jane* (Yes, really – *Dick and Jane, Book 1.*), and was sitting in the front seat of my row, just looking around. "Charles," it was Miss Elfring, "it's *your* turn."

I was dumfounded. My turn to what?

"My turn to what?" I asked.

"Read the next page."

"I read all the pages."

"You haven't read *any* pages."

"Yes I did. I read them all."

"No you didn't. Sandra read a page, Billy read a page and Jimmy read a page. Half the class each read a page and now it's your turn. Read the next page out loud."

"Out loud? Which page?"

"The NEXT page!" Teeth were beginning to grind.

"What page is that?"

"Come to my desk." I walk up to her desk.

"Hold out your hands." I hold out my hands, palms up to show that they're clean.

"Palms down." I turn my palms down.

"Charles," I look up at her and see that she has a 12-inch ruler in her hand. It doesn't register. "You have to learn to pay attention."

"Yes, ma'am."

"You have to learn not to sass."

"I wasn't sas..." WHACK! The flat of the ruler strikes the backs of both hands.

"...SING YOU!" I finish in a scream. She sends me back to my seat. My mother was not happy. She and Miss Elfring had a "conversation" about my first day. I remember nothing else about first grade.

CHAPTER 6

Piano Lessons and a Whizzer Motorbike

The summer of '48 I officially became a "big boy," and got my first (10-inch wheels) bicycle with *no* training wheels. A-a-a-and... I started piano lessons. Hattie Larlham was convinced that musical ability was simply a matter of knowledge and practice. The fact that I was tin-eared, tone deaf, completely arrhythmic and had the coordination of a disjointed puppet mattered not a whit. Charles would learn to play the piano.

A piano appeared in our house and there followed a sad succession of eight years of piano teachers, studios and recitals, with the inevitable result that I am now unable to play a single note of music on *any* instrument, a prediction made annually by whatever teacher upon whose tortured soul I was inflicted for that year.

Early in my musical career, I was removed from the studio teacher's purview, and a travelling music teacher was employed. Every week, rain, shine or snow, he would appear in our living room to wrestle with my obdurate unmusicality. And, except for the worst weather, he arrived on a Whizzer Motorbike... a wonder of imagination, entrepreneurial spirit and sheer inventiveness. This marvel was originally a motor and belt track kit suitable to be attached to a 24-inch Schwinn bicycle (Schwinn not included). Introduced during WWII to help people deal with gasoline rationing, the Whizzer had evolved by the late '40s into a wholly factory-manufactured motorbike.

The first time I saw Mr. Kelly, he was sitting immovably erect on the Whizzer, tooling down Infirmary Road toward our house at a steady 40 miles an hour, a peaked cap upon his head, from beneath which Einstein-like hair blew around his ears. He wore a greatcoat, with a short muffler (for fear of catching it in the spokes) and goggles.

My present-day translation of the mental image I still carry is that he was about 65 years old, six feet tall or more (he was taller than my mother, who stood 5 feet 10, and he weighed less than 130 pounds. He was the model for every image of Ichabod Crane I've ever seen. Every time he came, I badgered him about the Whizzer. I thought it the most wonderful riding machine I'd ever seen.

For his part, Mr. Kelly seemed distracted whenever I talked about the Whizzer. With the advantage of hindsight, I would say today that Mr. Kelly was bemused – a strange mixture, to my mind, of confused and amused. He would check his watch, and then turn an attentive ear to me, carefully phrasing answers to my years, for exactly five minutes. At the end of five minutes, he would stand erect, work his shoulders, put his hand on my shoulder and say, "It's time, Charles," and we would walk into the house together to begin our shared torture.

By the time his stint as a piano teacher was over, I knew more about the Whizzer Motorbike than I remember today. To my never-ending disappointment, the Whizzer had no rear seat. The platform over the rear tire wasn't meant to be ridden upon, and no one was making aftermarket buddy seats. Neither Mr. Kelly nor my mother would listen to reason. I could not, *would* not, be given a ride.

In the fullness of time we moved to the farmhouse whence we all, Giles, Lyndella and I, graduated into adulthood. The piano came with us and, until some time in my fifteenth year, I continued to abuse its plastic-surfaced keys. My paternal grandmother (Nina, of "Nina and the Tornado" memory) came to stay with us and, because she played piano, she took over teaching duties.

As a teacher, Nina made a great grandmother. Eventually, Nina left, and I was again sent to a studio to learn. At each juncture, the teacher of the moment would pull my mother aside and say something like, "Mrs. Larlham, it's not that Charles doesn't *try*..." And then they would refuse to teach me anymore. My brother, following dutifully if resentfully in my shoes (often *wearing* my cast-off shoes) fared no better.

But Lyndella did. She could sing, *and* she could play the piano, at least enough that if she could run through a piece a couple times, she could play it without embarrassing herself.

Once I got my driver's license, I used to drive her into Hudson Village. I'd drop her at her instructor's house and repair to the Village drugstore where I'd drink coffee and read (mostly their comics – but no one seemed to mind).

Eventually, my torture, and Giles' came to an end. Mother agreed that if after all those years we could play absolutely *nothing*, we were unlikely to ever do so. She was forever convinced that it was a lack of practice and interest, rather than ability, that caused the failure but she stopped forcing the issue. We gratefully abandoned our future as musical entertainers, and neither of us ever touched a piano again.

Epilogue:

About a year after piano lessons ceased to be a part of my life, I came home one afternoon to see Mr. Kelly's Whizzer parked outside our kitchen door. My heart sank. Mother had changed her mind. I went inside. She was standing at the sink, alone, cleaning vegetables for dinner.

"Mother, you promised!" I drew breath to argue the unfairness of it all.

"Mr. Kelly is dead, Charles. He died six months ago." She sounded a little sad but, oddly, a little excited. "The Whizzer is yours. He willed it to you. It just took his executor this long to find you."

CHAPTER 7

Of Grandmas and Nanny Goats

I saw an AFLAC commercial featuring a goat one night and it reminded me of a nanny goat that terrified me when I was a little boy of about eight. My mother's mother was living with us at the time and she was a goat's milk aficionado. Goat's milk, as a note of interest, is the second worst drink on *earth*! I say second worst only because no matter what one thinks is the worst of anything it has been my experience that there is almost always something worse. Grandma also loved goat's milk cheese, and made her own, in our kitchen... which guaranteed that the kitchen in summer was redolent of sour goat's milk, an odor which overwhelmed all else.

In order to feed her addiction, Grandma talked Mother into letting her bring a goat to the little red house. The Old Man, to the best of my knowledge, expressed no opinion on the matter, except to say, "That goat better not hurt my kids!" The nanny Grandma bought never hurt any of us, but...

The goat arrived in due course and the Old Man would move it each morning on his way to work. Because we had no fence around the yard, he would pound a half-axle with the gear end up, into the ground, through a ring attached to a heavy dog chain (not heavy enough, as it turned out), at the other end of which stood the goat.

Every morning and evening, Grandma would go out and relieve the goat of her milk, obtaining about a quart in the morning and two quarts in the evening. She would grab the goat by a horn and march it to the post, to which Grandma would strap the horn with an old belt. She would then settle herself on a stool, ram her head into the goat's flank, drop the bucket under the udder and proceed to *"zing"* milk into the bucket for a short time. Then she would release the goat and go inside with its milk.

Before long, the goat took to chasing Grandma as soon as Grandma started to walk away, so Grandma would hold onto the off-side horn as she released the one strapped to the old axle. Then she'd pick up her bucket and march the goat to the end of her chain and release her. This went on for some time with the goat making for Grandma every time she appeared in the yard. Soon she began making feints at Giles and me as well.

Grandma had a small garden on the far side of the driveway from the house and she worked in it daily, chopping weeds, cutting back overgrowing plants, picking vegetables when they ripened; all the things that have to happen to keep a garden happy. One day the Old Man chained the goat at one end of the garden, just far enough away that she couldn't quite reach the vegetables. Nanny was in a foul mood by the time Grandma showed up with her bucket and strap; she had decided that this wasn't funny anymore, and *somebody must pay*.

Once Grandma had finished milking her and taken the milk into the house, she ignored the goat and began chopping weeds, bent over in the garden, with her ankle-length gingham dress swaying a few inches above the ground. Nanny took a couple practice runs to the end of her tether. Then she stood there and glared at Grandma.

Finally, very deliberately, the nanny backed up. At about three paces to the far side of the axle, she lowered her head and headed for Grandma. Digging into the soft ground and throwing clots of earth like a racehorse just after a rain, she charged. When she hit the end of the chain... it parted as if it were made of aluminum. Nanny didn't even slow down.

Grandma neither saw nor heard her coming and the nanny hit her square in the buttocks. I was horrified. Grandma was *dead* – I just knew it. I began to bawl. But Grandma got up, grabbed the blade-end of the hoe-handle and went after the goat. She smacked it smartly at least once on every side. Despite being assaulted by an old woman *with a weapon*, and having broken the chain, the Nanny stayed within a chain-length of the axle. Finally, Grandma replaced the chain with a piece of heavy rope and went back to gardening.

A significant discussion ensued that evening between Grandma and her daughter. Grandma insisted she could handle the goat and Mother insisted her children were at risk. The Old Man insisted on staying out of it, which he did.

The next day, the goat was gone, and Mother and *her* mother were not speaking.

As I watched the AFLAC commercial that night, two things came to mind... the story you've just read, and the first couple of lines to a parody of "The Ballad of Hogan's Goat."

The Ballad of Grandma's Goat

(*With apology to the long-lost author
of "The Ballad of Hogan's Goat"*)

Well, Grandma's goat was feelin' grand
Hit th' poor ol' girl, square in th' can
She backed three steps, and set her eye
On the bright print dress, of red 'n' white dye

With a quiet snort, she dropped her head
Gramma flew so far, I thought she was dead
But Gramma got up, and she attacked
She gave that goat an awful whack
She tied that goat to a post and chain
Left Nanny standing in th' pourin' rain
She loaded up the Old Man's gun
She was goin' huntin', but not for fun
Poor Nanny Goat's in mortal fear
Shotgun Granny draws slowly near
Ol' Nanny goat, she's smooth as silk
Grabs a bucket and lets down her milk
Goat's milk and cheese were the reasons why
Grandma bought the goat that taught her to fly
She threw up her hands, said, "You can stay,
But do that again, I'll finish today."
Now Grandma's Goat is long since dead
She couldn't keep from usin' her head
So the very next time poor Grandma flew
There went Nanny... into th' stew.

CHAPTER 8

The Old Man Buys Two Farms

The year 1950 was a turning point in my life. It made all else possible, but that was far away. In 1950 I turned eight years old, and momentous events and life-changing occurrences befell my family (and, perforce, me). For starters, we moved... twice.

For two years I caught the school bus at the end of that driveway of the little red house on Infirmary Road. But at the end of my second-grade year, I said good-bye to the bus driver for the last time. During the famous "Last-Day-of-School-Picnic," I told all my friends that we were moving, and I would *never see them again,* causing thereby an amazing (and loud) outpouring of seven- and eight-year-old separation anxiety and grief.

As the news spread outward from the center, where I had told my closest cronies, the sobbing and hic-cupping advanced in waves. Even the kids who liked to bully me (I was a little fat kid) were crying; probably for the coming lost opportunities to hit me with willow branches at recess. Our teacher was first puzzled, then panicked, then angry, and finally, as she at last discovered the cause, comforting. The picnic was a rousing success.

That entire summer was an adventure. First we "moved" to a small farm with no house. There was a small barn, which, I was told, we would live in while we built a house. Even at not-quite-eight years old, I was skeptical. But the Old Man insisted it was so. So every morning, the Old Man would get into the 1942 turtle-back Oldsmobile with the bashed-in left rear fender (courtesy of a Model T that he pulled out in front of) and take my mother and me (along with my little brother and littler sister) out to the farm to work at getting it ready.

While she swept and holystoned the old barn (well, she scrubbed it with Fels-Naptha soap and a stiff-bristled brush), my brother and I played and fought all over the property. The back half was wooded and we usually played there in the heat of the afternoon. Mother would feed us lunch and, as the days wound down to fall, she would cut slices of King David apples (the biggest apples I've *ever* seen) and smear them with peanut butter for us. The Old Man and Uncle Bill, a master carpenter and husband to my mother's eldest sister Ella, would build two-by-four walls and set them into rooms. Plumbing was begun, and a couple teenagers from the area were busily digging a hole for the septic tank. Then, one afternoon, my brother and I asked...

"Daddy, what does 'Gas Line' mean?"

After much shouting and swearing, the Old Man had his money back. No one had told him there was a gas transmission line on the property, and he wasn't going to live with one. We were adrift, and the owner of the property we lived on wanted it for a relative to live in – immediately. So-o-o-o... we bought another farm; this time with a house, a four-car garage, a barn, a pig shed, two chicken coops, a milk-house and a granary.

The property consisted of twenty-five acres, give or take, of which the house and buildings occupied about two acres. Another two or three acres around the buildings were devoted to "domestic" uses like gardens, flower beds, additional lawns and the like. The remainder was about equally divided between productive and non-productive land, from a farm perspective. About ten acres covered the top and side of a hill. The soil was sandy loam underlain by sand and gravel. In fact, what we lived on was a glacially deposited pile of sand and gravel called a "kame" about forty-five miles behind the end moraine that marked the greatest south-eastward advance of the ice during the most recent glaciation of Earth.

At the bottom of the hill, what had been a "wet pasture" had long since become a swamp as the creek that ran through it silted-in downstream and water backed up and flooded the pasture. Later, a family of beavers moved into the swamp downstream of our property, and any pretense at being arable land ended.

About two hundred yards behind the farm buildings was a narrow forested strip of land. Our property line lay less than twenty feet inside the edge of the woods. Perhaps a hundred feet from the edge that faced us to its far edge, the woods ran from our swamp nearly a mile south, widening and narrowing depending on the desires of landowners, until it reached Ohio State Route 303. At its north end it did not cross the swamp but on the other side of the swamp, our property line ran about fifty feet inside a wooded strip that ran east-west between our road and the road behind us.

Much of this I learned as time went on. When we all piled out of the '42 turtleback Olds the first day, Giles and I were thunderstruck. The house itself was huge. We didn't know it, but it sprawled nearly ninety feet from end to end. Two sugar maples and a Norway maple tree (yes, of course we tapped them, but that was much later) stood in the front yard, and a wondrously tall Norway spruce stood near the road at the end of the driveway. Near each end of the house stood a massively large white birch, of Indian canoe fame, and to the rear of the house at each end stood a tulip tree. These last, birch and tulip, were destined to become part of the house.

Walking to the far (south) end of the house with the Old Man and Mother, who took turns carrying Lyndella, we found a large area of tall brown grass, above which waved roughly conical "ferns." "Asparagus," announced Mother, "a whole field of it. And all allowed to go wild. I'll have to do something with that next spring."

"Pat," began the Old Man.

But Mother was already striding away, trailed by Giles and

me. We circled the house, coming upon an apple tree nearly devoid of pale yellow, worm-eaten apples at the southeast corner. Mother picked one of the few remaining fruits. Inspecting it quickly, but with a knowledgeable eye, she tossed it away. "Transparents," she said with disgust. She headed for the north end of the house.

As we rounded the corner and approached the car, she pointed to a building perhaps fifty feet beyond the far side of the driveway. "Iris," she said.

"Where?" I looked all around, expecting to see a chubby little three-year-old, her sister Winnie's youngest daughter, running around the yard.

"Right over there." Mother walked toward the building. About halfway between the driveway and the building, she reached down and pulled a long, narrow flattened leaf from a fan of leaves erupting from the ground. "These will have gorgeous flowers in the spring." Between the small building and the driveway, hundreds of such fans were visible in a rectangular area between the driveway and the small building which I later learned was a chicken coop. Even later, I would live in it.

We went into the house.

The house was an amazing mix of styles and history. The center of it had been built more than a hundred years earlier, *much* more, I came eventually to believe, over a basement built of field stones; *large* ones. There was a concrete patch in one basement wall with the date 1866 on it – and the patch was newer, and made of better concrete, than the crumbling mortar between the stones of the walls. The first story floor of the center of the house was laid on logs of silver birch. We knew they were silver birch because when we went into the basement we could see them – and the bark was still on them.

The main room had been built by erecting in each corner a vertical, roughly square, 12-inch, adze-cut oak timber about 9 feet long. The timbers had been seasoned so hard while they stood for as many as a hundred and fifty years that a pilot hole had to be drilled to nail facing boards to them... or one could use square-cut iron nails (known also as "horseshoe nails" because they were used to nail horseshoes to horses' hooves), because the starting end of the nail was extremely slender. Being slender, it split neither hooves nor lumber.

Unfortunately, horseshoe nails had a problem we could not overcome. Uncle Bill actually visited a local farrier to buy some, and used them to nail Tulip Tree lumber to one of the corner timbers. But because the nails were iron, not steel, they rusted in the moist air of summer, in just a few days, too – and therefore they discolored the facing wood and had to be removed.

The original central, single-story building had been a schoolhouse. Later a second story had been added, with a stair against the back wall of the classroom *cum* living room, and the school building had become a house.

Much later, the house had also had "wings" added. The north wing, the earlier addition, was a kitchen with a dinette, behind which there was a covered porch (of which more later). The south wing was a two-room structure. There was a large room entered from the front yard, although it could also be entered from *our* living room, with a second, smaller, room off the south end of that. Its most salient features were a low-ceilinged "attic" entered from my parents' bedroom, and a steep slant of the entire wing structure from the "house" end to the far (south) end. This was the result of being built on a foundation created by placing large square-dressed sandstone blocks on the ground without benefit of soil compaction or spread of load. The north end, being spiked to the original house, did not sink. The south end, however, did... almost six inches.

The entire house was wallpapered, but the paper was discolored, soot covered, torn, written upon and, in Mother's view, generally totally unacceptable. Unfortunately for me, Mother actually *liked* hanging wallpaper. One of Mother's first tasks the next summer, with my reluctant help, was to re-paper the entire house.

There was little we could do that first summer, because there was little summer remaining. We had spent much of the summer working on the first house. Thus, little time remained for the second house before school began right after Labor Day, and Mother began working her winter hospital schedule again.

CHAPTER 9

The Magical, Mystical Barn –
And Other Wonderful Buildings

In addition to having a house into which we could move immediately, the new farm had... *buildings* – lots of buildings! There were two, count 'em, *two*, chicken coops. One was all wood and one was built of concrete blocks. There were no chickens – yet. There was a four-car garage at the end of the chicken coops and, across from it, a milk-house, right behind the rear kitchen porch. Upon entering the milk-house, one walked upon a concrete floor about four inches below the doorsill. At the far end of the floor (about eight feet from the door) was another sill, and beyond that was a "well" about four feet deep, as long as the building was wide, and about two feet wide.

When a farmer milked cows into a bucket, the bucket was emptied into a five- or ten-gallon milk can. When the milking was finished, the cans of milk were taken to the milk-house and placed into the well, which was filled with cold well water to just below the neck of the can. This kept the milk chilled until it was either used by the family (if they had only one or two cows), or until the dairy hauler came by to buy it.

Next to the milk-house stood a granary – a large, musty smelling wooden building with stiff wire covering louvers in the upper walls. Inside the building were rooms with strangely built doors and wall entries through which grain was blown or conveyor-carried into the rooms. The rooms were all empty at the time, but the main entry hall hosted a hand-operated, cast-iron machine that was destined later to be a great nemesis of mine... a corn sheller, designed to remove the kernels of hard field corn from the cob rapidly and efficiently... so long as the operator was capable of turning the crank and keeping the gears turning. Husked (bare) corn on the cob is fed into the top. Cobs fall out one side into a basket and kernels of corn fall out the other.

Finally, standing as a barrier between the back edge of the lawn and the hayfield, stood the barn... a magnificent two-story structure of many uses. Of true board-and-batten construction, painted gray and well-weathered, the barn guarded the rear of the living area of the farm. Board-and-batten construction consisted of wide boards nailed vertically across the length of the outside of a wall with a roughly one-inch space between each two. Then two-inch boards were nailed over the one-inch space. The smaller boards were nailed only through the gaps between the larger boards, creating a not-quite-tight overlap that moved with the expansion of heat and cold, but precluded the necessity to finish-plane the larger boards so they could be "butted" together. It also allowed for air exchange while keeping the wind out. You'd pay a lot for those boards today.

The barn became our playground, our fort, our monkey bars and mountain range. A third of the lower front was a large room in which we stored hay. We also had two upper level haymows, although the lower level mow extended all the way to the roof. Down in the rear of the lower level was a concrete-floored dairy room with milking stanchions and a second, smaller, dirt-floored room. In the two-thirds of the lower front not used for hay were three horse stables and an area for tack.

We bought a milking Guernsey every spring, milked her until about November, and when she dried up, she became steaks, roasts and hamburger. So we kept hay in the lower mow and, because it wasn't really full, we had steps and shelves of hay to climb up and jump down onto from the upper mow. Of course, the old square bales would break open and the Old Man would throw a fit about people who walked on someone else's (in this case, our cow's) food. But it didn't stop us. Clambering around that old barn was our favorite thing to do for many years. Of course, as we got older, there were more chores than play-days.

The cow was ours (Giles' and mine) to feed and milk as we got older. A Guernsey gave a good five gallons of milk from which up to a gallon of cream would rise while it sat in the milk-house overnight. The Old Man would assemble the cream separator every two or three days, and pour the milk into it slowly through folded cheesecloth (you don't want to think about what gets into hand-milked milk) whilst I cranked it. The nested centrifuges would spin at different rates and cream would pour out the top spout into a pitcher that sat on a built-in shelf, while milk came out the bottom spout into another ten-gallon milk can.

Once the cream was separated, it was poured into a geared butter-churn. The CIA had nothing on the guy who invented *this* torture device. The churn consisted of a square two-gallon glass container onto which a screw-lid containing a four-paddle device was lowered. A crank with a large cogged wheel was attached. The cogged wheel turned against a much smaller cogged wheel through which the churn paddle stem protruded.

When the crank was turned slowly, the paddle turned more rapidly... *forever*. And it was *hard* work. Churning butter was a slo-o-o-o-ow process. It took most of a day (wel-l-l-l... an hour, anyway), for the first little yellow blobs to show up. For another half hour, they would slowly coalesce, sticking to the wooden paddles little by little. And the more that stuck, the harder the paddles turned. Eventually, I would be unable to turn it rapidly enough to finish, and the Old Man or my mother would take over. It was a proud day for me when I could finish the job. I must've been at least twelve.

But we always had the barn. Well into our teens, that barn gave us a place to be when it rained outside, or stormed inside (the marriage of the Old Man and my mother was not a quiet one). We would climb and clamber, play knights against evil, cowboys and Indians, war games, and a host of imaginative things I can no longer recall. As we grew older, the games became more dramatic. One rainy Saturday, when I was maybe eleven, Mother called us to lunch. Lyndella and I appeared at the table, but no Giles. After a minute or two, Mother spoke up.

"Where's your brother?"

"Hanging out in the barn," replied little sister.

"Hanging out with whom?" Mother was losing patience.

"Not with anybody. He's just hanging out there."

"Just hang..." Mother exploded from her chair, raced through the kitchen door and headed for the barn. Lyndella and I just looked at each other. After all, Giles was the bad guy. If we'd cut him down for lunch, we'd just have had to hang him again, right? Anyway, we'd strung the rope under one armpit and tied it against the other side of his neck. He'd be okay.

Hattie Larlham, all five feet ten inches of her, quivered with appalled rage as she carried Giles into the house and laid him on the sofa in the living room. A raw streak lay across his upper chest and throat where the "rope," really baling twine, had rubbed skin away as he struggled to escape. She took a deep breath and stood, glaring down at two suddenly terrified children. "Don't. Ever. Put. A. Rope. Around. Someone's. Neck. *Ever!*" She turned and walked into the bathroom, from which came the sounds of quiet sobbing. It was years before she ever mentioned it again.

Behind the barn was a pigpen. No, really... a building and fenced yard for pigs. There was a large fenced area into which the cow was released and in the center of it stood a wooden shed, with its own chain-link fenced area. The building was filthy and it smelled of pigs. In fact, the only times we (Giles and I) ever entered it were the few summers during which we had pigs, and the two of us were assigned to feed them.

CHAPTER 10

Yardwork Beyond Our Means –
Gardening for Blisters and Sunburn

The Blackbird's Song

That first summer, my brother and I thought the farm a boys' paradise. I had just turned eight, he had just turned six and there was nothing for us to *do*, except play. The farm's primary purpose was to give us (the children, including our little sister) that most essential thing in life – the "farm experience." We would learn to be responsible for the farm, and we did... but not that summer; not that the Old Man didn't try.

There were no real "chores" for us to do. There were no animals yet for us to feed and water, except Bellsie, the old blind pony who came with the farm. There was lawn to be mowed but, as it turned out, not by Giles and me – yet. Nonetheless, the push mowers (there were two in the barn), were taken out, weed-whips were unlimbered, sickles were purchased, and a mammoth scythe (to be used by me years later) was discovered lying among a stand of burdock. All these devices of summer ruination were carried into the tiny burg of Mantua, Ohio, one fine Saturday, and sharpened.

The Old Man returned that afternoon and called my brother and me out to the car. "Let's see what you can do with these." He picked up the mowers, set them straight on the lawn and said, "Push!" waving in a generally forward direction.

Manfully, we stepped forward, grasped the cross-bar handles... and *pushed*! Reel (push) mowers have two geared wheels that make the curved blades of the reel spin more rapidly than the wheels turn. The reel blades trap grass between themselves and a straight blade set above the ground, where it is promptly sheared off. As the mower is pushed forward, the reel blades constantly sweep and trap grass blades against the rear blade. The height of the rear straight blade is adjustable, and is controlled by the height of the roller behind it.

Giles and I looked at each other. The handle on my mower, came about to the middle of my face. His was higher than his head. We pushed. I could, in thin grass, take short choppy pushes, at the end of which the wheels would lift and the mower would try to skid. At about the third push, thicker grass jammed in the blades, the wheels lifted, the mower stopped... and I did not. The pain was blinding... and red. Slamming one's nose into a wooden bar is never recommended. When you're eight, it's a hundred times worse. I squalled in pain, tried to breathe, sneezed... and squalled again. Giles laughed. Blood was everywhere, including Giles, and it poured down my shirt front.

Mother burst from the house, took one look at me, wheeled on the Old Man and demanded to know what he thought he was doing (as a nurse, she knew I would stop bleeding eventually). The pain slowly receded and I stood there, breathing through my mouth and listening to her rage and the Old Man trying to placate her. Eventually it became apparent that our mowing was done for at least *that* summer. Pleased with her victory, Mother headed to the house at a brisk walk and soon returned with a bowl of ice and water, a washcloth and a roll of cotton batting. The bleeding had slowed and she quickly had it stopped by applying the washcloth, wet and filled with ice, to the bridge of my nose. Cleaning my face, she plugged my nose with cotton and turned toward the house.

"All right, boys..." the Old Man wasn't finished. "Let's see how you do with these." He handed us each a sickle and a weed whip, their edges gleaming from the sharpener's stone and oil. "Hold it flat, like this" He took my sickle back, bent over and demonstrated a swing with the blade held flat to the ground. Grass fell behind the moving sickle.

"The whole lawn?" I was appalled.

"Dick, are you *insane*?" Mother had returned instantly upon hearing the clash of metal blades. "They're not old enough to handle those things!" She began collecting tools. As she collected, she cooled. "Dick, it's going to be at *least* a couple years before you can give either of these boys sharp stuff and feel safe with them."

The Old Man said nothing, but later that night they talked 'til well after we went to sleep. Neither of them sounded happy.

The upshot was, the first two years on the farm, we "helped" Mother relocate and plant asparagus, gardens and Iris bulbs (those Irises *did* produce gigantic flowers, once the root and corm masses had been properly broken up). Mother dug up the masses of Iris and broke up the "corms" (bulb-like roots). Then she replanted them in a far larger area, with a plan to identify colors and try to make a pattern. Came the next spring, there was a riot of color on what must have been half an acre of giant Iris. When she began talking about marking the colors the Old Man was stunned. "Pat," his voice was gentle, "don't. They're gorgeous as they are. If you try to make a pattern you'll spoil it." She never brought it up again.

For the asparagus, Mother called a farmer to come in with a tractor and four-bottom plow. Cutting four furrows at a time, with great difficulty he plowed the small field to the south of the house, in which only quack grass and asparagus grew. The soil was black and soft (mostly decomposed peat from a small bog), and the roots of the quack grass, and especially the asparagus, would grab the plows and slow the tractor, allowing the drive wheels to spin and dig in. He would raise the plows and try to rock the tractor out, sometimes shoving wads of grass against the tires... swearing monotonously but constantly.

Eventually the plowing was finished, and Mother made arrangements for the farmer to come back and disk the plot for a garden when she was done. After he left, she got a wheelbarrow and we went searching for asparagus root masses. There were hundreds, but she selected small ones. We made a pile and she covered it with straw and watered it heavily. The farmer came back and double-disked the plot, running both east-west and north-south, chopping the roots of both asparagus and grass.

After she had let it bake in the sun for a week, Mother began fashioning the plowed area into a garden. First, she dug holes and replanted chunks of asparagus roots. Then she took twine and pegs, stretched the twine between pegs and with a hoe cut a shallow trench below the twine. It kept the rows straight and equidistant from each other. Giles and I carefully planted corn, beans, peas and other seeds in the new garden. For the remainder of the summer, Mother spent days on end chopping at grass between the rows. Slowly, their roots died in the sun.

And we played – a *lot*. There were only a few play rules.

First and foremost was, never go into the road. Kent-Mantua Center (later Diagonal) Road was a dirt road with oiled patches in front of houses. The speed limit was 35 miles an hour, honored most often in the breach, and the dust raised often made visibility for up to a quarter mile pretty much nil.

Rule Number Two was as firm as Rule One: Never, never, *never*, go into the swamp – *ever*! The swamp had been a black-soil stream floodplain pasture until siltation and beavers flooded it. There were hummocks of grass, high-bush cranberry and other shrubs, and acres of cattails... all of it except the hummocks covered by about a foot of water. Beneath the water was black organic muck, in places as much as thirty feet deep, and it was saturated. Quicksand had nothing on this stuff. Little boys finding themselves in that swamp would be *shuddering breath* gone *forever*!

Rule Number Three was simple: always make sure you can see the house. We could go back to the woods (and we did, often) but we could not go *through* the woods. From halfway into it, we could not see out of it.

And so we played... the two of us. We had cap pistols and wooden swords, army gear (including wooden "drill practice" M-1s from the Old Man's failed Army-Navy surplus store) and toy bows with sucker-tipped arrows. Summer and fall on the farm was fun.

Then came winter: sledding and snowball fights, school and long bus-rides, roller-skating and church parties. Winter was fun – until it turned into March.

In March came rain, sleet and wet snow. Cold days without anything cool to do; every day a misery – trapping us in the house. Every cold school-day morning, we could be found standing at the end of the driveway, huddled under the dense branches of the sixty-foot tall Norway spruce, waiting for the school bus. And then one morning, as the sky began to lighten, there came a three-note bird's call – loud and raucous, the second note a long-held trill. I had *no* idea what sort of bird made such a call, but it was such a joyous, challenging song...

The Old Man had already gone to work and Mother was not dressed for the weather, so I waited. That evening, I asked the Old Man. I could not, of course, even whistle, much less mimic the bird's song, but the Old Man said, "I think I know. Come outside." Despite the cold and damp, winter was dying, and the sun was just setting.

We walked between the chicken coops and the garage to the top of the hill pasture. He pointed to the cattails in the swamp below and said, "Watch!"

I saw a bird atop the head of a tall cattail, illuminated by the last of the sun, open his beak, and that challenge poured forth into the evening, to be instantly answered by another... and another, and another.

"Redwing blackbird," said the Old Man, "first real birdsong of spring. When he shows up, you know winter's pretty much done."

Aside from the yellow-rimmed red shoulder patch, the redwing is not a particularly pretty or striking bird. But that song... hearing it turns the world around me into a small Ohio farm in the 1950s; a farm that I see, feel, smell and hear for just an instant, exactly as I did the spring that I first heard the magical, glorious, challenging three-note trill of the male redwing blackbird – my first and true harbinger of spring.

CHAPTER 11

My Little (Blind) Pony

As we left the house that first day, to return to the little red house and finish packing up to move, I heard a sound. Coming from the barn, a soft whicker built into a loud but high-pitched whinny. I stopped dead, nearly tripping Mother who was close behind me, carrying a sleeping Lyndella. I turned and looked at the Old Man. "I think I heard a horse. Did you buy a horse? Dad? Did you? Da-ad!"

The Old Man laughed. "That's not a horse. It's a pony. Her name is Bellsie and she came with the farm. But she's blind."

Blind? What did I care about blind? When the Old Man bought the farm, our new home came with... *a pony*! I was eight years old, and I had my own pony named Bellsie! Bellsie came with her own pony-sized saddle and bridle and a cozy stall in the barn, the cleaning of which, I soon discovered, was *my* job. Mucking out her stall was not the only drawback to owning Bellsie. As the Old Man had said, Bellsie was blind. One eye had been injured and the vet told the Old Man the other had gone blind in "sympathy." Today, I have serious doubts. I suspect a cataract that no one was willing to pay to have cured – and then it was too late.

The weekend after we moved in, the Old Man saddled her up, and led her around the yard with me aboard for several turns. Then he let go of the reins, showed me how to neck-rein her, and told me to have fun.

After a while (probably less than 30 minutes), he told me to get off. We led her to the barn and unsaddled her. The Old Man slung the saddle over an old over-sized sawhorse (he called it a saddle-horse), picked up a curry brush and showed me how to brush her down. That turned out to be a lot more work than I'd expected. When the Old Man was satisfied, he turned her loose in the fenced area behind the barn.

A couple days later, he pointed to the saddle and said, "Time t' saddle your own horse, Bud." I grabbed the saddle horn, picked up the saddle – and promptly dropped it. The single-hand sling-up wasn't gonna work for me. I was eight, short and fat.

"Two hands for beginners," the Old Man said, but he was grinning. "Here, grab it like this." He tossed one stirrup over the seat and lifted with one hand under each end. "Now you try." He dropped the saddle back to the saddle-horse. I performed each step as he had and turned to Bellsie... who stood higher than my chest! I could *barely* see over her back. I tried lifting the saddle up and, as Bellsie stepped sideways, the saddle hit the floor. As I picked it up, the Old Man said, "She's blind, Son. If you bump her, she can't see what it is, so she'll move away." I lifted the saddle as high as I could, and dropped it on her back. She started in fright and staggered sideways.

"Don't DROP it, Boy!" The Old Man was *not* the most patient of fathers. "I TOLD you... she's BLIND! Now, try it again!"

By the end of the afternoon, I could saddle, bridle and mount alone. The bridle was actually a halter (hackamore), because it had no bit. Bellsie wasn't about to run off with any of us aboard. "She's all yours, Son," the Old Man said. It didn't take me long to learn what "all yours" really meant.

For about four years, I rode Bellsie all over the farm, and the fifty acres we hadn't bought across the road. That was the fun part. I'd pull my little sister up behind me and ride around the yard. But "all yours" meant much more than riding Bellsie around all day.

Each morning I saddled her and rode her across the road, carrying a heavy hammer, an axle from a car and a light chain across the saddle in front of me. I'd dismount in what looked like good grazing, slip the small end of the axle through the ring at the end of the chain and pound it into the ground. The geared end kept the ring from coming off over the top of my "post." Then I'd clip the other end of the chain to the chin-ring on Bellsie's hackamore, and haul her saddle off.

I'd grab the saddle horn and sling the saddle over my shoulder (even a pony saddle weighs about 25 pounds – a pretty good load for an 8-year-old), grab the hammer and head back across the road. The trip was never more than a couple hundred yards, but it always seemed more like a mile. And it wasn't over when I got back... horses need to drink. I'd grab a pair of cleaned-out five-gallon paint buckets, put about two gallons of water in each from a hose (it's much easier to carry sixteen pounds on each side than thirty-two pounds hanging off one arm) and head back across the road. I'd lead Bellsie to the end of her chain and set one bucket down where she could reach it, but not dump it over, and pour the water from the other bucket into it. Then I was done... 'til evening when I did it all in reverse.

Meantime, I had to muck out her stall, give her fresh straw for "bedding" (horses don't lie down, but their stall is their bathroom), put fresh hay in the little manger and make sure there was fresh water in the bucket strapped to the wall. Even on school days, all this had to be done.

Owning a horse is a major business for an eight-year-old. Come winter, the ride across the road was out. Bellsie stayed in her stall, blanketed. Water was a problem. Every morning, the bucket was frozen, so I'd fill one with hot water and slide it into the strap that kept her from knocking it over.

As soon as I got home from school, I would boil a Dutch oven full of water and pour it into the bucket. The melting ice cooled the water. Later that evening, before bed, my father would do the same (my bedtime was 7:30), and come morning it started over. For four wonderful years, I did all this.

As my little brother got older, life became harder. I was short for my age, and fat. He was tall for his age, and skinny... and he could *run*! It was his great pleasure to frustrate me – make me angry, and then spend however long it took to wear me out, running from me, laughing all the while. I could never catch him. But, angry, frustrated and tearful as I might get, there was always Bellsie... until summer, 1954.

Two things I'll never forget happened in 1954. I had my twelfth, last and most wonderful birthday, and Bellsie became unrecoverably sick. She came down with what the vet called "The Heaves." Simply put, she seems in retrospect to have had something like TB. Every breath was an effort and she sounded like a busted bellows.

After about a month of pouring nasty smelling medicine down her throat, wrapping her in heated blankets, and spending, I'm sure, a lot of money on the vet, The Old Man sat down next to me one evening and said, "Son, Bellsie is going to keep getting sicker. We can't make her well, and it's not fair to make her keep suffering. We'll keep trying if you really want us to, but it's really not fair to Bellsie."

By the time he was finished, I was crying. But I managed to choke out, "Do we have to shoot her?"

The Old Man jerked his head up. "Shoot her? Us?" He was totally nonplussed. "Of *course* we don't have to shoot her. I'll arrange for someone to come and get her. You can say good-bye before she gets in the truck."

I choked out an, "Okay," and ran up to my room. I shared a room and bed with my little brother. He, of course, insisted on knowing why I was crying. When I told him, he began squalling. That brought the Old Man upstairs on the run; and Mother as well. Little sister chimed in, once there was a big enough audience. I think it took them a long time to get us calmed down and asleep.

That Saturday, while the Old Man was at work, a pick-up truck with slat sides and a drop-down ramp for a gate pulled into the yard. A man got out. "I'm here for the pony," he said as I came to the door, "I'll back up to the bank at the roadside (the road was about three feet below our front yard) and you bring it out." I don't remember where Mom and my brother and sister were, but I was home alone.

"Y-y-y-you weren't supposed to be here yet." I was stammering. The Old Man was supposed to do this, not me. He was coming home at lunch to meet this guy, and it was only ten o'clock.

"Yeah, Kid... I know; but one job fell through, so here I am. Let's get this show on th' road... waddaya say? Go get the pony."

I didn't know what else to do. He was a grown-up. Kids obeyed grown-ups in my world. I turned and stumbled to the barn, put Bellsie's halter on and clipped a short lead rope to it. I lead her out front and started to take her up the ramp, but the driver took the lead, and started to pull her up the ramp... too fast. Bellsie stumbled. "She's *blind!*" I choked out, and I looked away... and saw the truck door. There was a sign painted on the door of the faded old pick-up. It said "Lawson's Mink Farm." I started to cry.

The neighbor girl from across the road, a near-adult of eighteen, had come down to see what was happening. She snatched the lead from the driver. "You wait!" she barked, and gently took the pony into the truck and tied her off. She climbed out of the truck and strode up to the much larger driver. Using language I had no idea she knew, she spent about a minute and a half screaming at the driver. Apparently his heritage was not entirely human and he had not been born or reared in human habitation. There was graphic description of the environs of the rock from under which he had crawled.

The driver backed along the end of the truck, lifted the gate and latched it, and kept backing until he reached the door. By that time, the neighbor girl had run down. "He's just a *KID*," she hissed, "and he *loved* that pony." Then she took me in the house and stayed until I calmed down.

When the Old Man got home and heard what had happened, his jaw muscles bunched, and his eyes got flat and hard. He said, "I'm sorry, Son," put his arm around my shoulder and pulled me tight against him. Then he got in his car and took off. He never told me what happened, but his left hand was in a heavy bandage for several days, and he had trouble with it for the rest of the summer. He was always proud of his straight left jab.

CHAPTER 12

Tornado-built House – My "New" School

After we'd lived on the farm a couple years, the Old Man and Mother began an almost never-ending renovation of the old farmhouse; and got help they never expected.

It stormed all day the Saturday before Mother's Day; dark skies, thunder and lightning and rain coming down in sheets. We had no TV and soon no lights. The Old Man kept us all downstairs for fear of the tornado he was sure was coming. Abruptly, wind and rain swept down the stairs. The wind had "flipped" an eyebrow window at the head of the stairs. This window was narrow, wider than it was high and set horizontally with pegs that were pulled to allow it to be flipped to let air in. The constant rattling by the wind had loosened the pegs.

My brother and I raced up the stairs and flipped the window shut... and couldn't find the pegs.

"Boys," the Old Man hollered, "get back down here."

But there was no letting go of the window. I was sure it would follow me down the stairs (completely ignoring the fact that it hadn't come down the first time it fell out). Finally the Old Man came up, found the pegs and jammed them in and we all headed for the basement.

Our basement had an outside entrance at the back of the house with angled "batwing" doors covering the stairs. The wind rattled and banged the doors until, eventually, they slammed open. And there it was; an elephant's trunk just like the one Nina and Giles and I had seen on Infirmary Road; but this time I knew what it was.

"Tornado!" I screamed. It was black and it screamed back at me like a whole herd of Banshees (whatever Banshees were... I had no idea but I'd read that they screamed). It hovered over the woods spraying branches and small trees everywhere, and then...

...the end that touched the ground lifted and swung toward us. Slowly, like a blind snake searching for food, it homed on the house. As we cowered in the basement (well, we cowered at the foot of the basement stairs so as not to miss anything), my three-year-old sister screaming in fear, the tornado reached down and took...

...the milk-house. Black shingles and white boards spread from the house to the woods. The tornado shook itself and spat free the remainder of the small sacrifice the farm had made to save itself. And back it came. Its aim more certain, its direction truer, it came directly for the center of the house. The spinning, shrieking mouth of the dirty black tube swung again earthward... and took the granary! In the event, it actually took only the roof. The walls collapsed inward, having been pulled loose from the floor and each other. Finally, having spread the roof over several acres of the farm, the tornado gave up and headed east and ultimately south, bashing trees and power lines as it went.

As we later discovered, the tornado had come north along the ridge across the road, tearing up trees and creating havoc. As it came to the swampy creek that crossed into our "wet pasture," it swung to the east, and then around the house to the woods at the rear. All-in-all, it ran for about three miles, running north a mile and a half to our house, and then east and south nearly as far. When it came to us, it built our new kitchen/dining room.

Once the renovations began, my kid brother, Giles, and I were fascinated and we wanted to help... until actual work was required. After a few minutes of carrying or holding parts and tools or running and fetching, we rapidly lost interest in helping. But neither the Old Man nor Uncle Bill (married to Mother's sister Ella, and a carpenter and cabinetmaker – if the cabinets weren't too complex) would allow us to use the fun tools.

The Skilsaw, a vicious whirling blade of teeth, pushed through wood with ease and speed, or so it seemed. Uncle Bill was careful to point out that it pushed through fingers and hands even more easily. He allowed me to pick his up (unplugged), and I couldn't even set it up on a board to cut with. The early tools were powerful, and they were heavy. There was no way we could use them, much less use them safely.

As time went on, we grew older, and some work came our way. One of the early jobs when I was about twelve and Giles ten, was to replace the old, warped rear porch deck with the floor from the granary (collapsed, but the floor and walls were mostly undamaged). First, the original floor was removed and Giles and I were allowed to really help. There was nothing to save, so we were given crowbars and allowed to just tear into the porch. Half an hour later, Mother stopped the job. We had uncovered a hole in the ground filled with rocks and she knew what we'd found.

The old farmhouse had a well drilled right at the corner of the house, with a concrete-block pump-house that extended about four feet into the ground and about three feet above it. The pump-house sheltered the well-head, a pump, a pressure tank and a fuse box. The well casing went a hundred and thirty-five feet into the ground. The tank slowly lost pressure and the Old Man would disappear into the dank and dark pump-house through the manhole in the top every six weeks or so (of which I learned far more than I wished as I grew older). A loud, mostly unintelligible monologue would accompany his battle with the tank, bleeding water from it and pumping air into it. Liquids cannot be compressed so compressing air into the pressure tank was the only way to maintain enough pressure in the system to force water into the house without running the pump constantly.

Mother had recognized the predecessor to the well and pump. The "hole full of rocks" was a dug well. When it was abandoned for the drilled well, it had been filled for fear of children or animals falling into it. She decided we would empty it of rocks and turn it into a giant water butt for rainwater. Mother had a rain barrel, known to older folk as a "water butt," under a downspout, and she used the water collected in it for washing her hair. Her reasoning was that there are no minerals in the air through which rain falls so the water is "soft." Wells draw water from rock and soil and the water has dissolved minerals in it from the passage through that soil and rock making well water "hard" water. Without much effort and additives, it is not the water to wash your hair with. She hoped to use the well to store water enough to use for bathing.

For a week, Giles and I hauled rocks out of that hole. It was lined with larger rocks set in concrete, but the rocks we were hauling out in buckets were head-sized or smaller. The deeper we went, the fewer we put in the bucket, until the Old Man rigged a three-by-two block and tackle set for us. A block and tackle is two sets of pulleys, one set of up to four or five pulleys (in our case, three) set into the "block" attached to a fixed point, with a rope looped through those and another set of pulleys, the "tackle," that was attached to the load. In essence, a block and tackle is a set of levers that are circles rather than bars and fulcrums.

Eventually, despite the block and tackle, we reached a point at which it became obvious that two boys our ages weren't going to empty that well. We had no idea how deep it went and it also occurred to both Mother and the Old Man that there was no way of making that old well safe to work in. Giles and I were hardly disappointed. The fun was long gone from the enterprise, and all that was left was work.

In the end, the new porch was built over and around the old well (we didn't refill it with the rocks we'd removed) and Mother was left with her rain barrel and had to be satisfied with just washing her hair in it. Eventually the Old Man bought a water softener and she gave up the rain barrel.

To build the new floor and walls of the porch, now a part of the new dining room, the Old Man pulled a small bulldozer up flush against the edge of the walls of the old granary (now flat on the granary floor), wrapped chains around the walls or floor one at a time and around the 'dozer blade. When he lifted the blade, each piece, floor or wall, came up, level to the ground, and he slowly backed and filled the 'dozer, clanking finally to the place against the house where they would be placed. The granary walls and floor became the walls and floor for our new dining room, which extended out to where the porch floor, utterly rotted, had been removed and new concrete block foundations had been built. We had only to place, raise and level and square them.

Giles and I were allowed to participate in the renovation more and more as time went on, until we found ourselves full-blown carpenter's helpers. What had looked like so much fun became drudgery. Eventually, Giles simply refused to do it anymore. As the oldest, I had to be "responsible." The best I could do was use school as an excuse... but for the next six years, the Old Man, Uncle Bill and I rebuilt that house. OK, OK... the Old Man and Uncle Bill (and eventually Uncle Jack) rebuilt the house. I did what I could, which didn't seem to me to be all that much, and I had no idea how much I'd learned until I owned my first house and discovered that when things went south – I actually knew what to do.

That fall, a big yellow bus pulled up at the end of our drive and I got aboard. I waited anxiously for my first sight of my new school. As we got to the school and pulled into the bus lane, I sat in stunned silence. Everybody else got off, and still I sat.

"Gonna sit there all day, boy?" the driver asked.

"How did you find my old school?" I asked back.

"Stop being foolish, boy!" he said. "You have to get off. I have another run."

In a daze, I picked up my new three-ring book bag (with ruled notebook paper, built-in pencil case and zipper edge) and clambered down the steps. As I entered my "new" room (the classrooms were pre-assigned – we'd been sent a paper from the principal), I saw "Tuggy" and Donald, Rose Marie and Lynn, Connie and... I saw everybody I'd left behind on that weepy final picnic day. We had moved miles away (less than five as it turned out), but within the same school district.

CHAPTER 13

Taffy Pull

Everyone who's ever participated in a taffy pull, raise your hand. My, my not many of us, are there?

Well, back in the day, a taffy pull was one of our many substitutes for sitting on the couch watching stupid TV. We did not, in fact, even *have* a TV until 1955 or maybe '56, and this happened before that.

One evening, as I was doing my arithmetic homework, I came across a problem that was designed to teach us the progression of English measurements (ounces to teaspoons, teaspoons to tablespoons, tablespoons to cups and so forth). The problems assigned in the book included a recipe for pulled taffy!

I completed the problem, along with a dozen or so others, and took my homework to my mother to check.

"Charles," she said when she had finished, "I believe this taffy recipe is real. I think we could really make taffy with it." Before she gave me back the arithmetic book, she copied down the recipe.

And we did make it. I do not remember the occasion, but there were a bunch of kids at our house one Saturday afternoon. I don't think it was a birthday, but it might have been. In any case, a taffy pull was on the agenda.

My mother cooked up the candy mixture and we "pulled" the taffy.

Now, you have to understand, the taffy we're talking about here bears *no* resemblance to, nor is it related to, the saltwater "taffy" you buy in stores. Pulled taffy is a molasses candy that is cooked down into a stiff and sticky, sweet, brown mass. One takes a wad of candy, nearly hot enough to burn, in hands liberally coated in confectioners' sugar, and stretches it long enough to give an end to another child. The two then back away from each other until the candy pulls apart. It is quickly folded back together, and the process is repeated.

Pulling and folding continues until the candy can no longer be stretched. As the pulling continues, a magical transformation occurs. The candy begins as a rich chocolate mass of soft sugary goo. As it cools, it begins to stiffen, and to lighten in color. As it gets more and more difficult to pull, it becomes first tan, then beige, and finally nearly white. In fact, two people strong enough can pull taffy until it becomes translucent, although that is typically done by a pulling machine in modern candy manufacturing shops, if they make taffy at all. Before it fully stiffens, the taffy is rolled out into a rod about a half-inch to an inch thick, quickly cut into short chunks, and allowed to harden.

Pulled taffy is a hard sugar-candy – harder than a jaw-breaker and sweeter than any candy you've ever tasted, with a brown sugar back-taste that just perfects the flavor.

I wish I still had the recipe from that math book. I think it's the most use I *ever* got out of sixth-grade math.

CHAPTER 14

The Best Birthday Ever

The day I turned 12 (well, a day short of 12... my mother got the date she went into the hospital mixed up with the day I was actually born), my parents informed me that this would be my last birthday.

But on that day, the *only* birthday I have ever remembered, my father entered my bedroom and said, "C'mon, Son! Today's a big day. Breakfast is cookin'. It's eight-thirty and time we were up and doin'."

So I got up, wondering why I'd slept so late, headed downstairs to the bathroom, and the scent of bacon, eggs, rye toast (burned black and slathered with real butter) and coffee hit me. I rushed through my ablutions, ran upstairs to dress, back down into the kitchen and slid into my chair just as my father poured me a cup of coffee. "See if you like it black," he said, adding milk to his.

I took a sip of the over-strong brew, and swallowed it wondering how something that smelled like ambrosia could taste so foul. I took another sip and another. Mebbe not so bad. My mother shoveled four eggs-over-easy and a half-dozen slices of bacon onto my plate, smiling at my father – the most conspiratorial smile I'd seen up 'til then, or since. She pushed the plate of rye toast toward me, and sat down.

"You have a big day ahead," she said, "so eat up."

I dug into the eggs, shoveled yolk (I could never stand egg

white), bacon and toast into my mouth (now *that* was ambrosia), chewed and washed the whole wad down with a big gulp of hot, scalding coffee. My eyes bulged and teared up. I pulled air past pursed lips and panted it out again. I chewed and breathed frantically, and finally swallowed. I looked around.

Both my father and mother were very busy with their own breakfasts. Neither said a word about my near-disaster.

After a minute or two of silence, my mother said, "Happy Birthday, Charles!" She handed me a card. "We'll have a party with your friends this evening after you and your father get back, and the chores are done."

My father chipped in. "Bet you wondered why we let you sleep in," he said. "Well, because this is the last birthday you'll celebrate, we thought it should be special."

As usual, my rapidly maturing ability at witty repartee came to my rescue. "L-l-last birthday?" I stammered.

"Of course," my mother said, "you're grown now – twelve years old. We don't do parties after twelve."

First I'd heard of it, but "Oh," I said, "sure." And that was the end of it. I turned to the Old Man. "Where are we goin'?"

"Akron," he grunted. "Gotta pick up your birthday gift."

Now *that* was different. The Old Man and I were going clear into Akron and pick up *my* birthday gift. It must be something really special. I looked at the Old Man. He grinned and went back to eating. Oh-HO! Mysterious! Must be something *really*, **really** special. I dug into the eggs, bacon and rye toast (I had smartened up, though. I took the coffee in sips.) as if my life depended on clearing my plate in the next thirty seconds.

"Whoa there, Son!" the Old Man said, and he was laughing

– something he almost never did, "We'll get there. Making yourself sick won't get us there any sooner." He chewed deliberately and swallowed. Then he picked up his cup, sipped his coffee and set it slowly down. He picked up his fork and turned to speak to my mother, fork poised over his eggs.

I got the message. Sitting on a chair, the seat of which was suddenly filled with the pointy ends of straight pins, I realized that this was deliberate! The Old Man was *enjoying* this! I determined to give him no satisfaction.

I carefully scooped up a piece of bacon and a forkful of egg yolk, put it into my mouth, lifted a slice of toast, opened my mouth and...

"Charles, you don't need to fill your mouth like a dump truck," my mother admonished.

I stared at her, mouth half open. Didn't she understand? I was eating as deliberately as the Old Man. I...

A string of yolk, barely thicker than water, fell from my mouth to my lap. I looked down. A thick yellow splotch was promptly joined by a larger one. Realization hit! My mouth was still open! I closed it, chewed and swallowed and started to get up to change my jeans.

"Finish your breakfast, Charles," my mother said with a smile. "You'll have time to change before you go."

Oh, the humiliation. I had ruined my last birthday. I could feel my eyes start to prickle. I couldn't start to *cry*! I just *couldn't*!

"Yessir!" the Old Man said firmly, "Gonna be a heckuva day! Just you and me, Son. Just you and me." He slapped me on the back of the shoulder.

I gasped! "The chickens," I yelped. "I've gotta feed the chickens! And Bellsie!"

"Already done," the Old Man said calmly. "Fed and watered before I got you up; the pony too."

I gaped at him. The Old Man had done my morning chores! Unbelievable! Unexpected! Unprecedented! I ran out of "uns" and closed my mouth.

"Finish your breakfast," the Old Man said. "We need to get goin'. I've got to shave, and then we've got a couple things to do on the way."

"Don't gobble," my mother admonished, but she said it gently.

The Old Man took a last bite of toast, tossed back the last of his coffee and headed for the bathroom. My mother got up and began to clear the table. I looked down and discovered that I had all but finished the bacon and eggs (whites and all) and my coffee was gone. For a moment I felt cheated. A real man's breakfast, and I'd hardly tasted it. But I got up and went upstairs to change my pants.

As I took off the egg-spattered jeans, I actually laughed. I was going to Akron with the Old Man, and *we* had things to do on the way. I pulled on a new pair of jeans, stepped into and re-tied my high-tops (PF Flyers were *the* summer shoe) and headed downstairs for the kitchen. I could hear the Old Man's electric Remington shaver as I went by the bathroom.

I sat down at the table to wait. My mother looked up from the dishes and smiled. "More coffee?" she asked.

I grinned back. I couldn't help it. "Yeah," I said, "please."

She tipped the percolator and filled the cup. "Still hot," she said, "careful."

I blew across it and then sipped, making a slurping sound. "Excuse me," I said, as soon as I swallowed. My mother chuckled.

"It's hard to drink hot coffee quietly," she said. "Give it a minute or two."

As I sat and waited for the coffee to cool, the Old Man came out of the bathroom, toweling his face and neck. "Ready to go?" he asked. He tossed the towel into the laundry basket behind the laundry room door and reached over and hooked an Army chino shirt off the back of his chair (the shirt and pants were leftover inventory from his failed Army/Navy store). I watched the muscles ripple in his back and arms, and wondered if I'd ever look like that.

At twelve years old, I stood barely five feet three, but I weighed nearly 150 pounds (at sixteen I stood five feet eleven, and I *still* weighed 150 pounds – but all that was a silent future in July of 1954). The Old Man stood five feet nine, narrow-waisted and broad-shouldered and he weighed 135 pounds – all muscle. In swim trunks he looked like a wedge with legs.

"Hey!" he said. "You ready to go?"

"You bet!" I said, scrambling up from my chair. "Let's go."

We got into the black 1950 Studebaker Champion with the bullet nose and narrowed trunk, and backed out of the drive ("Couldn't tell if it was comin' or goin'," the saying went). As he put the car into first and headed down the dirt road, he looked at me and grinned. "You'll never forget this day," he said. "I promise you that."

I grinned back. I was sure he was right.

We turned north onto State Route 303 and headed for Streetsboro, at that time a three-road crossroads with a couple gas stations and an IGA grocery. As someone famous once said, "There was no 'there' there."

The Old Man pulled into one of the gas stations and said, "C'mon. I need an oil change and some new retreads (an oxymoron if ever there was one, but it made sense to us)."

We got out and went into the garage. While the Old Man talked to the mechanic, I wandered around and looked at everything. The Old Man looked up. "Don't get grease on those clothes, Son," he said. "Your mother'll skin th' both of us."

"Yeah," I grinned back, "she would, wouldn't she?" I carefully stayed half a foot away from everything I looked at.

The Old Man finally came over to me. "Wait over there," he said, pointing to a space with a desk. "I'll be right back."

The Old Man went to the car. He drove it into the garage and up onto a couple steel slats. The mechanic guided him to a stop, and the Old Man got out and came over beside me.

The mechanic pulled a lever, and the car rose into the air on a central pillar that erupted from the ground. I had never seen a hydraulic lift in operation before, but I refused to ask how it worked. The Old Man said nothing. We stood companionably, side by side, watching the mechanic remove the oil plug and spill the oil into a bucket with a tall funnel attached to the top.

Two hours after our arrival, we were on our way. Tire changing was a lengthy business in 1954. We headed for Akron.

As we drove into downtown Akron, the Old Man dodged electric trolleys, skidding on their steel tracks as he did so. The air was filled with the stench of ozone. The trolley arms reaching up and sparking as they slid along the criss-crossing power wires that fed their electric engines were hypnotic to watch.

We drove through the center of town and out one of the main arterials, while the Old Man seemed to be searching for something. "Here we go," he said, and swung into the parking lot of an Isaly's snack shop.

We went in and sat at the counter. The Old Man ordered

two coffees.

"That'll be twenty cents," the waitress said as she set them in front of us and slid a creamer our way. The Old Man gave her a quarter. "Keep the change," he said. While we drank our coffee, he asked the waitress if she knew where a shop was. I didn't catch the name because his voice dropped as he said it. She said to go back two streets and turn left.

We finished our coffee and headed for the car. As we got in, the Old Man muttered, "Last time I have coffee at Isaly's."

"Why?" I asked.

"Coffee was ten cents a cup," he said. "It's a nickel everywhere else. They've doubled the price." But soon it was a dime everywhere. The Old Man never understood inflation.

The Old Man started the car and turned back the way we'd come. He turned down a side street and pulled in behind a small store that said "Bill's Gun Shop" over the door. As we walked back around the front, I looked at all the flyers and signs taped to the window: "Hunting Licenses Sold Here! $5.00." "Fishing Licenses! $2.00." "GUNS – NEW AND USED – ALL MAKES – TRADES WELCOME!" "USED SHOTGUN SALE – FROM $10.00!"

We went inside – the Old Man striding with purpose. I, however, was thunderstruck. The smells of gun oil, dust, old paper, old wood and something indefinable were magical. I assumed this was one of the "things" *we* had to do before we picked up my present. The Old Man must've decided he needed a new gun.

We walked up to the counter and my world came to a stuttering halt. "I'd like to see a used shotgun to fit the boy, here," the Old Man said. I could not have spoken under any imaginable circumstance.

The counterman left the counter and returned with a small, single-barreled shotgun. "Bay State .410," he said, breaking it open, "single shot, chambered for 2-and-3/4-inch shells." He reached under the counter and pulled out a box of shells.

The Old Man took the gun and worked the release mechanism a couple times. He snapped it shut and shouldered it, sighting down the barrel. He cocked the hammer (which I hadn't even noticed until then) and pulled the trigger. The hammer dropped with a "snap" that echoed in the hard-walled shop. He brought the gun down and handed it to me. "Try it," he said.

I took the gun, hoping desperately I wouldn't do something stupid and make myself look foolish or inexperienced (although I certainly was). I did everything the Old Man had done. The stock hit my shoulder like it had been born there, and I found myself looking down the barrel to a small white bead, with the mounted head of a white-tailed deer on the other side. I pulled the trigger. The "snap" of the hammer hitting the firing pin seemed impossibly loud. I surely started, but I don't remember. I handed the gun back to him. I was grinning like a chimpanzee and I knew it but I couldn't stop.

"How much?" the Old Man asked.

"Twelve-fifty," the counterman said. Then, before the Old Man could respond, he asked, "Birthday?"

"Twelve today," the Old Man said.

"Tell you what," the counterman said, "twelve bucks for his twelfth birthday, no tax, and I'll throw in a box of shells."

"Done," said the Old Man, and handed over a ten and two singles.

The counterman wrote out a receipt, put the box of shells in a paper bag and handed them both to the Old Man. He handed the shotgun to me. "You take care of her," he said, smiling. "I think she'll do you just fine."

"So do I," said the Old Man, putting his arm across my shoulders and steering me toward the door. "So do I."

On my twelfth and last celebrated birthday (until I got married), I got the greatest present I *ever* got. I spent a day with the Old Man, and we were just two guys doing things together. *Nothing* could have been better.

Oh, yeah and I got my first gun.

CHAPTER 15

Boxing Lessons

What I learned from boxing lessons did not include, by any stretch of the imagination, how to box.

The Old Man was a boxing fan. Once we finally got a TV (a tiny 9-inch black and white in the center of a giant "entertainment center") we watched "Friday Night Fights" almost every, um-m-m... Friday night. Rocky Marciano, Carmen Basilio, Sugar Ray Robinson (the *first* Sugar Ray), all these were as familiar in our home as my mother's sisters (and a heckuva lot more fun).

As a teen and young adult, the Old Man had spent time in a boxing gym in New Jersey and claimed to have sparred with name fighters (whose names I did not recognize and have since forgotten), "Golden Gloves" fighters (did they even have Golden Gloves in the '20s and '30s?) and locals he called the "Jersey Punks." The worst of the Jersey Punks was a kid named Maxie... a skinny little jerk, according to the Old Man, with an extra-long reach, a half-dozen over-sized buddies always hanging around and threatening to "pound" anybody who hurt Maxie, and a wanna-be mobster attitude.

In the ring, Maxie was a "head-hunter," a fighter who always punched for his opponent's face, laughing at every hit and pounding away at any cut that appeared. More than one teen fighter went home and never returned after a round with that deadly looping right. But the one unbreakable rule in fighting Maxie was, "Don't touch his face!" Maxie was a pretty-boy singer in local clubs, claiming to be twenty-one from the time he was sixteen. Hitting him in the face earned the unfortunate puncher a "conversation" with a couple (or more) of his large friends.

Maxie's favorite targets were kids who weren't very good or who had physical limitations. That group included the Old Man's Uncle Hugh. Hugh was only about five years older than the Old Man and had been more of a big brother than an uncle while the Old Man was growing up. And it was he who first introduced the Old Man to boxing and the New Jersey gym. But Uncle Hugh had a problem: he was blind in his left eye. Everyone in the gym knew and a match with Hugh was a no-hook fight. Straight rights and left jabs only, to the head. Punches coming from wide left, looping rights, for instance, were invisible to him and, because he couldn't see them... he couldn't guard or duck. They wore no head-gear, so a bad punch to the temple could have killed him.

One stuffy, hot, New Jersey, summer night, Maxie goaded Hugh into a match, promising to abide by the no-hook rule. But a few minutes into the fight, Maxie made a mistake. He walked squarely into a flicking left intended to miss his face by inches. He was hit solidly in the nose with a straight left. There was a trickle of blood, quickly staunched by the gym trainer. Maxie's friends ducked into the ring, but he waved them back.

Hugh apologized and offered to forfeit but Maxie was having none of it. Three rounds was the fight limit and three rounds it would be; so Hugh agreed to continue. Thirty seconds later, Hugh was bleeding steadily from a cut over his left eye and Maxie was sending looping rights to widen it every chance he got. The gym boss came over to stop the fight, but the young singer's friends held him away. Finally, a left to the gut (Maxie was a head-hunter by choice... he knew what a good gut-punch could do, and he used it effectively when he used one), followed by a long, looping right, put Hugh down for good.

Maxie stood over Hugh, saying over and over, "Not in the face! I *told* you... *never* in the face! I'm gonna be famous!" Finally he left, and the Old Man and his friends got Hugh cleaned up and took him home. They never went back to that gym.

The Old Man gave up boxing but not fighting, as his missing left nipple attested. There had been a night, years earlier, as he and his three brothers celebrated the completion of a water tower, or perhaps a bridge or a ground-level tank farm, in a bar in a small town they'd never see again, when some local toughs decided to take on the out-of-towners. Words, whiskey and punches were thrown. Somewhere in the middle of it all, one of the townies bit his left nipple off.

Maxie was right. He became famous as both a singer and an actor. Ever after, when he came on TV, or one of his movies was shown, the Old Man would mutter, "Jersey Punk!" and do everything *but* watch him do *anything*. It took me years to get the reason why out of him. I think he was afraid word would get back to Maxie's friends. He was convinced Maxie was Mafia, through and through.

But the Old Man never lost his love for boxing, and when I was twelve or thirteen, my kid brother Giles and I got a joint Christmas present... a full-size, gym-quality boxing set. There was a speed bag with a mounting ring, just like in the movies, two pairs of "speed gloves" (black, leather gloves with padding at the knuckles) and two pairs of real boxing gloves. The Old

Man took us out to the barn Christmas afternoon and hung the speed bag. The good news was that I was short for my age. Giles, my "little" brother, was less than two years younger than I, but already taller, and much skinnier – advantages he retains to this day. In any case, at that time the same bag height worked for both of us.

We were each expected to work for thirty minutes daily on the speed bag. The Old Man showed us how, timing the swing, punching forehand and backhand, left and right, using both hands, singly by turns and then alternating and turning the swinging bag into a rattling blur. Then it was our turn. He kept us at it, taking five-minute turns for some time, and then he called a halt. We were both out of breath and sweating on a cold Christmas Day in northeast Ohio, but it was fun.

For weeks thereafter, we would get off the school bus, race through our chores, do our homework and head for the barn. The Old Man had added a gunny-sack heavy bag; two burlap sacks layered and filled with left-over chicken feed, which he suspended from the beams next to the speed bag. We took turns on the speed bag and the heavy bag, swapping from speed gloves to boxing gloves at ten-minute intervals, every night for an hour. For the first time in my life, I began to develop some muscle tone.

Spring arrived, followed far too slowly by summer, and one sunny Saturday, the Old Man called us outside, where he handed us our boxing gloves. "Time you guys learned to box," he said. He showed us how to stand, how to jab and how to move. Then he placed us facing each other, carefully positioned our gloves and feet, stepped back and said, "Fight!"

I lashed out with a left jab of blinding speed (assuming one was sight-impaired and had the reaction time of a drunken turtle) and my ever-quick, fast-as-lightning, always ready to hit me and run little brother... *stepped forward – right into it*! His right arm drawing back and his face twisted with determination, Giles forgot everything the Old Man had said about sparring. He saw only the opportunity to punch me squarely in the face, with the Old Man watching, and get away with it. If he had paid attention, he would have seen instantly what I didn't learn for years; I was way too slow to be a boxer, slipped the punch and hit me. Instead...

...he saw the punch coming at the last instant and turned around (I *said* I was slow)! I hit him squarely behind the right ear. The shock travelled up my arm and jammed my shoulder into my neck. Giles dropped like a stone, unconscious. I was terrified, the Old Man was exasperated, and my mother was furious. "Get up," the Old Man said, "and face your brother. The next time... don't turn away!" Giles remained silent and unmoving, but I swear I saw an eye open part way and quickly close.

"Dick, what do you think you're doing!" Hattie Larlham was furious. Coming through the kitchen door like a light cruiser in full battle mode, she yelled, "Get away from that child!" She pushed the Old Man aside and knelt by the inert form of her youngest son. He moaned, to all appearances waking up. A few minutes of recovery, and he began to get up. She helped him to his feet and said, "No more boxing! These boys do *not* need concussions; they're rattle-brained enough!" She turned and stormed back into the kitchen.

And that was the end of my career as a canvas-back boxer. I threw one punch, my opponent was knocked out, and the fight was called on account of mother-knows-best.

The bags remained in the barn, but slowly we quit using

them. The gloves were left on the hay, and eventually grew a fine patina of mold, and we returned to the days of my little brother hitting me and then running until I was too exhausted to chase him any farther.

I didn't learn to box, and I didn't learn to take a punch, but I did learn to throw one and to stand up to things I was afraid of – and I was *terrified* of my "little" brother, an emotion shared by many boys and men through the years. Little brother, it turned out, was *dangerous*. And I learned that the toughest guy I knew would quail in the face of an angry mother... especially if he was married to her.

CHAPTER 16

First Gun, First Hunt

I told you a couple chapters ago about the day I got my own shotgun. I was 12, it was the end of July, and the Old Man and I went on a road-trip to get her for me. She was a sweet little Bay State single-shot .410 with a hammer, made to be a woman's gun. But, because I was short at the time (and, truth be told, just a tad "husky"), that gun fit me perfectly. Three years later, I was six inches taller and it was more like an awkward, long-barreled pistol in my larger hands and longer reach.

But now, there was a problem. Hunting season didn't arrive until early November, and I had to wait. There were *three whole months* between me and my first hunt with my first gun. But we put that time (and a good many .410 shotgun shells) to good use. The Old Man was nothing if not creative. He threw clods of dirt in the air for me to shoot at. He pulled rabbit-sized targets bouncing through the tall grass and weeds behind the barn, while I fired, reloaded and fired again.

And that was my first discovery the little Bay State had a shell lifter, but no ejector. When you broke her after a shot, you literally had to pull the shell out. Not a difficult task in summer, but in winter, with gloves on? Well, I'd just have to wait and see.

Came opening day, and I was up at the crack of dawn to re-fire the furnace. We had an old lump-coal burner and it was my job every morning to go down, open the bottom vent, break up the banked coal (and hope it hadn't gone out), shake out the ashes and scoop them out of the ash pit, and finally, to open the flue to make the furnace draw, and put wood and coal in the furnace, making sure I didn't smother the fire. Then I would stand there, poker in hand, and move the coal around from time to time, until all the new coal was burning and I was sure the fire would last.

Of course, if there was no starter fire from the night before, it was my own fault, because...

Every night it was my job to go down, shake out and "pull" the ashes, arrange the remaining burning coal against both sides of the furnace, close the bottom vent and "shorten" the flue to reduce the draw. Then I'd go to the coal pile in the corner of the basement, choose head-sized or larger coal lumps, and arrange them over the remaining fire so flames could barely circulate, thus "banking" the fire.

Through the night, the fire would burn the bottom of those large coal lumps and, in the morning, breaking them up one would see a bright and cheery fire begin anew one devoutly hoped. If there was no fire, I had to build one from scratch and do it quickly. The Old Man was never pleased to get up to a cold house. And, of course, there were the water pipes to keep from freezing – but not this day.

The fire started easily, the bank the night before having been successful. I was upstairs, washed, dressed and ready for breakfast before anyone else was up. Which speed of effort did me no good at all. Hunting hours in Ohio began (and for all I know, still do) at nine o'clock in the morning. And all the rushing and dashing about would not bring them sooner by one tick-tocking second. I waited.

Eventually, the Old Man and my mother came downstairs

to the kitchen. He sat down next to me and we watched as my mother made breakfast. A hunter's breakfast was a thing of beauty in our household. I'd gone with my father before, but never for a whole day, and never with a gun.

My mother put bacon slices in a spider (a 12-inch cast iron skillet to those of you who have known only Teflon-lined cookware), and popped Beefsteak rye bread into the toaster. Then she filled the percolator and put coffee in the basket, and turned it on. Soon the bacon was turned, the toast popped and was turned end-for-end and reset, and coffee was perking away.

Mother never hurried, but as each item was finished, she dealt with it and moved to the next. Nothing was overcooked and nothing was raw. The toast popped up, black but not burned. She laid it on a plate and dropped in two more. She handed the plate and butter to the Old Man and scooped the bacon onto two slices of white bread to absorb the grease. She broke six eggs into the hot grease, and the toaster popped again. Once again, she flipped the toast, and grabbed a spatula. Turning back to the stove, she salted and peppered the eggs and flipped them. She took the toast plate from the Old Man, and within seconds, the eggs were on two plates, the toast plate and another, onto which she dropped the next two slices of toast as the toaster popped.

She handed the plates through to the breakfast bar. The Old Man gave me the one with the buttered toast and began buttering the new slices on his plate. Mother poured two cups of coffee and handed them through, giving the Old Man a small pitcher of cream to go with his. He poured some in his coffee and some in a Thermos sitting next to him, which he handed through to Mother. She filled it with coffee, closed it and handed it back. Then she started a new pot of coffee.

"Aren't you eating?" I asked.

"I will when you two are gone," she said.

As we finished breakfast, the Old Man collected rye and white bread, butter, lunch meat, peanut butter and jelly. "Make yourself a lunch," he said. "We'll be out all day."

We each packed a lunch, and it was near time. We stuffed the lunches, and in the Old Man's case, the coffee, into the game pouches in our field jackets, and booted up. Mine were buckled galoshes over work shoes. The Old Man wore Converse hip boots. This would be important on later hunts.

He checked me over; gun, shells, boots, gloves ("Here, put another pair in your pocket.") and hat. "You'll do," he growled. "Let's get the dogs."

We went outside and he took my gun and broke it. He handed it back and said, "Carry it broke until we get in the woods." I nodded and draped it over my forearm.

We rounded up the beagles (I believe the Old Man had three or four at the time), and walked on back to the woods. The field behind the house was about 200 yards deep, and ended at a woodlot about a hundred feet deep and a mile long heading south. To the east, it ended in a swampy floodplain, which a family of beavers later turned into a shallow lake and full-blown swamp. But this day we headed west.

One of the hounds bayed and a bunny popped out of nowhere and bounded away before we'd even fully entered the woods. I yanked the little .410 up and realized as it snapped shut all the shells were still in my pockets. The Old Man burst out laughing. "Easy, Son," he said. "They'll be back, and the bunny'll be ahead of 'em." And so it was. But I never saw the rabbit, and the Old Man shot him.

"You'll get one," the Old Man said, "just be patient. You have to watch at least a hundred feet ahead of 'em." I nodded, remembering what he had told me on hunts where I carried no gun. Cottontails run out ahead of dogs and then maintain that distance as the dogs track. It saves energy and they can make a big circle and get back home. The last thing they want to do is go somewhere they've never been.

The dogs bayed again. This time the Old Man stood next to me and pointed out where the chase was going. It didn't take long to learn how to figure where they were. The day was clear and a little warm and the dogs trailed well. You could almost "see" with your ears as they circled and returned.

"There!" the Old Man whispered, pointing, "right by that thicket." Yeah – right. "That" thicket was pretty much everywhere. But I followed where he pointed, and a cottontail obliged by taking a short hop forward.

I pulled the little .410 up and made a terrifying discovery. We were having an earthquake! The front site was jittering like a bobber on a fish-line and the rabbit was hopping about without moving. But I was determined. I pulled the trigger as the sight jittered past the bobbing rabbit. Silence! What th'...

The Old Man was laughing again. "The hammer, Son," he said, "cock the hammer."

"Oh, yeah, I know," I said sheepishly, cocking it. I raised it again. The jittering was much improved. As soon as I saw the rabbit over the sights, I yanked the trigger. Lord only knows where the shot went, but the rabbit took off.

"Reload," commanded the Old Man.

I shoved the break lever aside, broke the shotgun – and I couldn't get the shell out. I looked up, and the rabbit was just finishing a small circle and starting another one. But the jersey gloves I was wearing were both thick and slippery. The shell wouldn't come out.

"Wait a minute," I muttered. "Just a minute, darnit."

"Take your gloves off, Charles," the Old Man said, "but you'd better hurry. The dogs are coming."

I could hear them. I ripped off my glove and finally got hold of the shell. I yanked it out and promptly lost it. I rammed my hand in my pocket and pulled out a half dozen shells. As I tried to cram one in the chamber, I muttered again, "Just a minute. Wait. Wait a minute." A shell slid home, and I dropped the extra shells and snapped the gun shut. The rabbit took off and I raised the gun, swung past him and fired. The front of the gun was rock-steady. He did a flip, and it was over. My first kill.

The Old Man told that story for the rest of his life. He wondered forever at me telling that rabbit to wait. "And it did," he'd say with wonder, "it *did*."

CHAPTER 17

Christmas on the Farm, Part 1: The Days Before Christmas

Christmas shopping was organized chaos in our household. The Old Man worked a six-day week at the Standard Slag Sand and Gravel Company. The sand and gravel mine was on the next road east, a mile behind our house. He often walked to work in winter, taking his shotgun and hunting on the way home.

Mother worked at the Ravenna Hospital as a relief and private duty nurse, so her workdays and hours were often erratic. But she would reserve two Saturdays before Christmas for Christmas shopping. One Saturday was an excursion to Akron, often with one of her sisters. Our arrival at Main and Market Streets was a dive into a cacophony of horns and the clanging bells of the electric trolleys. The car would slip on the wet steel of the rails embedded in the brick streets, giving us children in the back seat a shiver of fear. And the smell! The odor of ozone from the constant sparking of the spring-elevated power bars on the trolleys pressing against the network of bare wires overhead was overpowering.

Mother would park in the covered garage at O'Neil's Department Store and she and her sister would head into the store. Mother, at five feet ten, erect as an evergreen, would stride forward, towing the sister of the day. We three would trail them through O'Neil's and Polsky's department stores while they shopped. They bought Christmas decorations, clothes and household items, and looked for bargains that had little to do with Christmas.

Mother and her sisters all sewed and the Christmas shopping expedition was an opportunity to buy new patterns and fabrics. So we would troop into the fabric department, and the agony would begin.

They would take their time, feeling the fabrics, testing the stretch, holding it to the light (I *still* have no idea why), laying one pattern next to another, re-checking patterns and all the while the Christmas shop and Santa waited on the ninth floor.

The Christmas shop was a magical place, even for a thirteen-year-old boy. It was a maze of hallways, flanked by lighted dioramas of animated elves making toys, miniature towns with miniature O'Neil's and Polsky's stores, drugstores, specialty shops and restaurants. People and cars moved through the towns, and if you looked carefully, you might even see two women with three children trailing them. And then there was *Santa*!

Resplendent in snow-white beard, bright red suit and polished black boots, he sat on a gilded throne, laughing heartily as each child sat on his lap. And children came by the thousands to do so. By the time we were eight, of course, Giles and I had been disabused of the notion of a *real* Santa, but Lyndella had not. We two, with the maturity that came with being thirteen and eleven, stepped aside with Mother and the aunt as she entered the last red velvet-roped aisle.

She slowly ascended the inclined ramp as child after child sat on Santa's lap, whispered in his ear, had a photo taken (mothers scribbled addresses on an order pad and handed over dollar bills to one of the elves) and ran down a side aisle to waiting family. At last, it was her turn. She strode confidently up to Santa, was lifted onto his lap, leaned toward him, wrinkled her nose and said, "You smell like pee."

With remarkable aplomb, Santa laughed heartily, ignored her comment and asked what she wanted for Christmas.

"A Flexible Flyer sled!" she declared, and hopped off his lap. Mother handed over her dollar and scribbled her address in an agony of embarrassment, and off we went to Polsky's, directly across Main Street, where the entire process was repeated in excruciating detail, even to the visit with Santa (where Lyndella announced that *he* did *not* smell like pee).

As the sky began to darken, we returned to O'Neil's, where we filled the trunk of the 1950 Studebaker with packages. Then we headed back into the store, where we ensconced ourselves in the store restaurant. O'Neil's featured a full-service restaurant on the second floor, and it was tradition to finish our shopping day with sandwiches and soup before heading out to ooh and aah over the Main Street store window Christmas displays.

O'Neil's and Polsky's Christmas windows featured, of course, the wonders available for purchase inside the stores. But they also featured dioramas even more elaborate than those in their Christmas shops (I had not yet realized that the Christmas shop displays were recycled from previous years' window displays). Many of the smaller shops along Main Street also featured animated displays, and we would walk, shivering, teeth chattering, from store to store, until the cold drove us back to O'Neil's and our car.

By eight o'clock, we would join the throng of cars exiting the garage and honking its way through the trolley-crowded streets. And, although it seemed to take forever to escape the traffic, we were home by ten o'clock, having dropped the aunt off, with her packages (except for the one that always seemed to get left for Mother to deliver on her next work-day at the hospital).

A week or two later, we would repeat the process, much less frantically, in Ravenna. This time, it was children's day. *We* were shopping for each other and our parents. Christmas lists had been exchanged among the three of us, and we knew the stores. At thirteen, I was old enough to shop alone but Mother took Lyndella and Giles was accompanied by an aunt.

For Giles, I bought a Spaulding Official Basketball and a Barlow pocketknife. This last had engendered significant conversation before the Old Man had given his permission. But I had one, and Giles was determined he would have one too. It seemed only fitting that I be the one to give it to him.

For Lyndella, I bought a doll and a make-up kit filled with pretend make-up. Almost-seven-year-old girls were *very* hard for a thirteen-year-old boy to buy for.

Mother received the traditional gift kit of bath oils and "perfume." The five-dollar per parent allowance did not extend to much in the way of imaginative gifts for a mother on the part of a young boy. But for the Old Man, well...

The Old Man smoked unfiltered Camel cigarettes and he hunted. Moreover, it had been announced that the next year would be the first year in a generation that Ohio would have a deer season. Christmas for the Old Man was easy. For three dollars, I bought a deer drag... a rope harness to be placed around the deer's front feet and looped over its head (There was a handy illustration right on the front of the package!).

For a dollar eighty, I bought a bright red carton of Camels, with a grinning Santa smoking a Camel instead of his pipe (yes, I *know* I said I was thirteen – nobody thought *I* was going to smoke them). In addition, I already had a gift for him. That summer, at 4-H Camp, I had made a leather cigarette pack holder in craft class. I kept the few cents change that had not gone for taxes.

Came the weekend before Christmas, the Old Man took Giles and me to choose a tree. There was a tree lot in Streetsboro and the trees were cut daily from the lot-owner's tree farm. The lot owner was the local Agricultural Extension Agent and my 4-H advisor. He and the Old Man would hold trees at arm's length and shake them, inspect the trunk for hidden curves that would make it hard to keep the tree straight in a tree stand, look for gaps and bare spaces, and generally beat the entire joy of tree-buying into the ground. But eventually we would have an eight-foot tree tied to the roof of the Studebaker and off we'd go for the four-mile trip home.

Once we were home, the tree was shortened two feet and the branches were cut from the butt. These would become wreaths (buying an eight-foot tree was *much* cheaper than buying a six-foot tree and branches for garlands and wreaths separately). My brother and I would be sent across the road to scour the woods for an evergreen vine called ground pine, the fronds of which looked much like the ends of branches of arborvitae. This vine was wound together with the wintergreen and bittersweet we collected with the ground pine to make garlands and wreaths of three shades of green festooned with bright orange berries.

The tree was set in its holder (filled with water daily), uprighted, and set in front of the living-room center window. We made construction-paper garlands, popcorn and cranberry drapes and hung those first. The Old Man would drape the lights around the tree, skillfully making sure that it was evenly lit. Then he would add the bubble-candles, and carefully unwrap the delicate glass balls of shaped and colored glass.

Once the glass balls were hung, Mother would begin draping tinsel (the real stuff – made of lead so it would actually *hang*) and we children would press static-held nativity scenes to the windows and spray around them with fake snow. The ground pine garlands and evergreen wreaths would be draped around and hung on the doors to greet visitors, and Mother would serve eggnog before sending us off to bed.

For the next week, we secretively wrapped our gifts and, come Christmas Eve, we brought out those gifts and placed them under the tree, knowing that in the morning they would be but a small part of the Christmas gift-opening frenzy. Then we went to the Christmas Eve church pageant, finally falling asleep, exhausted, at near-midnight. It was twenty years later when I had children of my own that I learned what happened between midnight and Christmas morning.

CHAPTER 18

Christmas on the Farm, Part 2: The Big Day

The Old Man had a problem... Christmas was downstairs, much of it was not disguisable, and his children would need a trip to the bathroom in the worst way come Christmas morning. And the bathroom was downstairs. As they turned from the end of the walled-in stairway, they would face the tree, and all the gifts, in the center of the living room. But the Old Man was not without resources...

***

As we pounded down the stairs and around the corner, we came face to face with the new center-wall bay window, decorated with sprayed-on snow, icicles and static-bond Santas, but of the tree which had stood there the night before, there was no sign. Every Christmas decoration we had hung on the window side of the room remained, in fact there were *more* decorations than there had been the night before – but *no tree!* Disbelief! Pandemonium! Outrage!

I recovered first. *"Dad!* Somebody stole our tree, with all the presents!"

"Really? Well, get done in the bathroom and come up here and get dressed." The Old Man seemed unconcerned.

Having had attention to our bursting bladders re-asserted, there was no possibility of ignoring them longer. Still, "But, *Da-ad..."*

"Do as I told you." Not the voice the Old Man used when

you could argue with him. This was the voice he used when obedience was the better part of valor.

Lyndella, being only almost seven, broke first. As she slammed the bathroom door in our faces, Giles and I squeezed our thighs together and yelled imprecations through the door. But soon we were all three back upstairs, scrambling into our clothes.

Mother had gone downstairs and the sounds and smells of frying bacon, hot sweet-rolls and percolating coffee drifted up. "Breakfast!" she called.

We looked at the Old Man. "Breakfast! Let's go," he said, shooing us toward the stairs.

"But, Da-ad, the tree!" we protested.

"Breakfast," he said, pointing to the kitchen as we exited the stairwell.

We trooped into the kitchen where bacon, eggs-over-easy, toast and sweet-rolls were piled on serving plates, and coffee and milk were being poured. I looked at the Old Man and took a breath.

"Breakfast!" He pointed to my chair. I sat; bacon, eggs and toast appeared on my plate. I ate.

***

To avoid scratching the new asphalt tile floor, the Old Man had placed a strip of carpet beneath the tree stand. Grasping it firmly, and with Mother steadying the tree, he pulled it slowly through the oversized door at the foot of the stairs into the south wing of the house. Once through the door, they reset the tree in front of the first window in the meeting-room sized parlor. Carefully, he and Mother rearranged all the presents under and around the tree, adding a few packages and some unpackaged gifts that had not been there earlier.

They returned to the living room. The Old Man got the garland and wreath from the kitchen door. They draped the garland around the living room window frame. He suspended the wreath from a hook in the center of the frame so it showed in the upper center of the window. He added more sprayed snow and rearranged the static-cling Christmas scenes so the window no longer showed an evergreen-shaped space where the tree had been. By four in the morning they were done.

The Old Man went to the basement, re-fired the old coal furnace, and went to bed after shutting off my alarm. Refiring the furnace in the morning was my job, and that would never do this morning.

At seven-thirty, we could wait no longer and went to their room, demanding that we go downstairs and start Christmas. But there had been no Tree!

***

Finally, I could no longer endure the silence. The elephant in the living room threatened all of Christmas. We three had bolted breakfast, but the Old Man and Mother were still eating with careful and quiet deliberation.

"Dad," I erupted, "the *tree*! It's *gone*! We *told* you!"

"Gone? Gone where? What tree?" Deliberately he wiped his mouth and rose. "Let's have a look."

We all headed into the living room. With all the drama of Charlie Chan exposing the murderer, I faced the family, flung my arm toward the window and announced, "See? The tree's *gone!*"

"What tree?" asked the Old Man. "Doesn't look to me as if

there were ever a tree in here."

I looked at the window. He was right! Giles was flabbergasted and said so. Lyndella was just confused. "Why are there pine needles on the floor?" she asked.

The Old Man exploded into laughter. "The little ones always see the trick," he said. "Bitsy, I think you've found me out. Come on." He headed for the south wing.

Giles and I looked at each other, understanding dawning. We surged ahead of him, threw open the door and ran into the room, sliding to a halt in our stocking feet. The tree was there, all right.

And it was flanked by all the wonders of a Christmas beyond our best dreams. There was not one, not two, but *three* Flexible Flyer American Eagle sleds, the steerable, steel-runnered wonders of the slopes. And there were *skis*! Two pair of skis crossed at the tips and arranged with their poles in tee-pee fashion. Within the "teepee" was a stack of packages (which proved to contain nothing but clothing, but we expected that – there remained packages *under* the tree).

I received an Ansco snapshot camera and, when I looked outside, it was the perfect gift. It snowed that Christmas Eve, a soft, fluffy, damp snow that built up on branches and limbs so that all the trees looked white and wooly against the bright blue sky. I shot an entire roll (24 shots) of film trying to get the perfect picture of one of those trees. I wonder if I did. The film is long since lost in the mists of moves and life changes.

Mother expressed great joy at the three bath-beads and perfume sets she got from her children. The Old Man was pleased with his cigarettes (he lit one immediately), the cigarette pack holder (he never used it after that day) and the rope halter that the box showed being used to haul a freshly killed buck (it came in very handy the next winter).

Giles was happy to receive a Spaulding Official Basketball, but his joy was unmistakable and his thanks beyond effusive when he opened the oversized box and dug through the crumpled tissue paper to find the Barlow pocketknife. I really liked the Wilson Tru-Shot basketball he gave me, a much better ball than I'd been able to afford for him after I bought the Barlow. Lyndella thought the doll was "awful pretty," and the pretend make-up was "very nice." She promptly took a bite of candy lipstick.

There were new winter coats, hats and gloves, and boots, all of which had to be tested. But the wonder of the day was the cluster of three American Flyer sleds two full-length sleds, at least four and a half feet long for Giles and me, and one "shortie," about three feet long for Lyndella. We pulled on the coats, hats, boots and gloves. We grabbed our glorious sleds and headed out the door.

Soon we were across the road, coasting down the back of the hill in the pasture, flattening snow and grass. Well, sort of. The area of northeast Ohio in which we lived was where the last glaciations stopped. There were hills, valleys and pothole lakes that made no sense, unless you understood that as the glaciers retreated, they left giant blocks of ice that contained gravel, sand and soil, and other blocks of mostly ice. As they melted, they left piles and holes. It was down one of these small hills called kames that we attempted to sled.

But the grass was tall and uncut – and dry, with the snow piled as much beneath it as on it. The sleds wouldn't move. We stomped up and down the hill, burying grass in the snow, and finally created a path down which the sleds would at least move, but slowly. Giles went looking for a better spot, and he found it! In the woods where the hill swept around to the west, there was a two-track path, established by the loggers who followed the 1952 tornado. There was also an open-strip cut that ran to the top of the hill, probably as a skid by those same loggers. There was less snow under the trees, but the leaves had wetted and refrozen and that path was streaky fast, with a jump where the two-track ran.

We spent the next two hours speeding down the track, taking turns getting Lyndella's sled going on the lower part, and generally having more fun than winter ought to be. The sleds were all they'd been cracked up to be fast, flexible, steerable – and *fun*! The skis? Those we left for another day. I never did master them in the slightest degree. Giles got to be pretty good on his.

It got to be noon, and we were called into the house. Every Christmas, the Gadd sisters got together at either Edna's or Ella's for a gigantic potluck meal and gift exchange. Each cousin had pulled a "Secret Santa" name from a box, and purchased an appropriate two-dollar gift. Aunts got presents for each other's children, and Grandma Gadd got presents for us all (mine from her that year was a snow shovel).

Once the dinner was eaten and gifts were exchanged, there was the family photo to do – Grandma Gadd, surrounded by three generations of her descendants.

After the photo, the children were shooed outside (with me as the eldest admonished to keep everybody else out of trouble). We had brought one sled but there were no hills at Aunt Edna's, so Giles and I played horse and gave everybody else rides around the yard on the sled. I took more photos (also long since lost in the mists of time and house moves) and basked in the responsibility of being the oldest and "in charge."

There may have been better Christmases at the farm, but I don't remember one.

CHAPTER 19

Measles, Mumps, Chicken Pox and Fear

"Dick! Dick, come here and look at Charles' face!" Mother was an RN, a registered nurse, and she knew full well what she had seen on my face. But she didn't want to see what she was sure she saw.

The Old Man walked into the kitchen where I was eating breakfast (and feeling poorly, truth to tell), took a quick look, stood back and then bent close to take a better look. "Measles," he announced, stepping back. "I'll pack a bag."

In America in the '50s, measles meant quarantine. The Old Man had to be out of the house before the doctor got there or he'd be locked in with us. Locked in, as in no going to work – as in no money – as in no job by the time he got out, if they were nine-day measles. As it turned out, they were. As it also turned out it didn't matter.

Doctor Knowlton showed up later that day. Mother had me in a darkened room (measles can cause serious vision damage if one's eyes are exposed to full light) and my brother Giles was playing in the yard. Lyndella, only six, was downstairs with Mother. None of us had been allowed to go to school. Mother had given the bus driver a note for the principal.

Doc Knowlton peered into my eyes, ears and throat. He said, "Mm-m-m. Hm-m-m," a lot, turned me over and looked at my back, said, "Mm-m-m. Hm-m-m," some more and stood up.

"Nine-day measles, Pat," he said to Mother. "Where's Dick?"

"He went to work," Mother said, carefully not mentioning that he'd known about the measles before he left.

"Can you get hold of him and leave a bag outside the door for him?"

"Of course," she said, "I can call the company."

"The other two will get it," he said, "but they should all be okay." They left the room.

Thus began the most frustrating three *months* of my life.

The Old Man went to live with Aunt Edna and Uncle Orville for the couple weeks it would take the measles to run their course for the three of us.

First Giles and then Lyndella came down with the nine-day measles. Giles waited nearly a week. Lyndella sprouted a rash three days later, as I was in final recovery. I faced yet another ten days of isolation.

Each day of my incarceration, my teachers would put together a "care package" of homework for me (and for Giles, of course Lyndella got a pass). While we were in the darkened room, Mother would read our assignments to us and write out our answers to questions and tests. We were in essence home-schooled. Mother was a good teacher. She had taught me to read before I was four. She'd never heard of "phonics," but she knew what syllables were and she taught me the skill of what she called "syllablatics" (a skill that drove at least two of my early teachers to distraction). It was a relief to come out of the dark room and do my schoolwork at the kitchen table until the day my sister came down with the measles and I woke with a VERY sore throat.

As Doc Knowlton and Mother left the others' darkened

rooms I said "Mom, my throat hurts."

"Well," said jovial Doc Knowlton, "let's have a look." And have a look he did. More, "Mm-m-m hm-m-m-ms," with a couple "Well, wells," tossed in, and he straightened up. "Pat, do you have any orange juice?"

Mother produced a glass of orange juice (which I despised anyway) and handed it to Doc Knowlton.

"Down the hatch, Charles," and he handed me the glass.

I took a swallow and shrieked as I swallowed. Crying and choking, I said miserably, "It hurts, Mom."

"Thought so," said the good Doctor; "mumps." He turned to the sink to wash his hands.

Mother was aghast. "Mumps! How?"

"Dunno, Pat." Doc shrugged. "Maybe brought in on the schoolwork. Some of the kids I'm seeing have mumps."

What he didn't suggest was that *he* might be the carrier.

Days passed. In the fullness of time, each of my siblings came down with mumps. Lyndella suffered both mumps and measles together. Then each of us came down with three-day measles, and then *chicken pox*! And of course there was no structure. There was never a time for weeks when we could break quarantine. And then...

Giles came down with something new. His face was shrieking red. He spiked a high fever and Mother was obviously frightened.

Doc Knowlton came out of Giles' room. "Pat," he said, and his voice was somehow different, "I think Giles has Scarlet Fever."

Mother just looked at him.

"We have to keep Charles and Lyndella away from him, Pat, and you have to really be a nurse for this one. Rubber gloves, mask, separate laundry the whole nine yards. This one's really dangerous."

Mother set up a tight regimen. Doc Knowlton brought several pairs of rubber gloves and a half dozen surgical masks for Mother, which she literally boiled every couple days. She would not enter Giles' room without gloves and mask. Lyndella and I could not pass through Giles' door frame at all. She carried his food in and his dishes out. Giles ate on "picnic plates," which she burned when he was done. And she made it her business to entertain him. He was going to be essentially alone in that room for at least a month, and this was late February.

Then, Mother found a large, bright green chrysalis on a bare bush in the back yard and brought it inside, still attached to the branch. She put it in a small fish tank that she arranged to have delivered, and gave it to Giles, along with articles about and color pictures of the caterpillar that made the chrysalis, and the *huge* green Luna Moth it would become. The chrysalis became his focus. He would talk of nothing else as Lyndella and I stood in his doorway (Lyndella seldom stood long).

Mother did not tell us until later how frightened she was. In the '50s, Scarlet Fever killed children. But Lyndella and I knew nothing of that. We were, in fact, more than a little jealous of Giles. He got his own radio in his room (we had a nine-inch TV in the middle of a huge "entertainment cabinet," but TV time was much restricted). He got comic books that were *burned* after he read them. Balsa-wood models came to the house for him to build. But he, of course, could not go outside and play in the barn, or go sledding.

In April, Giles began to recover, and Doc Knowlton was puzzled. "Pat," he said finally, "I don't think Giles has Scarlet

Fever. I think he has Scarletina."

Scarletina was a Scarlet Fever mimic. It lasted longer, but its effects were much less dramatic. Most important, it didn't kill children.

Within a couple days, Giles was out of bed, quarantine was lifted, and the Old Man returned. Sunday, we prepared for the next day's school.

Monday, the Old Man met us in the kitchen. "Don't tell anybody," he said, "but your mother has mumps. If you tell *anybody*, they'll quarantine us again, and I *can't* spend another day in the same house with your Uncle Orville and Aunt Edna!" We all nodded and trooped back to our parents' room.

Mother didn't tell us how much worse Mumps could be for adults. She looked at us and said she'd be okay. Lyndella was sent to live with a neighbor who also had a six-year-old girl, because the Old Man didn't think he could take proper care of her. The Old Man and I shared cooking duties and Mother was nurse for herself. By the end of the week, she was up and about and so far as I know we carried her mumps to no one else.

The cocoon began to split one Saturday in late May. Giles took the little square fish tank outside and watched. The wonder was agonizingly slow to complete. Hours after it began, Giles started screaming for us to come out and see. Minute after minute the back shoved through the split in the cocoon, until finally the insect stood on the outside of its winter quarters and transformation station.

We were all thunderstruck. Giles was devastated. "It's broken," he sobbed. "It's gonna die."

But Mother knew better. "Remember the book," she said, "the wing veins have to fill with air. He'll be all right. Keep watching."

So we watched. Slowly, oh painfully slowly, the wet, crumpled, broken-looking wings began to straighten and flatten, as the great moth pumped air into their veins. And then it was there, huge, green and complete – wings flattened and slowly flapping, testing... then abruptly it took off, flitting to a perch on a maple branch, resting but a few moments and then leaving.

We never saw the great green night-flyer again, but Giles talked about it for a long time – a *very* long time – thereafter

Later on, it became apparent in the community that the carrier had *not* been schoolwork handled by sick but unsymptomatic children. The medical profession figured it out too. Doctors making house calls expanded epidemics. We were not the only family with a rolling thunder of disease.

Doctors don't make house calls any more, largely because their patients have transportation options we didn't have back then and because house-to-house medicine is gawd-awfully inefficient, but the spread of the diseases they were treating was a part of the reason too.

CHAPTER 20

Pullets, Eggs and Judges, Oh My

The front yard of our farmhouse comprised two Sugar Maples, one Norway Maple, one Norway Spruce and two White Birch and almost *no* grass from the front of the house halfway to the dirt road. The Old Man spent the next twenty years at war with that lawn trying to get grass to grow under the maples, with no success at all. The shade was simply too dense. Even weeds didn't grow in that packed soil. The back yard was large, open and a mass of dandelion and plantain. Grass fought gamely for space, but it was years before we could call it a "lawn." Nonetheless, I shoved the old reel-type mower across it every week, beginning the summer I turned ten years old.

And the year I turned ten, I did what nearly all the farm kids did. I became a member of an organization called 4-H. We were given the opportunity to be responsible for small-scale farm activities: raise a small garden, raise 25 chickens, build a "trouble lamp," and so forth. In 1954 (I was not yet twelve, though I would be before the summer was out), after a couple years of small projects, I chose the lamp and chickens. The lamp was a simple and basic device and I had it built soon after the instructions and parts were delivered. But the chickens...

"Charles, twenty-five chickens will be nothing but trouble. It'll cost more to buy them, house them and feed them than you'll make off the eggs and selling them for roasting hens." My mother was farm-reared and she thought in terms of profit.

into the coops, with exit windows at floor level to allow them into the "run" between the buildings. I got larger feeders and watering cans and set up fewer throughout the coop. My mornings went faster and I had time to eat breakfast *every* morning.

I began finding crushed eggs here and there. I greatly feared there would be no eggs for me. I shouldn't have worried. Small eggs ("pullet" eggs) began to show up in the laying boxes. The Old Man and I built a "candling box." Eggs must be candled before you sell them. If you hold an egg up between you and a light, you can (sort of) see inside it. You can see enough to tell whether the egg has been fertilized, whether it's old and needs to be thrown out and whether those seeming cracks are real, among other things.

We built a box out of 3/8-inch plywood and one-by-two boards to nail it to. We cut a hole in the top, and built a base with a short lamp attached to it, into which we inserted a light bulb. To "candle" an egg, one turns on the light, places each end of the egg by turns against the hole, and slowly rotates the egg, looking for spots on the yolk (which would indicate a fertilized egg), cracks in the shell, off-center yolk, double yolk (a prize, indeed), and so forth.

I began peddling eggs to the neighbors and the little store down at the corner. The Old Man went to the local Farm Bureau feed store and bought a hundred dozen-egg boxes. Back then the egg spaces were arranged three deep and four wide. He went to the local stationery store and bought rolls of sticky labels that said:

Chuck's Eggs

Along with the labels he bought a crockery "wetting wheel" to avoid licking the labels (no such thing as self-sticking labels in 1954).

Once we were past the pullet egg stage, we also made a "sizing board" out of heavy cardboard with lath to stiffen it. Eggs are size-graded by girth, so the smallest hole through which an egg would pass endwise was the size of the egg. The Old Man bought more egg boxes and labels that said:

Farm Fresh Eggs

Size _____

It was my responsibility to write in the size eggs for each box. We sold six sizes (although the first two faded fairly soon): Pullet, Small, Medium, Large, Extra Large and Jumbo. There were often enough double-yolkers to make up a box or two. Those brought a premium from Mrs. Nelson.

Along with the chickens came 4-H responsibilities. It was up to me to track expenses and income for the birds, including the cost of the chicks, feed, coop renovations, vet visits, egg boxes, labels and everything else. I was given an accounting booklet and a short course in double-entry bookkeeping.

But it was the chickens themselves that were truly the talk of the town. With one small exception, these hens were identical to Leghorn Hens. They *looked* like Leghorns (relatively small white hens that lay large white eggs prolifically) and they laid eggs of pure and dazzling white as prolifically as Leghorns. But these chickens were *black* with the exception of one tiny hen who we named Brunhilda, much as a very large man may be nick-named "Tiny."

Brunhilda was a "Polish sumthin-or-other," and she was *tiny*! She was not half the size of the other hens, but she was boss of her little coterie of hens. All chickens will form into groups of about a dozen and establish a "pecking order" within each group and between groups. The term "pecking order" comes, in fact, from observing flocks of domestic chickens. They establish dominance by literally pecking each other. Low-order hens will be pecked, by *everybody*, until they bleed, mostly from the tail.

The cure was to cover the tail with tar, and that was a daily chore. I had a six-foot length of steel wire, one end of which I bent into a narrow "S." I would walk among the hens as they ran and squawked, and sweep the S-hook around the leg of a chicken, pull her in (her attempts to escape kept her locked into the catcher). It was about a half-hour's work every evening to catch and tar the bleeding hens.

Brunhilda was a terror. Instead of a comb, she had a topknot of floppy black and white feathers, each about an inch-and-a-half long. She was mostly black, with a white breast and tail, and she was the top hen in the coop. When both coops were out in the fenced "run," Brunhilda was Number One among 250 other hens, and "her" girls could peck *anybody*. She did her share, too. She appropriated the window-end laying-box in the top row, and there was an egg in that nest every day.

All 4-H projects had to be exhibited at the County Fair to be "complete." I took my Black Leghorns (and Brunhilda), along with all my accounting. The judges came by, asking each boy or girl a question or two, giving the account-booklets a quick look-see, and picking up a chicken or two, and handing out ribbons of various colors. Once they finished, all first-place winning "laying hens" would be re-evaluated, and one of that elite group would win the coveted "Champion" ribbon.

When the judges got to me, everything stopped. Nobody had warned them and they'd never seen shiny, black hens before. And they had *definitely* never seen a hen like Brunhilda. I hastened to assure them that she was just there to keep order (the exhibit hens were from various coteries), and that only the black hens were part of my project. It didn't seem to mollify them.

I showed them eggs laid during the night and proved that they were wonderful producers. I was already in the black, even considering the cost of renovations, and I hadn't even *begun* selling the hens themselves as "roasting hens." When they said that none of it mattered, I was crushed.

"Charles," the head judge's voice was kind, but bad news was coming, "I can't tell whether they're equal to, ahead of or behind others like them, because I've never *seen* others like them. Because you get more eggs every day than you have chickens, I'm going to assume they're doing well. You're showing a profit. You'll make even more when you sell the hens. But what I *can't* tell is, 'could somebody else have done even better?' I just can't *tell!*" He wound down.

I was near tears. The Old Man was near apoplexy. His normally pale skin was blotchy red, and his voice was *very* quiet and it shook, just a little, when he spoke. "Show me," it wasn't a request, "where it says they have to be a breed you know. Show me where it says you can't judge these birds on their own condition and by their own production."

"Well," the judge had *no* idea what to do next. "Well, I guess we can judge them against general condition and production." He looked at his fellows. They nodded. "They all seem to be in excellent condition even her." He pointed to Brunhilda. "And their production is definitely higher than average, even for Leghorns." He looked to his fellows again. "Judged against those factors, I believe these chickens have earned a first place ribbon." The other judges nodded, but I was too busy gawking at all the people, my fellow 4-H members and their parents, who had gathered to watch. As the judge hung the bright blue first-place ribbon on our cage, they all clapped and cheered and laughed. I beamed. The Old Man looked surprised.

"However," the judge was using the "kind voice – bad news coming" voice again, "I'm afraid you won't be eligible for the Championship ribbon."

There was a garble of sound, moving rapidly from confusion and uncertainty to anger, as people told each other what the judge had said. A man wearing a 4-H armband stepped up to the judge and whispered in his ear. They left, and the other judges followed. I felt deflated. I just *knew* that wasn't fair. People commiserated and left, and soon the Old Man and I were alone. "I'm sorry, Son," he said sadly, "it's not fair, but there's nothing I can do."

"You don't have to 'do' anything, Mr. Larlham," it was the 4-H official who'd led the judge away, "it's taken care of. Charles' chickens are eligible." He shook the Old Man's hand, and then mine.

I stammered some sort of thanks, and he just smiled and left.

The Old Man looked at the black hens, and then at me. "If they're fair, you'll win, you know."

"What if they're not?"

"Then you set your jaw, smile and say, 'Thank you.'"

I nodded. It hadn't really been a question. I didn't think I'd cry.

The judges came back. All the first place winners brought out their records, their best birds, and their eggs. I put the best hen to sleep (tucked her head under her wing and swung her in a big slow circle) and handed her to the judge. He took her without speaking. My heart sank.

They inspected every chicken, every egg, the accounting booklets and everything they could touch or see. They asked interminable questions about our care methods, our salesmanship, how much help we got (none, once the re-modeling was done), and a million other things, it seemed. Finally, they stood to the side and talked, and talked, and I was wondering whether they'd forgotten us when they came back.

The judges called a girl forward, and my heart sank. After a seemingly endless speech about how well she'd done, he presented her with *Reserve* Grand Champion! Now I *was* ready to bawl. It wasn't fair; they wouldn't even give me *Reserve* Grand Cham... Had someone called my name?

Oh, indeed someone had. My "Black Leghorns" were Grand Champions of the 4-H laying hens!

Brunhilda was so proud, she laid an egg.

CHAPTER 21

Misadventures in Horticulture – 4-H Redux

I remained in 4-H until I was 18 (Once I turned 14, it was mostly about the girls who owned horses – not that they paid *me* a blind bit of attention. I didn't have a horse). Once the last of the hens had been delivered to Forney's Meat Market, I was ready to never see (or eat) another chicken (or egg) as long as I lived.

The next morning, over a breakfast of bacon, rye toast (burnt) and eggs over easy (okay, when it comes to food, my resolve has been known to weaken occasionally), I was informed that next year's project would be half the garden my mother usually planted. "Why half?" I asked plaintively, thinking that was an awful lot of garden. A half of Mother's garden, after all, meant a half acre of garden. Perhaps I could negotiate down to a half of a half, still a lot, but...

"Because your brother will have the other half," came the crushing response. Giles, upon reaching the appropriate age, had been tossed into the 4-H blender without as much as a thought. Of *course* he wanted to. I wasn't so sure. Giles was even less enthusiastic than I about farm activities. In any case, the two of us were gonna each be responsible for a half-acre garden.

"And," Mother was on a roll, "for your second project..." My heart sank. I could feel it coming. If she was choosing next year's projects in October, I wasn't gonna like it. Mother had a knack for getting the most out of any situation, and having a 13-year-old and an 11-year-old in 4-H was definitely a "situation." "...Giles will raise rabbits, and..." Well, that wasn't so bad; Giles had been talking about rabbits ever since Aunt Ella had shown him hers. And rabbits *were* a 4-H project. "...you will have chickens again." So much for hope.

When we had moved to the farm, Mother had stood at the edge of the front yard that first Saturday morning, gazing toward the south property line. "Asparagus," she said, pointing to a low area consisting of couple acres of tall grass and feathery weeds between us and the property line, "...a *lot* of asparagus." I had no idea the ubiquitous six-foot tall "feathery weeds" were the end product of those eight-inch spears of foul-tasting plants we bought at Kroger. But they were everywhere. There were at *least* two acres of them. The bad news was that the same two acres were home to a plow-eating species of grass called "quack grass."

Early the next spring, a small red Farm-All tractor was in the quack grass pulling a four-bottom plow. For the uninitiated, a "four-bottom" plow is a frame to which four plows are attached. Horse-drawn plows were generally single plows. A heavy team or a team of mules might pull two. But those plows were straight plows, creating a furrow into which seed was dropped. Soil was not turned over. It took a tractor to pull four plow blades through the soil, not only cutting it, but turning it over so the soil ten inches in the ground came to the top.

Twenty minutes after the plowing began, the tractor was buried to its rear axle, and the farmer was growling into our telephone, "Yes, this *is* an emergency! You need to give me the line!" Party lines were the norm, and we had learned early that Mrs. Nelson, our new next-door neighbor, believed hers were the only important calls on *our* line. But she eventually gave him the line (and promptly picked up to listen and to tell him that needing his tractor pulled out of our garden was *not* an emergency!) Her canning discussion with her sister was, of course, *far* more important – to her.

Before long, a huge green Oliver tractor appeared to pull out the much smaller Farm-All. The dirt where the wheels had sunk was black. I'd never seen black dirt but Mother had, and she was ecstatic. Black soil is highly organic and will grow *anything*! Asparagus seemed to love it because asparagus creates a flat root mass, normally a foot or so in diameter and a few inches deep. *This* asparagus had grown root masses up to four feet in diameter and more than a foot thick, and they had even grown together. When the four-bottom plow dug into it, the plow *stopped*, perforce stopping the Farm-All (but not its rear wheels, which promptly dug themselves down into the muck).

Between the two tractors, a pair of towing chains and some skillful operation by the farmer and his son, the field got plowed. Asparagus root masses were separated and relatively small ones were planted at one end. It then became the Mother, Charles and Giles show to pull roots, asparagus and weeds from the plowed and disked soil. The garden became a war between Mother and quack grass for the next two years, with Giles and I her soldiers. Finally, it seemed that, if not conquered, the grass was at least submissive. Now the garden would be a 4-H project for Giles and me.

The next six years saw Giles and me as the primary providers of vegetables for the family. The black soil grew tomatoes so large and fast they would often split. In deference to the Old Man's appetite for fresh tomato slices on his lunchmeat sandwiches, we grew a Burpee's yellow variety that was oval in shape, like a slice of Jewish rye (the Old Man's bread of choice) and not terribly juicy. Mother would wrap two or three slices of one of them in a couple layers of waxed paper, and the Old Man would open a sandwich at lunch, slap on a tomato slice, salt it enough to make a salt lick and put the sandwich back together. The tomato would extend beyond the crust in all directions.

Corn rows extended the length of the garden. Half of each row would be yellow varieties (that ripened in succession – giving us corn all of late summer into fall), and half would be white or bicolor. Beans climbed six-foot poles, and carrots as large as bananas were the norm. I would grow tomatoes while Giles grew bell peppers. If I grew broccoli, his assignment was cauliflower. If mine was peas, his was lima beans.

We planted, hoed and weeded; killed giant green tomato worms and maintained the rabbit fence; and we fertilized that garden every spring with whatever last summer's milk cow or other animal had left us. Now, fertilizer is a wonderful thing – makes the plants (including the weeds) grow wonderfully. But natural fertilizer *does* have its drawbacks, not the least of which is trying to work great clumps of straw and fertilizer into the soil by hoe and rake. Year after year, we struggled, Mother right there with us, and the Old Man telling us at the end of his twelve-hour days how proud he was of us.

One Saturday, the Old Man returned from an errand and he brought with him a wonder of machinery, a *tiller*! And not just any tiller! This was a dismountable tiller that was but one of three attachments, the other two being a *power rotary lawnmower* and a (mostly useless) snow thrower. A belt-drive snow thrower was simply not up to the rigors of the northeast

Ohio snowbelt. But we used it for anything less than four inches.

This wonder of ingenuity consisted of a main body that included the motor, handles and a belt drive-wheel. The tiller was attached by two flat bars that extended from its rear into slots in the main body, where it was held in place by friction plates snugged by bolts. This arrangement was essential, because the belt stretched as it heated during use, and it was necessary to stop work, loosen the bolts, pull the tiller away from the body, thus re-tightening the belt, and re-snug the bolts. Despite its drawbacks, it cut our work tremendously, and Giles and I were forever grateful for its arrival. Actually, given the size of our yard, the age of our boy-powered reel mowers, and the sharpening they received (once a year, during winter, only), we may have been even more grateful for the lawnmower attachment.

Every August, we took blue ribbons for virtually every vegetable we entered in the 4-H fair, including exotic squashes and gourds, and decorative kales and cabbages. It became a challenge for us to find *something* in the Burpee seed catalogue the judges weren't likely to have seen. Our only real competition was the children of the muck farmers. They had the same soil to start with that we did, but they didn't have milk cows, sheep or horses. Giles and I were, hands down, the champion 4-H gardeners of the county for at least four years.

And remember, we did all this while running those second projects of chickens, steers, hogs, sheep and rabbits.

CHAPTER 22

Misadventures in Animal Husbandry 4-H Re-Redux

While we were chopping weeds, hauling manure, planting seeds and generally turning the half-acre of black bottom land assigned to each of us into prize-winning, eatable, can-able and freeze-able vegetables, we were required to have a second significant project each. The Old Man and Mother had an absolute horror of the idle hands of children. Neither Giles nor I were athletic in the sense of being coordinated and capable of playing organized sports (I tried both football and wrestling with humiliating results), and there were no summer leagues of "everybody plays" soccer, basketball, baseball, and other such. Thus projects.

The year after the two-hundred fifty hens had made the first of several significant deposits into my college fund the Old Man looked through the projects list and discovered that if a boy were to wish a second year of chicken-raising as a project, instead of twenty-five chickens, fifty were expected. Thus, because I had raised two-hundred and fifty hens... yes, you see the math. *Five hundred* chicks showed up in the mail – all cockerels. I was going to raise five hundred *roosters*?

Well, no it turned out that what I *was* going to raise was five hundred capons. Capons are the steers of the chicken world male chickens whose um-m-m-m maleness has been "removed." This involved a near-all-night session with Giles, the Old Man and me capturing chicks from one brooder and handing them to the vet. Dr. Rogers had a syringe into which a large number of little "pills" had been dropped and which had a needle that looked as big as a pencil. Under the neck skin of each chick he injected one "pill." The "pill" was, of course, a compendium of filler and female hormones. The testosterone production of each chick was immediately arrested, and the testes atrophied. I had five hundred capons by morning.

It turned out that these chicks were a cross of Rhode Island Red and New Hampshire Gray breeds, both large chickens in their own right. But these birds put large to shame. The four I took to the 4-H fair weighed over fifteen pounds each and precipitated another confrontation with judging officials. This time there was discussion about whether cross-bred chickens were eligible and whether we were allowed to buy from out-of-state. That last was quickly resolved when it became apparent that, at least a third of the chickens on display had been purchased out-of-state. The Old Man got red again, the 4-H officials talked to the judges again and I took another championship ribbon home.

When I sold the last fifty capons to Forney's Meat Market, they weighed twenty pounds or more, dressed out, and he sold them at half-again the price of turkeys. I took them in late in the day, on Saturday before Thanksgiving, and they were sold out by Monday evening.

Giles raised rabbits that year and, yes, we learned a great deal about rabbits and multiplication. He began with three pair and sold over a hundred to Forney's. Today, we couldn't do that. Back yard abattoirs are unlikely to pass muster in today's world.

We also, as the years went on, raised sheep (nasty, vapid animals), pigs (evil smelling, mean, entirely too intelligent escape artists) and steers.

To raise sheep, I had to have a half dozen of them. I had to build a fence around five acres of our "pasture" beside the barn and I had to get them docked (tails removed) and sheared. There is *no* money to be made with six sheep. No one wants their wool, they won't eat tall grass (I had to *mow* their pasture *and* buy them hay) and mutton is not a favored meat in the USA.

For the pig project, we began with a pregnant sow in winter and had our "projects" in early spring. Because these were intended for sale as meat hogs, the males had to be castrated, which resulted in infection, which meant we could not show them at the fair, even though it was months away. The sow and pigs were moved from a building behind the barn to a fenced pen at the rear of the property next to the "wet pasture." This was *not* the Old Man's finest hour. Pigs dig. Pigs inside a pen in soft soil equal pigs everywhere. Chasing pigs through swampy grass, cattails and high-bush cranberry, learning an iron-worker's vocabulary from the Old Man, became a regular event. In the end, some money went into the college funds, but not much.

We each raised a steer the summer I turned fourteen. The Old Man bought a Hereford steer for me and an Angus steer for Giles. Unfortunately, Giles' steer still thought he was a bull. He was never docile enough to take to the fair and could not be touched, curried or cared for except through the slats of his stall. The only thing he *did* do was *grow*. Came the end of summer, he was half again the size of my Hereford and could well have been fair champion had we been able to take him.

My steer, on the other hand, was docile as a Labrador retriever. I named him Red Feather and I could actually ride him (and did, upon occasion when the Old Man wasn't around). He too, grew large, but looked small next to the Angus. He was well behaved (except for the hour he spent in Mother's strawberries) and easily learned to stand for extended periods – a requirement of steers in the judging ring.

Came the fair, and I joined two or three dozen other 4-H steer owners in the barns, and I discovered to my horror that Red Feather was the only non-"steer club" steer in the barn. Every other boy there belonged to a club where they specialized in steers. They shared knowledge. Their club meetings didn't waste time discussing vegetable parasites, chicken diseases, the best feed for hogs, or anything else. They talked about *steers*, only *steers* and nothing *but steers*! I was doomed!

Still, I was there, so I made the best of it. I bathed, dried and curried Red Feather. My father had given me a true Malacca cane, with a silver knob at the top and an ivory tip, around which he had wound stiff wire, leaving an inch protruding. So long as I scratched Red Feather's belly with that wire, he would stand. I made every preparation I could, even practicing looking straight ahead and not moving when the steer club boys were announced the winners.

Several officials came by, collected us and our steers and accompanied us to the ring. I made a last-second decision, and slung myself up on Red Feather's back. We trailed the clubs and their steers out of the barn. As we entered the judging ring, a low hum of conversation began and grew rapidly louder. Finally, I realized everyone was talking about me. No one had ever ridden a steer into the judging ring before.

I lined up at the farthest end from the judges, slid off Red Feather and waited. Two men walked slowly, one in front of the line-up, and one behind. As they passed me, they walked on a few yards, stopped and spoke. They returned to me.

"Come with us, son," one of them said.

I swallowed and nodded. I didn't dare speak. I'd chosen the wrong end of the line. The *other* end was where the lesser steers would be placed. Red Feather and I were but the first to be relocated. Eyes prickling, a thousand eyes in the stands following me, I trudged behind the two men. We reached nearly the end of the line, when one of the men tapped the second steer from the end and said to his owner, "Follow Mr. Smith, please."

As the boy led his steer out of line, I looked at it. That was a *huge* steer nearly as large as Giles' Angus. The man still with me motioned me into the empty slot. As I passed him, he whispered, "His steer was too old. Good luck."

I was stunned. Somebody was cheating? How could you *do* that? Wouldn't your father kno... Oh. I watched as the boy and his steer were led out of the ring.

Somebody was asking me a question. I stammered a request for him to repeat it. He did. Three men went up and down the line, asking questions, moving steers from place to place, checking hooves, looking for botfly wens and generally creating...

Did you ask, "What's a "wen?" Um-m-m-m... a wen is... er-r-r-r... it's a uh-h-h-h... how do I do this delicately? Oh heck, this is a farm story. Well then, a wen is normally just another name for a cyst, a raised lump of flesh or skin that begins in a hair follicle or a sebaceous gland. However, botflies lay their eggs under the skin of cattle and other mammals, usually along the spine and, as the larva grows, it raises a lump that's commonly called a "botfly wen." I searched daily for these on Red Feather, opening any I found with my trusty Barlow, removing the larva and dusting the cut and interior liberally with sulfa powder supplied by our vet.

Now, where was... oh yeah, ...and generally creating interminable and unendurable suspense.

Finally, they repaired to a small raised platform. After a short speech about how well we'd all done and how important it was to compete fairly, and a few terrible jokes about the tons of meat just standing around in the sun, the awarding of ribbons began. Ribbons were awarded from fifth place to first, and it took three awards before I realized they were moving up the line *toward* me. But when the steer to my left was awarded the blue ribbon for first place, I was completely lost.

"And now, would Charles Larlham and (I've utterly forgotten the other boy's name) bring your steers forward please."

I looked at the other boy. "C'mon," he grinned, "we're the best."

We walked our steers to the front of the platform. "Reserve Grand Champion goes to..." he paused – forever it seemed, "...Charles Larlham and Red Feather."

We had beaten them. Red Feather was Reserve Grand Champion! So one boy and steer were ahead of us... who cared? We had beaten all the rest of the "steer clubs' " steers!

As they led us out of the ring, I scrambled onto Red Feather's back and raised the Malacca high. There was general laughter and clapping as we exited the open end. Red Feather followed the other steers to the barn, where I was met with glowers and grumbling. It had never occurred to them that someone from a lowly "general" club could beat them.

But we had. Oh, indeed we had!

CHAPTER 23

Cook's Forest Summer Vacation –
Bears, Canoes and a Unicorn Horn

I have, most of my adult life, self-initiated vacations in late winter. We leave in bitter cold, come back two weeks later to melted snow and ice (or the soon expectation of same) and cheat thereby the deepest cold of winter.

In earlier days (*much* earlier), others organized my vacations and they were always in summer. Any vacation the Old Man took had to be within driving distance. A winter vacation meant going somewhere warm and that would have required train or (unlikely) plane tickets for five. That was *not* gonna happen. So, what can you do with a family in the summer? For *two weeks*? Heck, for even *one* week?

Yup – camping it is, and camping it was. *Fresh air* (We lived on a farm – why did we need that?). *Hiking* (We didn't get enough exercise working on a *farm*?)! *Outdoor living* (Well, the only thing different was outdoor *sleeping*.)! But you know what? It turns out camping is a lot of fun when you're a kid.

I can't tell you the year for sure, but based on the photos of me and my brother and sister, I'm gonna say I was about 12 or 13, so-o-o-o – summer of '54 or '55.

I had never heard of Cook's Forest in Clarion, Pennsylvania. It was (still is) a Pennsylvania State Park, replete with WPA-built log cabins (of which I made great use later in my life, when I had children) that were available only to

Pennsylvania residents from Memorial Day to Labor Day. We, of course, were not eligible to use the cabins, so-o-o-o...

The Old Man borrowed a pop-up trailer.

We arrived at Cook's Forest about mid-day and the first thing we needed, of course, was a photo of the arrival. Out popped Mother's old bellows Kodak 120 (hence, the square snapshots), and *snap,* first photo. The car is a 1950 Studebaker Champion, and you know we've just arrived because the car-top carrier is still loaded.

Oh, why does the sign say "No Picnicking"?

Black bears.

Once camp was set up, we drove around, mostly to get oriented.

We visited Scenic Overlooks

Which, oddly enough, overlooked Scenic Vistas!

We climbed trees (the sign on the tree probably says to stay off the tree). That may, in fact, be a real signal tree – a tree bent to shape by Native Americans to "signal" to all who passed that at this location people gathered or that a certain distance in a direction indicated by the arms a trail began or something. We played in the (probably polluted) Clarion River. At night, we drove around and spotlighted deer (and a couple bears, who took off as soon as we spotted them). The Rangers had a habit of shooing them away from the campgrounds and cabins for all the good it did. They'd learned to disappear when a spotlight hit 'em.

137

We hiked through the dense Hemlock-White Pine forests of the Pennsylvania Appalachian Mountains. The trees grew closely, the shadows were deep and dark, and my little brother could disappear into them in seconds. We'd look around and no Giles. The Old Man and Mother would call for a while and then the Old Man, hurling imprecations at small boys who thought it was funny to scare people, would charge into the woods. We'd watch him until he was no longer visible, and then look around for a place to sit and wait. Giles would ask, from his perch on the nearest fallen log, "Where's Dad goin'?"

We fished. Wel-l-l-l the Old Man fished. He tried to teach me to cast a fly, but I was (and remain) approximately as coordinated as a random motion generator. I did learn to use a spinning rod and we had to settle for that. He never believed that "spin-casting" was truly fishing. Real fishermen used flies; boys used straight cane poles. *No* serious fisherman used a spin-caster, or a *shudder* bait-casting rig. That was all right with me; I was never a serious fisherman.

By the end of that trip, I had come to deeply enjoy the place called Cook's Forest and I would, when I had children, return there for many years with a couple we knew from college and their children. Because the cabins were restricted to residents during summer, we took our families in late April or May before Memorial Day, and often again in September or early October. We would rent, for a four-day weekend, a large cabin for two families with children, and give them the run of the cabin area until one day...

We and our friends piled into our car for a trip to a destination I have forgotten – but I will never forget the start of the trip. As we started off, our then six-year-old son was demanding to know what we'd do if we met a bear. I explained that the best way to deal with a bear was always to make noise in the woods so as not to surprise them.

"Yes," he wanted to know, "but what if you do anyway and she wants to eat you, and you already said bears run faster than us, so what should we do, Dad? Huh? What should we do?"

So I explained that people should wave their arms and jump around and yell a lot to try to make themselves look and sound as big and bad as possible.

Whereupon, number one son jumped forward against the dashboard, bounced on the seat, and pointed out the front window of the car and yelled just as loudly as he possibly could, "**BEAR! DADDY! BEARS!**"

I looked up and sure enough, we were rolling slowly down the main cabin drive, directly toward a black bear sow and two cubs. The female, having apparently heard my son, promptly turned away from us, collected her cubs, and herded them into the river. The three swam away, and we never let the kids outside at Cooks Forest without us again.

One of the half-day adventures we always went on was a canoe trip down the Clarion that included a trip through a short stretch of relatively flat rapids. Most years the rapids were just a fun, fast ride but one trip included a short swim for me. Our canoe became jammed between two boulders and, after some struggle, it became evident that the only possible rescue was to lift it out.

I climbed out over the tail of the canoe, bent down, took a firm grip and stood up... sort of. The picture in the water differed somewhat from the picture in my head. As I stood up, lifting the canoe and thrusting it forward, I fell victim to a reality of river boulders – they're slippery as all get out. A fellow by the name of Newton pointed out that "every action has an equal and opposite reaction," a basic tenet of physics that I proved as the canoe shot forward and my feet shot backward!

The rushing water rammed me into the space that had trapped the canoe and, for a moment, I was trapped. But I had an advantage over the canoe – I had hands with which I could push myself out of the wedge. I shoved hard against the rocks that held me. A moment's resistance and I was free and tumbling. But the water wasn't deep, and I was able to orient myself, spot the canoe and take off after it. Charging down the river, swimming, walking and sometimes hauling myself from rock to rock using my hands, I soon caught the canoe. Th' Luvly Laura was having little luck controlling it from the front and it was sideways across two rocks as I caught up.

Matt was having a great time but Laura was terrified that the canoe would turn over. I looked the canoe over as I approached it and decided I agreed with her. I grabbed the front, hauled it about ten feet to shore and pulled it up on the sand. I got my family out and looked around. Our friends had passed us and were well on their way to the pick-up point. There were no cell phones and I needed them to tell the canoe rental we were done. I looked around. We had come ashore on a little beach of sand just off the main drag through the park. Beachside amenities drew my attention. There was a hamburger stand, a frozen custard stand, a towel rental and changing room and a couple other places. I went over, ordered three custard cones and asked to use the phone.

I called the canoe livery and arranged for pick up. I grabbed my cones and headed back to Laura and Matt. They were involved with some sort of sand drawings and, as I got closer, I realized that neither of them had noticed the ugly green welt moving across Matt's upper arm. It was some sort of caterpillar with spiky protrusions and this old farm boy knew that meant bad things.

How did I know? Caterpillars (and other creatures) wear bright colors to tell predators that they're dangerous. It's a tad late for one's predator to find out about the poison *after* one has been eaten. Lumps and spikes reinforce the message, and they often carry a load of formic acid (wasp venom) in those lumps and spikes.

Well, so long as no one messed with it there should be no problem and, once I got the cones handed out, I'd just brush... Oh, no! Laura had spotted the caterpillar. For some reason she jumped up. Then she grabbed Matt's shoulder with her left hand, scaring him, and he began to cry. She pulled back her other hand and, before I could yell, *"Honey, don't!"* she had smacked the caterpillar. Matt screamed and I made the last ten yards to them in about two bounds. Matt's arm was already swelling, but I had a fix for that. I shoved the cones at Laura, grabbed Matt and ran to the river. I scrubbed all the remains of the caterpillar off, along with the poison and carried him, still screaming, back to Laura. People had gathered to see what the commotion was about.

"Could somebody go over and get us a cup of water?" Before I finished asking, a half-dozen people were running for the hamburger and custard stands. I turned to Laura, "Give me the cones." She handed them over, "I need your Benedryl." She started to protest, looked at Matt's arm, and understanding dawned. Laura was allergic to bee venom so we always carried Benedryl for her. Matt's arm was swelling just as hers did after a sting and she scrambled for her purse. Meanwhile, I handed Matt a now-dripping cone. His screaming cut off in the midst of a squall. He hiccoughed as he took the cone, but he managed to quiet down and begin eating it. A boy showed up with water and Laura handed me the pills. I gave them to Matt, who hardly noticed because of the ice cream.

Our friends showed up, along with the canoe livery truck, and demanded to know the whole story. "After dinner," I said. "I don't want to sit here *another* half hour." We all climbed into their car and headed back to the cabin.

Laura had been fortunate not to break the skin of her hand when she squashed the caterpillar. It would have been as dangerous for her as being stung by several bees or wasps.

On a later trip, after our daughter was born, we took the long trail over the mountain to the park headquarters. Although the forest was mostly Hemlock and White Pine, which has little undergrowth, there was a varied edge growth of azalea, hazelnut and other mountain deciduous shrubs and small trees. I was pointing out the various plants and the birds that specialized in them when it began to rain. We huddled under a hemlock while we sorted out umbrellas and Laura pulled out the hood on the back-carry I was using to carry Elizabeth who was about two at the time.

While all that was going on, I looked down at a pile of reddish punk that used to be a hemlock a generation ago. Punk is what remains of a softwood tree after bacteria have eaten all the organic material away from the lignin in the wood, leaving the world's best fire-starter. In the middle of all this lay a rock-hard, sharp-pointed something. On the large end, it was apparent that it was a tree branch that had been broken and then burned. I picked it up. Upon closer inspection, it was a "pine knot," the beginning end of a branch, so compressed by the tree as the tree grew outward along the branch, and the branch attempted to expand, that it had been impervious to bacteria.

"What's that, Daddy?" Matt was peering at it from under his little collapsible umbrella.

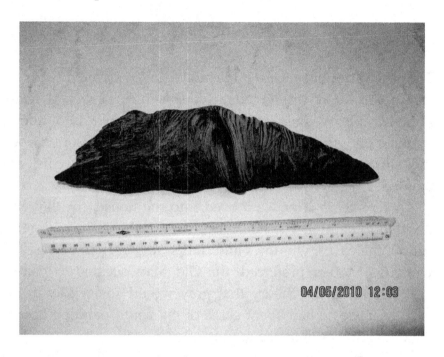

04/05/2010 12:03

I held it up, wrapping my hand around the large end. "This?" I announced, my voice filled with all the questioning wonder several years of stage training could give it, "This is a unicorn's horn, Son. We must protect it, for we may never find another." I never spoke a truer word because we never did. At home three days later, as I tried to dry it out (impervious to bacteria it may have been, but it was saturated with rain), I filled the bottom of Laura's oven with pine tar. All in all, not a bad week – I found a unicorn's horn, and Th' Luvly Laura got a new stove.

CHAPTER 24

My "Little" Brother

The old farmhouse was huge and it was covered with cut shingles of wood. Unlike cedar shakes, which were hard, nearly impenetrable wedges of wood that were split into uneven surfaces and sizes; these shingles were cut out of softer wood, the surfaces machine-scored in narrow, shallow cuts, and painted.

A few years after we moved into the house, the Old Man decided to paint it. The house was a battleship gray, with white trim at the eaves, windows and doors. Rather than change it to white, as Mother preferred, the Old Man decided to paint it gray again, on the theory that gray would cover gray in one coat. Because he had spent some of his youth painting houses, the decision was deferred to him.

In preparation, the Old Man dug out an old gasoline-fired blowtorch. These little hand-bombs were probably responsible for burning down more houses than any other single item except women in wool skirts jumping out of fireplaces in flames, and that was already generations behind us when the Old Man showed Giles and me how a blowtorch worked and why it was standard house-painter's gear.

Exterior paint from the '40s and '50s was oil-based enamel. Yes, it contained lead in significant quantities. But that was only a problem if you ate it – much less likely than with indoor paint. At any rate, the exterior paint of the day did not soak into wood well, and gripped only onto other paint – a special primer that provided a surface for the final coat. Unfortunately, wood absorbs moisture, no matter how well covered, and those shingles were better at absorbing moisture than any other wood.

Paint pulls away from moist wood. It blisters, hangs in strips, splits and generally looks like heck within a few years of the initial work. The blowtorch is meant to burn away all the loose paint. But the generation of blowtorch we were using was fired with gasoline. The pot was filled with the liquid gas and a small button at the top attached to a shaft with a plunger at the other end was pumped rapidly until pressure built up. A small amount of gasoline was poured into a tray under the mouth and lit. The Old Man opened a valve, and gasoline blew out under pressure, catching fire immediately. The pump had to be manipulated at very short intervals and the gasoline would run out with no warning. Worst of all, the blamed things blew up with appalling regularity. But the Old Man fired it up.

Adjusting the flame to a low-pressure burn, he began to play it slowly over the side of the house. Three minutes later, accompanied by words I'd never heard the Old Man say before, he played water from the garden hose over the flames crawling up the side of the house. Mother came out to watch.

"It'll be OK, darlin'," he said, "as long as it just scorches the paint. See?" With a wire brush, he rubbed the now-wet shingles. It was immediately apparent that more than paint had burned. Charred pieces of shingle lay on the ground around his feet. More new words. He picked up the blowtorch and opened the valve. Standing back, he gingerly played the flame along a row of shingles.

The Old Man turned to Mother as he continued to char the

paint. "See," he grinned, "it's gonna be..."

"Dick!/Dad!" It was a dual shriek from Mother and my little brother. He (and I) whirled toward the house.

Flames once again licked the bottom edges of shingles. An expanse of about ten feet long and three or four shingle rows high was burning steadily. I grabbed the hose while the Old Man went to work with the wire brush. When we had finished, it was apparent to both of us that *several* bundles of shingles would be required. It was apparent to Mother that the Old Man was done with the blowtorch.

"But, Pat," the Old Man was fighting a losing battle and he knew it, "it's been a long time. I just need practice."

Mother said nothing more. She simply stood there, five feet, ten inches tall, reed slender and iron-straight. There was a silence. Finally...

"All right, Pat, I'll do it another way. But it's gonna take a *lo-o-ong* time."

"That's all right. We'll still have a house." She turned and went inside.

The Old Man gathered my brother and me up and we headed for the hardware store. We purchased scrapers, wire brushes, gloves and other pre-painting gear and headed home. For the next month, Giles and I during the day and the Old Man weekends and evenings, with our help, brushed, scraped and scrubbed loose paint off that house.

As we came to the front of the southern wing, we found "Bumble Bees." Large yellow bees with black thoraxes, bees the size of the end of a boy's thumb, lived between the giant sandstone blocks that substituted for a foundation under that wing. The Old Man got the pump sprayer we used in the garden and pumped insect poison into the crack from which

146

they had emerged.

Bees boiled from a space three feet away. It was apparent that they lived under the house and the spray was simply making them change their access. The Old Man stood there, swatting at bees with his hat. I ran for the rear of the house. Giles ran *into* the house. It wasn't long before I heard, "Boy, what the HECK do you think you're doing?"

"Killing bees!" The boyish reply, amidst choking laughter was definitely puzzling. I went to see what my little brother was up to.

He was standing halfway to the road, ping-pong paddle in hand. He trotted back to the Old Man by the house. Picking up a slender limb he'd broken from one of the maple trees, he shoved it into the slot from which the bees had come. And out they came. Giles took off running toward the road. Abruptly, he stopped and turned, swinging. There was a sharp "crack!" as paddle met bee. He ducked, leaned far enough back that I thought he'd fall, snapped the paddle out and another "crack!" and a bee sailed past my head.

The Old Man allowed him to do that a few more times and then he pointed out that even Bumble Bee hives contained several dozen, if not several hundred, bees. Killing them one at a time with a ping-pong paddle wasn't gonna get us anywhere.

Giles, having tired of his game (and simply tired, for that matter) agreed. We moved away from the bees. The Old Man brought home an insect sprayer and eliminated the bees a few days later.

Once the prep was done, the Old Man ripped out the burned shingles and replaced them; and when *that* was done, he hand-painted them with a gray base-coat. Finally, he covered and taped all the trim. Then he rented an air-driven paint sprayer. In the '50s, this consisted of a paint-covered air tank, a compressor and two hoses connecting the air tank to the paint tank attached to the bottom of the sprayer head. The paint tank contained about a quart (two pounds) of paint, and the entire rig in your hand weighed about six pounds. The trigger was gummy and stuck, and at first, paint went everywhere. After a couple hours of cleaning, the Old Man was ready.

Slowly waving the sprayer back and forth, feathering the trigger, he painted the entire house in one afternoon. It was obvious, even to a youngster that the Old Man had done this before. There were no blotches, runs or missed spaces. Except for the occasional insect trapped in the sticky paint it was a beautiful job. The next weekend, he removed the taping from the trim, and painted it white.

Years later, I painted a house I owned. It took me *weeks*, and I could only remember with envy the speed and simplicity with which the Old Man had done the same job.

CHAPTER 25

Year of the Horse(s)

The Old Man spent a fair amount of time, off and on, trying to get horses for us. After all, what's the point of having a big barn if you can't put a horse or two in it? Oh, there was Bellsie, the blind pony, but she was gone after four years and the Old Man thought every boy ought to have a horse to care for and ride. Giles and I agreed wholeheartedly (well, about the riding part anyway).

One Saturday morning in May 1956 (I was about to turn 14), I went to the barn to feed and milk the cow, and heard a whinny, which was strange because there had been no horse or pony in the barn since Bellsie was sent to the mink farm. I raced to the small room off the end of the dairy and there stood a full-sized brown and white horse! I raced for the house. The Old Man was bringing my brother and he laughed as I skidded to a stop. "I see you've met our new friend," he said.

"A horse," I gasped, looking at my brother, "a *real* horse!"

"His name's 'Pinto,' " the Old Man said. "I swapped the twenty-two for him. Want to saddle him up?"

For the rest of that week, my brother and I rode Pinto. And then, Friday, when we got home, he was gone. The Old Man was in a thunderous black mood. He paced the house and swore. He called his friend with whom he'd traded, and swore at him. He went outside and smoked and swore some more. Finally he sat down. "Boys," he said, "Pinto's gone." We started to babble, and he held up his hand. "Stolen," he said, "Pinto was *stolen*! Jimmy sold me a stolen horse." He shook his head at the profound betrayal. But there was worse to come. "And he sold the twenty-two."

We were stunned. That he had traded the twenty-two for the horse had been almost unthinkable. The Old Man had spent hours on winter nights, carving hunting scenes into the maple stock and forestock of that rifle. Cottontails fled beagles on the forestock and, on the stock, a brace of pheasant cocks exploded from in front of a spaniel and shotgunner on one side, while ducks flared in over decoys on the other. When we asked, he'd said, "I wanted a real horse for you, and I was done with that old gun." But now he wanted it back and Jimmy had sold it. "He told me for years," the Old Man mourned, "how much he wanted that gun. And he sold it in less than a week."

The Old Man remained convinced ever after, that his friend Jimmy had stolen that horse just to get that rifle away from him. They never spoke again.

But, the Old Man wasn't done. Oh, no not by a long shot. He kept looking as the summer wore on, and he found us each a horse – one for him, one for Giles and one for me. But there was a catch. We couldn't have the horses in summer! The horses he found were stabled at a day camp for the children of urban wealth. The camp opened in early June and closed in late August. For the other months of the year, the camp was closed and the horses were boarded to local farmers, with the understanding that they were to be ridden regularly and fed only the hay the day camp delivered to us.

It was now mid-September and the available horses were a limited bunch. The Old Man chose for himself a rescued pinto mustang named Domino who was, upon occasion, known to attempt to discourage riders. For my brother, he chose a retired trotter named Tango; a sorrel standard-bred prone to nosebleeds if pushed too hard or too long (hence the retirement). For me, he had selected a rangy, burnt umber-colored horse named, with no originality at all, Umber.

Umber, we were told was the best horse in the camp with older children. I was apparently not old enough to qualify. As we stood in the paddock with the three horses and several of their fellows, Umber walked away. None of us paid any attention, until Mother suddenly cried, "Charles!" It was but an instant later I was flying over the paddock fence and Umber was prancing across the paddock, neighing defiance. Mother later said that the horse broke into a rapid trot, dropped her head almost to ground level ("Looked like a giant snake," she said.) and headed straight for me. Just as Mother finally got my name out, Umber grabbed me by the left buttock and threw me over the fence (the bruise was a beaut).

There was a short angry discussion between the Old Man and the camp director, and it was agreed that Umber would *not* be part of the package. Giles would still have Tango, but I would have Domino. The Old Man would ride either of them as time allowed.

The horses, along with their hay and feed, were delivered the next day. Giles and I stacked the hay in the lower mow, with the straw that would be their 'bedding.' Horses don't lie down, but they need straw that is replaced daily around their feet to capture waste.

Giles and I were each given a pitchfork. His was a five-tined, long-handled fork, while mine was short-handled and resembled a coal-scoop with tines instead of a blade. These were to be used daily and woe-betide the young man who shirked. The Old Man was not about to return those horses with hoof-rot.

Each morning, we provided fresh water in a five-gallon pail to each horse and dropped a couple "leaves" from a bale of alfalfa hay into the small manger in each stall. Each evening we did the same, plus a scoop of feed. We also mucked out the stalls and hauled the used straw to the rear of the barn, where we stacked it on top of the pile from the cow (a practice that led to near-disaster the next spring), and forked new straw back in its place.

When we were done feeding and watering (and cleaning), we'd saddle the horses and ride all over the fifteen acres of the farm in all but pouring rain and blizzard. The Old Man insisted on at least an hour every day, with a good variation in gait. We learned to sit a western saddle at a trot (very hard to do), and to "post" in an "English" saddle at the same gait – much easier to learn, but tiring on the legs.

Domino had a nasty habit of trying to bite the left foot of his rider. I broke him of that by smacking his nose with a quirt every time he tried it. He also would grab the bit and run if one didn't keep tension on the bit. One day he got the bit and headed for the woods at the back of the field at a dead run gallop. When we got to the forest fringe, densely packed with brush, briars and young trees, I stepped off. Domino plowed ahead, until the reins tangled in the undergrowth, whereupon he, perforce, stopped as well.

I found a passage through the tangle, caught up the reins and led him out to the open ground. I tried to remount. Giles, having followed me with some unformed idea of rescuing me, was now roaring with laughter as the little mustang turned in a constant circle, leaving me with one boot in the stirrup and hopping after him on the other. Fuming, I swore black oaths against the black and white devil's mother, father and siblings, reached under my left arm and rapped him at the base of the nose with the butt of the quirt.

Domino stopped instantly! He spread his front feet, lowered his head and shook it violently, during which exhibition I remounted, booted him in the ribs and pushed him to a gallop. He promptly grabbed the bit again, but I was ready. I rapped him between the ears with the butt of the quirt, and he dropped the bit. I hauled him to a stop and repeated the process. Within half an hour, he no longer tried for the bit.

From then on Domino was well-behaved under me (and the Old Man, who had no trouble with him at any time), but Giles refused to ride him. Tango was regularly subject to nosebleeds, but was an easy horse to ride and control. We rode at every opportunity and, when it came time to return the horses, they were well fed, well groomed and fit.

On a Saturday about two weeks before the horses were to be picked up, the Old Man decided that he and I would ride them back to the camp. We had run out of alfalfa, and were short of grain. We had some timothy hay, but it was ours and the Old Man didn't want to put money into the horses. So we saddled up and got about five miles down the road. A storm appeared to be building, but the Old Man said we'd reach the day-camp before it broke.

Flash! Crack! Blam! It appeared the Old Man was wrong and the horses wanted no part of this. He was riding Tango, who spun 180 degrees and broke into her racing trot toward home – *our* home! Domino reared and pranced, but he seemed confused. I got him turned and galloped after Tango. But there was no catching her. She was racing, and Domino was no racehorse. The dirt road was partially oiled and the footing wasn't good, but he'd have had no chance anyway. And then the rain came in sheets.

. The Old Man leaned forward over Tango's neck, took a short hold on the reins, sat back and hauled. Tango resisted momentarily, but settled down in short order as I backed off Domino and there was no further competition. Once Tango settled down, I rode up beside her. We rode together toward home. After a little while the Old Man spoke. "What were you doing?"

"I thought she was running away with you, and I was going to catch her." It was true. I'd had this cowboy vision of riding up to her head and grabbing the reins at the bit.

The Old Man laughed. "She's a *racehorse*, Son. That little mustang couldn't catch her unless she bled to death." He looked at me. "I was riding horses when I was six, Son. Thanks for the thought, but I didn't need rescuing."

"Yeah," I mumbled, "I could see that."

We rode the five miles home in off-and-on rain. They did fine for two weeks on timothy hay and the feed that was left. When the day-camp trailer came for them, the driver complimented the Old Man on their condition.

For reasons good and bad, we never had horses again.

A word to parents who would send their children to a day camp or summer camp that boasts horseback riding as an activity – day and summer camp horses don't like your children. It is not outside the realm of reality to say they hate your children. Just sayin'...

CHAPTER 26

School Daze – Consolidation Frustration

I turned twelve July 29, 1954, my last fully celebrated birthday (until I got married), got my own shotgun, spent a wonderful day with the Old Man and began a year of great confusion. I was about to enter seventh grade in Shalersville Township school. I didn't know it, but seventh grade was about to change, and with it the rest of my school life, and it was all Mother's fault.

Mother had been campaigning tirelessly for consolidation of our Shalersville Township school district with the Mantua Village and Mantua Center school districts, ever since my first day of school in September of '48. Finally, after six years, consolidation was well on its way to happening. I had no idea how badly that was going to screw up my life – no idea at all.

All three school boards had finally agreed to put the question on the November 1954 ballot and Mother's campaigning stepped up. The three school districts bordered each other and they all had the same problem; each needed a modern middle school (junior high) and high school and not one of them could afford to build either one, much less both. As a consolidated district, they'd be large enough to finance both schools together.

Mantua, Ohio, was a typical little northeast Ohio farm town. It was home to about a thousand people, sat at the border between Mantua and Shalersville Townships and served as the farm-town center for both of them. Building a middle school and high school for all three districts in Mantua Village would put them smack in the middle of the consolidated district.

Ohio schools were and, for the most part still are, funded through a property tax millage (still the most common method of funding schools across America). Property tax millage is a charge against the value of property figured on a per thousand dollars value basis. One mil (thus "millage") is one hundredth of a cent or one thousandth of a dollar. An eighty to a hundred and twenty mil property tax brings in eighty to a hundred and twenty dollars per one thousand dollars valuation.

Mantua had the fewest number of students but much of the most highly taxable land in the three districts. Farmers, on the other hand, tended to produce more kids than they could afford to build schools for, because agricultural land was (and still is) taxed at an artificially low rate.

Consolidation was the only chance of survival for all three districts and Mother embraced it enthusiastically. She spoke at small gatherings and large, criss-crossed Shalersville Township handing out fliers and speaking with our neighbors one-on-one except for Mrs. Grassmutter. Mrs. Grassmutter let it be known as soon as Mother handed her one of the brochures she always carried, that she wanted no part of consolidation. "Communist propaganda!" she spat. "It's a plot to take our schools away from us."

Mother opened her mouth to plead her case but Mrs. Grassmutter was quicker. She opened the house door and said, "Sic 'em." Three large bull terriers boiled through the opening and headed for the car and its passengers, Giles, Lyndella and me, passing Mother before she could react. She raced after them and kicked one of them aside as she yanked open the car door.

As she ducked into the seat, pulled the door shut and slammed the little Studebaker into reverse, the dog she had kicked tried to get back in the car and was caught between the body of the car and the edge of the closing door, which bounced back open, releasing him but breaking his foreleg. Another dog tried to bite a tire, got a broken jaw out of the deal, and had to be put down.

Mrs. Grassmutter tried unsuccessfully to sue. In deposition, she described the entire confrontation in explicit detail, whereupon she was advised (by her own lawyer) that she had just admitted to assault with intent to do great bodily harm, or worse, and could be charged with a felony and would likely go to jail if she was. Mother asked her lawyer to see to it. The deposition was adjourned, the women were sent home, the lawyers met and there was no more talk of a suit. Once the threat of a lawsuit was gone, Mother told her lawyer to forget the whole thing.

Despite the best efforts of the forces of anti-Communism in all three districts, the consolidation passed in all three districts. The new district was named the Crestwood School District. Our high school sports teams were named the "Red Devils," a point of dismay with some of the more fundamentalist Christian groups in the community. All three communities largely ignored them.

Once the consolidation was official and the district name was registered, it was time for the hard part – divvying up the students. The Shalersville Township School that we attended had been, until 1952, made up of two structures. The one I attended for as long as I went to school there was a low, sprawling brick elementary and middle school that was too small the day it was finished. I had first and second grade classes in "classrooms" created in the gym by setting up rug-covered panels made by volunteers to separate one class from another.

Higher grades had their own actual rooms. When I entered seventh grade, I was technically a middle school student and I expected to be moving from room to room. But in Shalersville, all seventh grade students had only a single room and the same teacher for all courses except gym and music; and gym class was strictly a fair-weather, outdoor event. When the high school students showed up beginning in 1952, things did not improve.

The reason high school students showed up in the overcrowded school was that the "other structure" was condemned in 1952. The original school had to have been the worst part of Shalersville Township's schools for a long time, from the parents' perspective. High school classes had been held in an old two-story wooden schoolhouse with a single staircase connecting the floors, one entrance/exit (with a fire exit at the far end from the main door, and another at the side of the building). It was heated in winter by a coal-fired steam boiler.

Built in the early '20s (perhaps earlier), there were no fire codes to which it acknowledged allegiance. I have seen photos that show both the original school before it was demolished, and the elementary school built in the late 1940s, as well as the addition to the Elementary School that was built during the demolition of the high school.

Every parent of a high school student in the Shalersville School District must have spent more than one night fending off night terrors and nightmares of the horrors of a fire in the old wooden school building. While it was being demolished during the summer of 1952, an extension was built onto the elementary school, and high school students were crowded into the newer, already over-packed elementary/middle school. Despite the extension's additional space, some classes had to be held across State Route 303 in the Grange Hall *cum* Township Meeting Hall.

Immediately after Christmas break, implementation began. For Shalersville high school students changing schools, a double bus ride was necessary. They changed buses at the Shalersville School, and were transported to the other two schools. Shalersville became a K through eight school for the remainder of the year.

The lower grades were a different matter. For the remaining half year, nearly all the students in the first six grades would remain. Grades seven and eight would lose half their students. When school began in the fall of 1955, Shalersville would become solely an elementary (K thru six) school.

Parents were polled and teachers were asked to create classes. No one, parents or children, wanted to start a double bus ride in January and no one asked me anyway, but it had to be done by *somebody*. I was told that I would be staying at Shalersville, and I was happy enough with that, until I was betrayed by my best friends. I had two duties that came with having good grades, which let me get out of class. I had not attended kindergarten, but Shalersville instituted it not long after I began school. It was half-day and buses took the kids home at noon.

I rode one of the kindergarten buses on its home delivery route every other week, getting off at each stop, walking across in front of the bus and holding out the Triple-A Safety Flag, the magical powers of which stopped all traffic in both directions for up to ninety seconds as my little charges trudged across the street toward his or her waiting mother.

On alternate weeks, I was a crossing guard at the State Route 44 and State Route 303 intersection in front of the school. When students approached to go home for, or return from, lunch, we guards would step bravely into the street and hold out those self-same Triple-A Safety Flags, stopping all traffic as before. Tuggie, Lynn, Jimmy and I shared these duties, along with the team with which we alternated. The four of us were so tight our teacher called us the Four Mouseketeers.

The Triple-A Safety Flag had a design-flaw. Its staff was of a perfect length and balance to be a fencing sword (none of us knew the word "epee") for a boy of twelve, and when no one was coming, they darned well **became** fencing swords. Unfortunately, their staffs were made of pine and, in every case, the grain ran at an angle to the length of the sword.

Within a month, every sword, er-r-r staff, was broken. Soon we were summoned to the Principal's office. I was the last called. He asked no questions. He simply told me that because I had seen fit to break all the flagstaffs, I was off the detail, and would receive no award. I tried to protest, but he cut me off, telling me that all three of my friends had told him I deliberately broke all four flagstaffs. I found Tuggie in the boys' room and asked him why they'd done that.

He looked at me as if I were stupid. "It had to be somebody's fault, and you weren't there." Somehow, the other three had been called together, leaving me to face the principal alone, and the three of them had done this to me.

I went home and announced that I wanted to be part of the

transfer. I refused to say why. I insisted I thought it would be an adventure. Neither Mother nor the Old Man was buying that, but I would say nothing else. The battle raged (well, the wheedling and whining continued) for days, but finally Mother threw up her hands and agreed. The Old Man shrugged and said it was my funeral and Mother sent a letter to Shalersville Elementary and my teacher saying I could be part of the transfer.

Sure enough, I came home for Christmas break with a letter that said I'd been assigned to Mantua Center Middle School (Mother had been hoping for the Village, but...).

Came the end of Christmas break, I boarded a second bus at Shalersville Elementary and rode in silence, along with about forty-five other kids of various ages, to Mantua where we stopped, discharged three-quarters of our riders and picked up more to go to Mantua Center. Another ten minutes brought us to the Township center, a desolate square alongside State Route 82, with no other public or commercial buildings in sight. The square was filled with and surrounded by sugar maples, although I didn't know that until the trees were tapped in the spring. The bus pulled up to the school, where a man and a woman (the principal and a teacher it turned out) came out to welcome us.

We piled out of the bus and stopped in front of them. The man said, "Hello, I'm Principal Smith. This is Mrs. Baker. Welcome to Mantua Center School. It's cold out here, so please follow me to where you're supposed to be." He turned and went inside. We trooped after him

We wound up in a gym, with a great many other students of various ages and grades. The principal had a nice enough manner as he called names and identified locations. Finally he got to us and told the seventh and eighth grade students (now officially Middle School students) in which rooms they would begin each day. Teachers stepped forward at his behest, and we followed them to homerooms.

For the first time in my school life, I had separate rooms and teachers for most subjects. It was an exciting prospect. But by the end of the week, I had come to a depressing conclusion – no one had sent their best and brightest to these new teachers and classes. With the exception of about six of us, everyone in the new classes was a C student – or worse. They were unruly, asked questions that had just been answered, demanded all the teachers' time, and were generally obnoxious and a pain in the neck.

When my grades kept being held up as examples for the rest of the (failing) class, not all my fellow students shared the teachers' pride in my accomplishments. One boy in particular constantly demanded that I come outside at lunch and fight. Finally, fed up with staying inside just to avoid a fight, I said, "OK, wise guy, let's just do that," and headed for the door. Once we were outside, he said that if I wouldn't hit him, he'd tell me a joke. I didn't. He did. I asked what was up. Turned out that he'd always been the class clown – nobody had ever taken him up on an offer to fight. He was scared to death (as was I, truth to tell). We went back inside. His family moved before the school year was over.

Worse than the riding by students who saw me as somehow deliberately trying to make them look bad academically (a task at which most of them needed little assistance), was the dumbing down of the curriculum. The challenge of school was gone within the first couple weeks. Most of the kids simply couldn't keep up with the standard lesson plan. That was a problem when they were a few students in a class, but when they were the entire class, it was a disaster. The second half of my seventh school year was a no-learning zone. By February, I could do most of the classes with my eyes closed, and did it so often the Old Man heard about it.

Mother had received the phone call about me sleeping in class, but she felt it was better if the Old Man handled it. I got a two-hour lecture on respect, disrespect, learning under adversity. Then I got the rest of it. I would be receiving extra work daily, from *every* class. Whoever had called had recognized the problem. They couldn't run away from the entire class just to give me a challenge, but they could set me an independent learning course that would eat my evenings whole. It was only for about four months, but it was a terrible four months. For all practical purposes, I taught myself for the second half of seventh grade.

There was one odd incident that became a family legend. The Old Man was fond of calf's liver and onions. Giles and I – not so much. Our dislike notwithstanding, every once in a while we had that most unpleasant of surprises when dinner would be liver 'n onions. And so it was one famous Sunday night when, not only did we have liver and onions, we had mashed potatoes and liver gravy; liver concentrate if you will. The next day at about eleven in the morning, I began to itch. I asked to see the nurse and, when she stripped off my shirt, there was no question... I had a monster case of hives. Mother was called, decided on the spot that it was from the liver gravy and I never had to eat liver again. I spent a miserable afternoon, even after Doc Knowlton gave me a shot of adrenalin to ward off the worst of it, but it was worth it to eat a hamburger the next time Giles had to choke down the dreaded liver 'n onions.

I slogged onward and the next year I wound up in the Mantua Village complex. On a hill within sight of many of the upper story classrooms, new junior high and senior high buildings were going up. The entire class structure was revamped in 1956 and, as a ninth grader, I was a freshman, a high school student, so I never took a class in the new junior high building. Middle School/Junior High became the sixth, seventh and eighth grades and K through fifth grade was our elementary – for a while, at least.

I have no idea how those students got distributed, but in the 1964-1965 school year, a neighboring school district's high school roof collapsed and my sister's junior class grew instantly from barely a hundred students to more than three hundred fifty. The next year, the Hiram district, with a Senior Class of five straight A college faculty's children, and no other students, joined her senior class. She went from valedictorian to sixth in her class overnight.

I had graduated with only perhaps seventy-four or five other students in 1960 and I was not valedictorian. Neither was I anywhere near as high as sixth in my class.

CHAPTER 27

My Kid Brother's "All-Shalersville Pet Show"

I think it was the summer I became a teenager, or maybe the next.

I had never seen my kid brother so excited. Where he got the idea, I don't remember, but before he was done, he had the whole family into it even the Old Man, who, as he constantly explained, worked overtime and was *tired* when he got home.

"I'm gonna have a pet show," Giles announced entering the kitchen at a dead run, his primary gait during summer.

Mother was unfazed. She turned from the sink. "Where?"

"In the barn."

"Well, we may have to talk about that, but tell me about the show."

I was appalled! What if nobody came? What if it rained? What if *everybody* came? "Mo-om!" It sounded plaintive, even to me.

She turned from Giles. "Yes, Charles?"

"Well..." I was beginning to sink. "Uh-h-h-h er-r-r-r-r... What if uh-h-h-h... What if it doesn't work?"

"It'll work, Mom, it'll work. *I pro-o-omise!*" Giles saw his great idea for a summer event disappearing.

"Of *course* it'll work." She glared at me over Giles' head. "Now, we need to talk about events, classes..."

"Classes? What classes? It's *summer*!" Giles wasn't quite up to speed on his own idea, but Mother was not easily panicked or distracted.

"Classes of animals, Giles. Like, oh I don't know hunting dogs, family pets, working dogs, big dogs, little dogs, tiny dogs those are classes."

"Oh." Worries all gone. "Great! You can set up the classes. I wanna do the prizes."

"Well, we need to have the classes first so we know how many prizes to get. Some animals might enter two or three classes, so we'll have to have extras."

"Oh, OK." Giles was a little deflated. He brightened. "I wanna *make* the prizes!"

"Make the prizes? How?" Now Mother was truly puzzled. She was envisioning little awards on plastic stands, with dogs and cats on the platforms atop the little columns. Giles, however, had a better idea (really – he did!).

"Plaster of Paris," he said. "We have all *kinds* of animal molds."

And we did. We had a dozen different breeds of dogs, several different cats, horses, cattle, chickens you name a farm animal and we could make a little statue of it.

And so it began. Invitations were drawn up by Giles and me, and delivered up and down the country roads. We rode for *miles* on bikes and Mother took us to places too far to ride. After all, a township in that part of Portage County, Ohio was five miles wide by five miles tall. That's a lot of miles of road, by-ways and pathways paved and otherwise. I'm sure, although I never heard her and she never said, that Mother spent *many* hours on the telephone.

And we made Plaster-of-Paris statuettes by the *dozens*. We mixed plaster and water until we couldn't grip the spoons to mix any more. We poured the plastic into the molds using small funnels, and carefully squeezed and massaged them to get the air bubbles out. Then we topped them off, set them on waxed paper to cure, and repeated the process again, and again, and again, and...

And, of course, the molds had to be stripped, oh-so-carefully, from each statuette. It was at this point they were most vulnerable. Unpainted, they were eminently scratchable. Being handled and inspected, they were most likely to be dropped, and, worst of all, the "molds" were stretchable rubber that had to be peeled off the statuette – a great opportunity to lose a foot, a tail or even a head.

But it was finally done. Even Lyndella had proved invaluable in filling and removing molds. She, at the tender age of seven or eight had the capable hands of a girl much more mature. Came next the painting.

Mother had bought every bottle of gold and silver and tan model paint in three stores, and brushes to match. Freezer paper was laid over the kitchen table and the floor around it, and we began. Until then, when we made statuettes, we had taken great care in color selection, the proper look of eyes and other special appendages such as manes, tails, coxcombs, and so forth. But now, all was gold, silver or tan. Eyes, mane, comb none were any color save the color of the animal.

For days we painted. We had estimated as well as we thought we could, the number of attendees, and allowed for two events each, understanding that some would do more, and some only one. Then we'd made one additional set of first, second and third prizes for *everything*! Finally, it was done. We were ready. Came Saturday morning, we were busily staking runs and race-courses, setting out the statuettes, laying out equipment and supplies (there were several shovels, spades and trowels with attendant trash receptacles), as well as large bowls of chips and pretzels and a brand new garbage can filled with ice and every flavor of Nehi and Norka sodas known to the grocery store.

And then we waited – Giles with confidence; Mother with absolute equanimity; Lyndella with impatience. And Charles? Well, all my anxieties were back. After a short while, I went into the house and hid behind a book – always my refuge. I was sure no one was coming.

The Old Man came in. "Charles," his voice held some amusement, some exasperation, and a lot of understanding, something of which at the time I thought I heard and saw very little.

I looked up from my book. "Nobody's coming, are they?"

"Well," he said, laughing outright, "if they aren't we've got a *lot* of new dogs."

I jumped up and heard for real the cacophony of barking and howling that I'd been ignoring for the last half hour.

We went outside, where it seemed every dog, cat, chicken and rabbit in Shalersville Township had gathered in our yard. There was a good-sized front yard, overspread by sugar maples, and a larger rear yard, overspread by nothing. The Old Man, Mother and several neighbor adults were arranging kids and animals into groups and areas.

I realized that there were nearly a hundred pets and at least seventy-five kids there, and a few parents who stayed to help. For the rest of the afternoon, I judged dogs, cats, chickens, rabbits and anything else that hopped, ran or flew, including turtles, salamanders and frogs. The Old Man and Giles set up time trials for dogs (they tried one race and it took them ten minutes to get the dogs separated) and timed them with an old pocket watch of the Old Man's that had a stop-watch feature.

They tried to time-trial cats. I'd never heard of herding cats at the time, but if I had it would have fit. Cat time trials were abandoned in favor of several weight classes. One old Tom weighed in at a little less than sixteen pounds. If he'd had both ears he'd have made sixteen pounds easily. One female had a litter of eleven. They'd brought them all, because the kittens were only three days old.

At the end of the day, every child had at least one prize, and if the Old Man and Mother fudged a couple of the classes to insure that, who was harmed? The kids were happy, the animals were confusedly excited and my brother was the hero of the day even with the teenagers who'd come on a Saturday, I've no doubt, at the ear-twisting insistence of their mothers.

Even the Old Man was expansively pleased. Much as he'd grumbled at taking a Saturday for such foolishness, he'd enjoyed himself, and so many people had seen him do it he couldn't even pretend he hadn't.

And me? I spent the day in amazement. My kid brother had pulled it off. He'd come up with the idea, he'd followed through, he'd stuck with it and he'd made it work. Heckuva day!

CHAPTER 28

Thanksgiving Cat

Hattie Larlham was the best doggone cook West Virginia ever produced. Her Thanksgiving meals were celebrations of the joys of her kitchen and affirmations of life. Ours was the spread of thousands, the quintessential Norman Rockwell *Saturday Evening Post* cover.

From the range came twenty pounds of turkey, golden in its glazed glory, fragrant of celery and giblet stuffing. Hours had been spent drying bread – white, wheat, rye, French every sort we could find in the "day-old" bins – in the oven at low heat to make this perfect stuffing. The bird itself had been basted in soup stock and slathered with butter, then placed in a deep roaster and covered. Four hours of low-heat cooking, followed by an hour at much higher heat, with constant re-basting, created a masterpiece of edibility.

The bird was placed on a giant carving plate on the throne of the king of birds – the center of the table. Flour gravy was made from the bastings in the pan. The bird was surrounded by bowls containing potatoes whipped with milk and butter, green-bean casserole, stuffing, yams with a brown sugar sauce reduction and tiny marshmallows. Farther out in a secondary orbit were plates of rolls and butter, jellied cranberry and whole cranberry sauces, a sectional plate of olives, both black and green, celery, carrots, tiny tomatoes with a bowl of onion dip in the center.

We all bowed our heads as the Old Man said grace, in the tone of a Baptist minister praising the Lord for the wonders of life. When he had finished, we all raised our heads and gazed upon the feast before us, and its crowning glory; old Tom Turkey – from inside of which, through the great space from which the stuffing had been extracted emerged the head of *our gray farm cat*!

Pandemonium! The Old Man grabbed at the cat, which erupted from the turkey beneath his arm and streaked the length of the table, leapt over my mother, and turned left. The cat was betrayed by the grease on its feet and the linoleum floor. Sliding and scrabbling she bounced off the bottom of the stove, dug in with her claws and ran in place on the greasy linoleum long enough for the Old Man to reach her.

With one huge swoop, he had her by the scruff of the neck, yowling and unable to reach him with her claws. Continuing forward, he flung open the rear door and flung the cat spang into the screen door! From which she rebounded over his shoulder and into the sink-full of dirty dishes. I grabbed her as she abandoned ship, the Old Man opened the screen door and I heaved her out. Silence.

We looked at the turkey. We looked at each other. We looked at the grease and soapy water on the floor. We looked again at each other. Mother began to laugh, and it was contagious. Even the Old Man laughed.

When the laughter died down, we all sat again. "Well," said the Old Man, "we don't eat anything from the inside anyway." And he began to carve.

CHAPTER 29

Farmed Out

As my brother and I grew older, we began to be "farmed out" to neighboring farmers to assist in haying, milking, barn clean-out, etc. Whatever a neighbor needed to have done the Old Man would "farm us out" to do. Pay was not usually expected, but we could accept it if it was offered. However, there were specific instances in which it was part of the deal to begin with.

For instance, potato farming was big business in Portage County and several neighboring farms had large potato plantings and contracts with Frito-Lay (just Lay's at the time), Better Made and other local chip makers. Come fall, migrant workers performed the ultimate stoop labor of following the digging machine and picking up the potatoes and putting them into a bushel-sized basket they hauled with them. If a farmer were short of workers, he would call for us and for every child over ten within the immediate area. We would get the same pay as the migrants, which was thirty-five cents per basket filled. Of course, the migrant workers, having done this for years, could triple our output, but the farmers were scrupulously fair. Every picker got the same piece-work scale.

Haying, however, was another matter. The phone would ring and Giles and I would be on our bikes, heading for a day of heaving eighty-pound "square" bales of clover or lighter alfalfa hay. These square bales were tightly wrapped endwise with two strands of baling twine. Some baler ejection chutes extended to the wagon while others were designed simply to drop the bales to the ground. Depending on the day and weather, a farmer might remove the longer chute to get the hay baled ahead of rain, or to have it ready for after-school assistance.

If they were dropped from the baler onto the ground, a wagon was pulled from bale to bale. As the wagon approached the bale, one of us would grab the two strands together in both hands and heave the bale up to the brother on the wagon, who would place it for stability. If the wagon were pulled behind the baler, each bale came off a chute and was grabbed by Giles or me and handed off to the other brother who placed it onto a stack of bales growing from back to front. It was essential to cross-pack the bales for stability, because the load might be as high as ten or twelve bales by the time we headed for the barn, and spilling a load meant busted bales and an angry farmer who wasn't likely to be generous at the end of the day.

Some farmers used a different technique and created smaller round bales, most often of timothy, a much lighter grass baled primarily for horses. These bales were rolled into a tube, with the twine following the roll, making it impossible to handle them by hand. Each of us had two steel hooks, each about three-eighths of an inch in diameter, and ten inches from the wooden crossbar handle to the center of the curve of the hook. The point of the hook was amazingly sharp. It was honed every time it was used.

As a bale came off the baler, a hook was slammed into each end. The bale was lifted by the ends, and taken by the hooks of the next man (boy) and swung into the growing pile on the wagon. These could not be cross-stacked, so could not be piled nearly as high as the square bales. This required extra loads and a haying job with round bales always went slower than a square-bale job.

Unloading at the barn consisted of grabbing a bale from the wagon stack with two hooks, and swinging them upward with one end leading. The man in the mow would swing his hook into the top of the bale and haul it up. On one hot August haying day, our last load got to the barn near dark, and it *was* dark in the barn as I grabbed the last bale and slung it above my head toward the haymow door. I was tired, and perhaps didn't swing it far enough. The farmer was tired and perhaps didn't strike accurately.

The shock of the hook striking the back of my hand was more a surprise than pain. Everything stopped. I knew instantly what had happened, and so did the farmer. I held rigid and he made no move. "Let go of your hook, Mr. Gutterman," I said. I wondered at the lack of shaking in my voice. "Just open your hand." He opened his hand, and as I felt the tension leave the hook, I opened both of mine, letting the bale fall to the barn floor.

"I'll call your Dad," he said, climbing down from the mow. "We'll meet him at Doc's." The Old Man agreed to meet us at the Doctors office (in the back of his house) and we took off, Mr. Gutterman, Giles and me in his '47 Ford quarter-ton pick-up.

Our local Doctor was a classic small town GP. He made house calls, kept an emergency surgery in his office, tended the sports teams and occasionally drank too much. It was mid-August, full dark and hot. I was covered with barn dust and sweat, I was tired and my hand was beginning to throb. I was in no mood for foolishness.

We got to the office, which was still dark, at the same time as the Old Man and my mother. "He should be up," the Old Man said. "I called him before I left." He pounded on the door.

Eventually the doctor answered the door. "Sorry," he mumbled, "guess I went back to sleep." He turned on the light. "C'mon in."

We trooped into the office. The doctor took up a position half-sitting on the edge of the surgery sink. "Heard you got a hay-hook stuck in ya," he growled. "Let's have a look."

I raised my left hand, with the hay-hook hanging from it. Blood dripped from the point and ran down the shaft. "Just how," he asked owlishly, "do you expect me to fix the hole in your hand with that thing in it?" He drew himself upright.

"Good point." I grabbed the belly of the hook and yanked. It came out and sent a splash of red onto his shirt.

The doctor turned puce, spun on his heel and vomited into the sink. There was nervous laughter, but not from the Old Man. The Old Man was unhappy, and he was of a mind to share.

"You're drunk." The accusation hung in the air while the old doctor washed out his mouth. "You're stinkin', fallin' down drunk."

"Not 'ny more." The doctor belched, picked up a bottle of green liquid, threw some of the contents into his mouth, gargled and spat into the sink. "I'm sober now. Boy!" He turned to me. "Let's see that hand."

I lifted it to him. We'll pass on the details of the next few minutes. Suffice to say that I learned I was a bit less stoic than I might have hoped. At the end of the ordeal I had Iodoform gauze (gauze saturated with an iodine solution) stickin' out of both the palm and back of my hand, a quarter inch to be pulled out each day so the wound would heal from the inside.

He gave me a tetanus shot, gave my mother a vial of penicillin and told her to shoot me in the backside every day for five days (a task in which she took entirely too much pleasure). The Old Man forked over some bills and we left.

My left hand swelled to the approximate size of a softball, and it *hurt*! For a day or two, I contemplated stabbing it to deflate it, but it already had a hole in it and it wasn't deflating. I waited it out, and it began to reduce in a couple days, but my haying was done for the summer. I was reduced to one-handed chores for the better part of a month, a circumstance much bemoaned by Giles, who had to do all the rest.

CHAPTER 30

Work-a-Day Summers – First Paying Job

The Old Man did not believe in lay-about summers nor did Mother. Children were meant to learn to work. So summers on the farm in the '50s were not the idyllic boys' escape they've been painted to be. It was seldom I got to sit in the shade with a grass stem in my mouth and a straw hat upon my head. Oh, we had the shade and the straw hats and there was plenty of grass. But the shade did not cover the garden, and the straw hat was there to shade my eyes while I chopped the grass out of the garden with a five-inch hoe.

From the summer I was ten, there were animals to feed and water (and clean up after), eggs to gather, gardens to tend to, lawns to mow and neighbors to work for. Not long after, there was paying work caddying at the local "Country Club," weeding, picking and planting in the local muck farms, potatoes to pick (and later sweet corn) and hay to load and stack. The days were long, hot and busy, and I envied my friends who complained of "nothing to do."

My kid brother Giles, not quite two years younger, was tossed into the same roil as soon as Mother deemed him old enough. Soon we were caddying together, haying together and fighting over whose turn it was not to mow the lawn. I might have been older, but he was taller, leaner and faster by the time he was twelve. We could do about the same amount of work in the same amount of time.

Although we were still available to any neighboring farmer who called the Old Man or Mother and asked for help, there came a day for each of us when first I, then Giles a year later, was told our lives of summer ease was over. Work that paid actual wages had been found for us. Unsure what, exactly, was the "summer ease" we were losing, we ventured forth, each in his own time.

My first foray began the summer I turned twelve. We lived on the hills and potholes left in the end moraines of the glaciers that covered North America 12,000 years ago. Unlike the hills and valleys of unglaciated areas, these hills were piles of easily eroded soil and gravel and the potholes were blind sumps, however large some of them were. Over the twelve thousand intervening years, the potholes had filled with water, which could not drain. The water became loaded with vegetation, mostly sphagnum and peat mosses. The water became anaerobic as oxygen was used in the digestion of dead plants, but not replaced by water flowing through. Slowly the lake filled with anaerobically digested vegetation that became earth as it completed its biological breakdown.

But this soil was a special kind of soil. Not being made from ground up rock dust, its texture was gel-like when it became wet. When dry, it had the texture of talcum powder. But whatever its physical state, it was akin to pure fertilizer. The soil was called muck, of which there were two types, Carlisle and Linwood. The soil itself was a rich black and perfect for growing vegetables. But it presented problems. It didn't drain, for it had no more particle separation than clay, and it was lowland, with nowhere to drain *to*. So it had to be artificially drained and those drains had to be regularly dredged, which brings us to problem number two – no shear strength. That meant that wheels tended to spin and sink in even the driest conditions because the soil just sheared off in sheets under the lateral pressure of a turning wheel.

In northeast Ohio, celery farms, sometimes called "muck farms," were often a boy's first chance to do regular labor that paid a wage. And so it was with me. Mother took me to meet a grumbling, grumpy old man who owned a small celery farm. He employed several boys and he offered full pay for half-days, the munificent sum of seventy-five cents an hour; three dollars for a four-hour day. Mother had found other work for me in the afternoon, so a half-day was my allotted work time. The farmer grumbled, but agreed. I don't believe he felt that Mother had asked him for a job for me. It seemed to me he was following orders.

And so began my sojourn as a truck farmer's helper. The farm grew mostly celery, but there was a fairly large area devoted to cantaloupe and another to summer squash. Most garden vegetables would do well but he had a small farm, less than fifty acres plus the five acres the buildings occupied, so he restricted his output to three or four things, but always mostly celery.

And it was celery to which I was assigned, it being judged the easiest to deal with. Celery is planted in long rows, far enough apart for tillers (that would be me) to pass between them on hands and knees.

On *what*? Hands and knees? Seriously?

Yep, hands and knees, seriously. I would crawl along, scooping muck and weeds bare-handedly from between and alongside the celery plants. Crawl forward, scoop left, scoop right, crawl forward. My back screams at the very memory. As I scooped and crawled, the black dirt caked in the knees of my jeans, dusted into my mouth, nose and eyes, soaked into my skin in the sweat that erupted like an instant bath as the sun rose above ten o'clock. And have I mentioned that I was crawling? Back screaming in protest, I crawled and scooped. At the end of the second set, as we approached the farm buildings, the farmer appeared with iced soft drinks and jugs of ice water.

I soon learned that the farmer's gruffness was nothing more than his accent. He was a German immigrant who had not learned English until his teens. German is a guttural language, and he spoke English with all the rolled r's and glottal stops of his native tongue, a language that he, ironically, could no longer speak. He and his wife were always nice to us. They understood the dangers of overheating and the advantages of hydration.

Once the celery plants were twelve inches tall, twelve-inch-wide strips of black tarpaper were rolled out along each side of each row. When the strips extended the full length of several rows on both sides, packs of wire loops that resembled nothing so much as croquet hoops, were dropped at intervals along the rows. Then it was my job to lift the strips to vertical, drop two loops across both of them a couple inches apart, and push the ends into the dirt, denying the sun access to the chlorophyll in the celery stalks. When harvested a couple weeks later the celery stalks were pale white... what? You thought they just grew that way? *Au contraire', mon amie.* It takes work to make all that green white.

So why do it?

Well, chlorophyll is bitter, that's why. And the more sun it gets, the more bitter it becomes, so celery farmers hide it from the sun. When chlorophyll doesn't see the sun, it uses itself up, and the cells containing it cease to be active. The plant turns white.

What are you talking about? The celery I buy isn't white, and you're right, it's bitter.

Yep, commercial truck farms on a scale of multi-thousands of acres probably can't, or at least don't, field-blanch their celery the way we used to. It's just not economically feasible.

Harvest was a fairly straightforward process. One person crawled between the rows, pulling the wire hoops and dropping the tarpaper. We then crawled the rows, pulling up celery from the loose black muck and dropping it roots and all into boxes that were picked up by another crew and tossed onto a flatbed wagon. The wagons carried them into a packaging barn where the roots were cut off and each celery plant was run through a spray hood where water at high pressure came at them from three directions, knocking all the dirt off.

Once they were placed in plastic-lined boxes on ice beds, they were delivered to local grocers the same day. The farmer's wife ran a small fruit (apples and pears purchased from local orchards) and vegetable stand at the roadside. A shed with tables in front under an awning, the market was primarily run for the benefit of neighbors. I doubt she made enough to more than cover her costs. We would be sent from the barn to find out what stock she might need, and the farmer would take her whatever she needed.

We all chipped in at squash and cantaloupe harvest. Fishing through the tangle of vines for green zucchini and yellow summer squashes was back-breaking, skin-tearing adventure. No crawling here – one had to step around and over the vines and unripe fruit to get to the pickable stuff. Then too, the vines were closely covered in tiny short spikes that tore at skin as one reached through and over and under, seeking squash and cantaloupe. As soon as picked fruit and vegetables reached the barn, they were transferred to the spray hood and then sorted by size and ripeness for sale to the local A&P, Acme, Kroger and so forth. Once the cantaloupe were ripe, a big sign went up in the yard, and many more cars filled the pull-off as men stopped on their way home to pick up a melon for dessert.

The cantaloupe and green honeydew melons in most stores today are all about the same size, not fully ripe, and trucked from southern states and California. They average maybe six inches in diameter. The cantaloupes and honeydews we sent to local stores back in the '50s were a wee bit different. They varied in size from six inches diameter to twelve inches, they were fully ripe, had about a two-day shelf life and they came from the farm down the road.

The final difference is flavor. Today's commercial cantaloupe has a flavor reminiscent of the flavor of a vine-ripened melon. Our melons *were* vine-ripened. They didn't taste like cantaloupe – they suffused one's mouth and senses of taste and smell (a big part of the sense of taste) in the totality of cantaloupe.

I worked the muck farm until I was sixteen (it was within bike-riding distance) and I always worked only mornings. In the afternoons, I caddied at the Aurora Country Club, or picked strawberries for my seventh-grade teacher, or was back to the "spare kid" business of haying and other local farm work. Mother would take me and later Giles as well, to the country club or the teacher's berry farm, but getting to local farmers was by shank's mare or bicycle. But for a first job, nothing could have beaten the muck farm.

CHAPTER 31

Sweet Corn Pickin' Daze

My last couple years at home, Giles and I picked sweet corn. I had earned my driver's license and getting to the sweet corn picking job required a better ride than a single-speed, fat-tire Schwinn. Commercial picking meant filling a farm wagon, and quickly. A barn filled with conveyor belts, ice blocks, sharp-eyed women and packing bags awaited. The picking began at five o'clock in the morning. On our first day we were assigned two rows each, right next to the wagon. These, we were assured, were the "easy" rows.

Five minutes into the morning, Giles and I were dropping steadily back, nearly next to the tractor pushing the wagon. Suddenly we ran out of corn. The rows had been stripped ahead of us by the men in front of the wagon. These two men had three rows each to pick, and apparently had time to pick two rows to the side for at least a hundred feet. Giles, ever reticent and reluctant to cause a scene caused a scene. "What the heck happened to my corn?" he demanded. "Somebody thinks he's funny?"

We kept going and, every so often, we'd find ourselves picking empty rows. It was embarrassing. At nine o'clock, the wagons were stopped and the farm's owner showed up with a pickup truck carrying pints of ice cream, a huge coffee machine and cold drinks for the non-coffee drinkers among us. As we ate our ice cream, Giles pulled me aside.

"There's a trick to it, and I've got to find it." Giles was frustrated and angry and Giles frustrated *or* angry was not a good thing. "If I don't, somebody's mouth is gonna be selling tickets he can't cash." I looked at my skinny fourteen-year-old kid brother. One of the front guys, an ordinary looking college student in his early twenties, had been riding us pretty hard. Suddenly, I was worried for him.

"Faster," I said, "we have to move our hands faster, and we can't worry about the corn we miss. Throw at four or five, not every couple." I hadn't enjoyed being hazed any more than Giles had. I just hadn't been planning anyone's demise. I'd been watching our fellow pickers. I looked up at the sun. "Drink a lot of pop or water. It's gonna get hot and you're gonna sweat – a lot."

We loaded up on water and the wagon started. We began to sweat and peeled off our shirts. The wagon stopped and the tractor driver collected shirts. Giles and I were keeping up. In fact, we were going faster than the wagon. Well, I was, and I hoped he was. I couldn't see him on the other side of the wagon. As the day wore on, we began to learn about the worst part of the job.

Corn leaves have sharply toothed edges and we were a mass of scratches and shallow cuts, into which our salt-rich sweat poured. In addition to salt, our sweat carried pollen from fields in which live pollination was allowed, meaning the tassels remained, and they still released pollen at every jiggle and jog. We sweated and burned, burned and itched, and there was nothing to be done about it.

Reach, grab, yank downward, slide fingers around the silk – reach, grab, yank downward, slide fingers around the silk, repeat, repeat and toss repeat cycle – endlessly. Giles began to swear. Being only fourteen, his vocabulary was limited and he knew it, but he was not deterred. For the rest of the morning we heard, more than a little repetitiously, exactly what he thought of working in his own sweat, being cut by corn and burning without relief. But he never quit picking.

By the second week, we were the wagon leaders, and only the most experienced pickers could stand the gaff behind us. We set a pace that sent two to three extra wagons to the barn each morning.

Came noon, and picking was over. The corn would lose moisture and wilt (yes, sweet corn kernels wilt) in the sun, so the last wagons were sent into the shade of the barn. Pickers were offered space at the sorting conveyors if they wanted the extra money. Most did not. Giles and I often did. The sorting room was filled with noise. Dozens of people talking, the clatter of cogwheels driving conveyors, a huge ice chipper in which three-hundred pound blocks of ice were reduced to one-inch chunks to be poured into large paper bags after each dozen ears. Each bag held five dozen ears in alternating layers with the ice.

The summer after my senior year, I was wearing my class ring while I sorted corn. The corn-sorting table consisted of two chains of flat, squared links that were pulled along a narrow flat table. At intervals of about eighteen inches, a flat bar of wood was attached to the chains by a small tongue of steel at each end. One of those tongues had a raised corner and, as I grabbed an ear of corn off the conveyor, the raised corner caught my class ring, nearly taking my finger off. I leapt up and raced alongside the conveyor, screaming for help. My hand was about to get pulled into the cogwheels that drove the chain when someone slashed the drive belt.

I told the picker foreman I'd be back in the morning, and Giles and I took off for the jewelry store in Streetsboro. The jeweler, after some argument, agreed to remove the ring. He produced a small, hand-turned circular hacksaw, slid the grooved sawing bed between my finger and the saw, and slowly turned the blade. After an eternity, the saw-blade settled into the groove and he pulled it away. Taking two small needle-nosed pliers, he slowly separated the cut ends of the ring and eased the ring away from the cut in my finger. He agreed to braze the ring and Giles and I went home.

I soaked the hand in Epsom salts that evening, and the next morning, it took me about fifteen minutes to flex it into usability. Then Giles and I went to work.

CHAPTER 32

Potato Pickin', Caddyshack and All That

Every teenager in Shalersville Township dreaded potato harvest. It was piece-work stoop labor and backs and knees bore the brunt. Tractors pulled digger machines along the rows, digging up soil, potatoes and rocks, shaking the soil down through a screened chute, and dropping the potatoes and rocks, often indistinguishable, off the back end of the chute onto the finer soil. We worked in a pervasive haze of fine dust, our knees raw the first hour and our backs screaming in pain by noon.

The potatoes were picked up by hand and tossed into a slatted wooden basket. As each basket filled, it was emptied into a bushel basket. A tag was inserted in the rim of the bushel basket by the picker who filled it. You got paid by the number of tags with your number the foreman had at the end of the day. Migrant worker families worked along with us, laughing at the pathetic efforts of the local teens. Any migrant child of eight could out-pick any local teen by at least two to one. I thought a ten or fifteen dollar paycheck at the end of the day was pretty good (at thirty-five cents a basket), but the migrant families were pulling from twenty to seventy-five dollars a day per person, including their kids. Still, it was money, and the farmers needed all the help they could get.

I started caddying at eleven (turned twelve that summer), carrying a single bag for two dollars and fifty cents for a two and a half hour walk around nine holes of a golf-course. The tip was usually fifty cents and half a day was all the caddy master would let kids under fourteen work. As time went on, I graduated to full-course days and, when I turned fourteen, I began carrying two bags at once. The bags were heavy leather bags with fourteen clubs, a couple dozen balls, miscellaneous devices for improving the game of duffers (these never worked – they just collected in golf bags) and a pint of whatever potable was favored by the player. The whole shebang weighed from twenty-five to thirty pounds. Carrying two of them provided balance, but at a total weight of fifty to sixty pounds, they made the last couple holes exercises in torture.

I learned a lot about people at the Aurora Country Club. I had clubs thrown at me (once, I chased the offending golfer back to the clubhouse with them), balls hit at me with no "*Fore!*" as warning (I toed them into the ground) and was sent into poison ivy infested woods to find balls (fortunately, I am not affected by poison ivy). I was stung by hornets in my shoe (I stepped into a nest hole climbing out of a creek bank after retrieving a ball and every hornet in the nest dived into my shoe) and chased by a coyote (the golfers drove him off by throwing clubs at him).

The members were mostly middle-management types who knew they'd topped out and were bitter about it. They took their frustrations out on bartenders, towel-boys, the shop pro and most especially caddies. I carried my last bags a month after I turned eighteen. There were few caddies left. Golf carts were replacing us and few courses would allow a caddied foursome because they slowed down play. I saw a couple guys who'd always been nice to me and persuaded the caddy master to send me out with them. At the end of the round when they pulled out their wallets, I waved them off. "My last loop," I said. "I picked you guys for a freebie."

Once I went to college, work became a more formal business. One summer, I worked nights as a busboy and fry-cook at a Howard Johnson plaza on the Ohio Turnpike. For part of one summer I worked afternoons as an orderly in the local hospital. Eventually I worked as a rough carpenter. But from the time I was ten, there was no lay-about summer.

When I had children, I was appalled to discover that there was *nothing* they were allowed to do to earn money on a steady basis. They weren't allowed, by law, to do anything I'd done until they turned fourteen, and then they were severely restricted. Lay-about summers, it turned out, had become the law while I wasn't looking.

CHAPTER 33

The Beast in the Basement

The hammering rhythm of my cheap, '50s (no great surprise there... it was 1956) electric buzzer alarm wakes me. It's four-thirty on a cold January morning in northeast Ohio. Thirty miles northeast of Akron, our house lies in the northeast Ohio Lake Erie "lake-effect" weather zone of big cold, big winds and big snow. This morning the temperature out in the wind and snow is probably about fifteen degrees Fahrenheit, and about fifty inside. Down in the basement of this century house waits "The Beast." And this beast is my charge. Like the animals and chickens in summer, I feed this beast, clean up after it and generally keep it in good health. Simple enough no?

My brother, Giles, with whom I share a bed grunts and turns over – ramming an elbow into my ribs. Enough! I'm awake! Time to get going. I sit up, swing my legs over the bed and stand barefoot on a *very* cold floor. I grab jeans, shirt, socks, underwear and shoes and head downstairs. Waking the Old Man is not recommended. He gave me this task because he works twelve-hour days as a welder and heavy equipment operator in a nearby sand and gravel mine. Getting up an extra hour early makes the work and drive home risky.

In the downstairs bathroom, I drag my clothes on. Shower and shave will come later. I'll need it. I head for the basement, a dark little room with walls made of small boulders set in mortar for lack of brick or block, and with silver beech logs for ceiling (living room floor) joists. I know the kind of tree because the bark is still on. The floor is old, damp and broken concrete and The Beast squats on that floor against the wall to the right of the stairs.

The Beast is a lump-coal-fired furnace. There is no fan... the heat from the furnace is gravity fed to the house. The Beast comprises a large cylinder of galvanized sheet metal covering an inner structure of heavy cast iron. From the galvanized cover sprout ten-inch sheet-metal arms extending to crawl spaces under the wings of the house, joints sealed by asbestos tape. Cold air "return" registers are placed near outer walls. Air chilled by the cold walls falls into the registers and is carried to the bottom of the galvanized case surrounding the firebox. Heat from the firebox is transferred through the cast iron into that same space. The cold air, being heavier than warm air, enters the bottom of the space and, as it slowly heats and expands, it forces the hotter air at the top out heater registers in the various first-floor rooms.

The front of The Beast sports a mouth – a wide iron door leading to the firebox. The door is opened and closed with a drop latch operated by a hanging handle that looks like a spring narrowed at both ends. A handle attached directly to the drop latch would have been too hot to touch, but the iron loop attaching the "spring" handle to the latch doesn't transfer enough heat to matter.

Below the central door, a second door with slots with a sliding panel behind them leads to the ash pit. Between the two sections, a heavy, moveable grating allows ash to be shaken from the firebox into the ash pit by sliding the end of a handle onto the squared end of a protruding rod and levering it smartly left and right, causing the grates to move and shake out the ash.

The slots in the ash pit door are there to control air flow into the firebox. The more open the slots, the more air to the firebox and the hotter the fire. This mechanism is controlled by a small chain attached to a mechanical thermostat in the living room. Turning the thermostat dial moves the panel behind the slots and controls the heat to the house. It's a very inefficient system, and the house is never truly warm in winter.

I grab a coal scuttle and use a scoop shovel to fill the scuttle with small and medium-sized lumps of sulfur-rich bituminous coal from the pile beneath the eyebrow window set high in the back wall of the basement. Back at the furnace, I insert the shaker handle and vigorously shake the fire-bed grates, dumping ash into the ash-pit beneath it. Some of the ash glows red, which tells me I won't have to light the fire from scratch today.

Grabbing another scuttle, I scoop ashes out of the ash-pit into it with the coal scoop, coughing in the sulfurous fumes. I run up the back stairs, fling open the lay-over shed doors covering them, and carry the ash out and dump it on the gravel drive that circles behind the house.

Back at The Beast, I open the door at the foot of the chimney and shovel soot into the ash bucket. If I get a good fire going and it catches the soot in the chimney afire, we could lose this old wooden house. I finish and go stand in front of The Beast, poker in hand. Opening the door, I can see flames encouraged by the air I've let in through the ash pit licking the vestiges of the large coal lumps I'd used the night before to bank the fire. In "banking" a fire, the fire is pushed into a tight mound against the furnace wall, and large lumps of coal or wedges of split wood are laid against and atop the burning coal, packed closely enough to keep oxygen out, while the air feed is closed in the ash-pit door.

Having burning coal in the furnace is good and bad. Good, because I can use the poker to create a burning coal bed out of the remaining coal, and cover it with the coal in the scuttle. Bad because it's already *hot* in that thing and, as I pull the bank apart, it's likely to flare. I pull on the welding gloves the Old Man gave me for this job, and proceed.

With the poker, I drag flaming coal from against the furnace wall out into the middle of the fire-bed. Then I fill the scoop-shovel with coal and spread it as best I can over the burning coal. A puff of hot air hits me and I step to the side as flame bursts out the door. I repeat until the coal is gone from the scuttle and finish by tossing the soot into the flames. I never do *that* again. I have never heard about combustible dust, but I learn that day. The explosion is impressive to a teen-aged boy, but it's not really all that big. Fortunately, the furnace is not harmed.

I open the air gate in the ash-pit door, set the flue in the pipe leading to the chimney and head upstairs. It has taken me a half hour, and the house will take another hour to warm and, with no fan, simply a gravity fed hot air distribution system, warm is a relative term. Now that the work is over, I'm cold. Nonetheless, as I look into the bathroom mirror, I know I dare not go out into the house carrying all the soot and ash I'm wearing. And Mother isn't going to be pleased with the missing eyebrow. I hadn't been quite as quick as I thought to avoid the first big gout of flame.

I strip and shower, stepping out from the enclosing curtain into what feels like a sub-freezing bathroom. I towel off in record time, brush the Greaser DA pompadour into shape, brush my teeth, pull on clean clothes and head outside to take care of the few animals we keep in winter (a few chickens, two pigs and a pair of turkeys), before the family gets up for breakfast.

At five-thirty, I get Mother up, and go to gather up my schoolwork. Then I sit down at the table and wake up only when Giles snaps my ear with his finger. I jump up, ready to fight, but the Old Man barks, "When I told you to wake him I didn't tell you to start a fight. Now sit down and eat!"

Bacon, eggs over easy, buttered toast all appear on serving plates, and we pass them around. Mother brings coffee for the Old Man and me, while Giles and our sister (only eight at the time) have milk. As we finished and put on our coats, Mother calls, "I see the bus!" Shoving our arms into sleeves and grabbing books, Giles and I race for the end of the driveway, arriving just as the bus does. We step aboard and head for school. Another ordinary day begins.

When the Old Man bought a coal stoker that would fill the furnace two years later, it meant I could sleep another hour each morning.

The stoker shows up in mid-August and the Old Man and I, and Uncle Jack who now lives a quarter-mile down the road, install it and its attendant fan (Glory be! Wonder of wonders, we finally have a furnace fan!). The stoker comprises a box, an Archimedes Screw Conveyor and a fire-grate.

The box is shaped like a somewhat elongated, inverted, truncated pyramid. At the bottom it narrows to a slot that runs along the longest dimension, and from which protrudes a steel tube. Within the tube, beginning at the end of the box farthest from the furnace and ending in the center of the ash pit, lies a device called an "Archimedes Screw." Millennia ago, a "natural philosopher" (today we'd call him a scientist) named Archimedes discovered that if a screw were built without taper (essentially an auger), and encased around the bottom and at least part of each side, it would, as it turned, carry from one end to the other anything that would fit between the flights of the screw and not extend beyond the encasement. In our case, it would carry coal.

At the end of the screw, an inverted cone filled with coal, and at the top of the cone the coal spread out over a firing grate, the shaker grates having been removed. The stoker was filled with stoker coal, which had particles no more than one-and-a-half inches on a side, and a load of it included everything from that size down to dust.

Once the stoker is installed, along with the fan and a new electrical thermostat that simply turns on the motor that drives the screw, my morning becomes much simpler. I fill the coal scuttle and empty it into the stoker box. When the box is full, I pour five gallons of water into it to lubricate the coal and close and latch the lid. The bituminous coal we burn is fairly hard and very abrasive. If run through the tube surrounding the screw without lubrication, it will grind through in short order. Water reduces the ability of coal to abrade the tube. It doesn't affect the fire, because it is evaporated by the fire's heat before it ever reaches the actual fire.

What changes for me is the building of the fire – it doesn't occur. With a motorized screw filling the firebox on demand, there is no banking of the fire. We simply set the thermostat to add coal less often (we set it for a lower temperature). In the morning, I need build no fire, burn off no eyebrows or build no new fires in a cold furnace. I need only remove the clinkers that are blocking the fire grate after I've filled the stoker.

There is no ash in the ash pit. Instead, the heat of the fire fuses the molten ash into clinkers that collect on the fire grate. I have three tools: a long, straight poker made of steel rod about three eighths of an inch thick, with one end formed into a flattened loop as a handle; a similar rod bent at the end into an "L"; and a two-rod grasping set. The graspers are made of two rods held together by three steel rings, each welded to the same rod with the other rod inside the ring as well, but kept from moving vertically. On one end, each rod has the formed handle. The other is bent ninety degrees, and then formed into a partial arc. With some practice, I learn to manipulate the two so that the graspers will actually grasp.

With the straight and "L" rods, I break a clinker and move the pieces into a pile. Using the graspers, I pick up each piece and drop it into a coal scuttle. Once the scuttle is full, the race up the stairs surrounded by sulfur fumes is the same as before.

I could've kissed the Old Man but dignity prevented any such display of gratitude.

CHAPTER 34

Diggin' a Hole

The battered old dump truck backed through the snow toward the basement window frame – a narrow slot about a foot high and thirty-two inches wide. The driver braked, set the parking brake and climbed down from the cab. I had removed the window from its frame. The driver slid a steel chute through the window frame. He dropped weld-reinforced holes cut into the other end onto pegs at the bottom of a sliding door built into the base of the truck's tailgate. Then he pulled a lever that raised the door in the tailgate, and a few blocks of cabbage-sized and smaller coal rolled down the chute to break on the old cement of the basement floor.

The driver jogged to the side of the truck and pulled a lever that activated the hydraulic ram of the dump body. As the front of the dump body raised up, more coal rolled down the chute, but the small gate soon choked. The driver poked a steel bar into the coal jammed in the gate, and more coal tumbled down the chute. The process of poking and waiting for pluggage continued for about twenty minutes, until the truck bed was nearly empty. The driver lowered the bed, hoisted himself up into it carrying a large shovel, and proceeded to clean the truck bed into the chute.

When he was gone, I went down into the basement, leaned a ladder against the coal and clambered up to the window frame, where I pulled the window from its storage rack, dropped it into place in the frame and locked it shut with the turning blocks at each end.

My last job was to take our coal scoop and chase all the far-spread coal back to the pile sloped against the stone wall of the basement. By the time I'd finished, I was coal-black as a miner from the coal dust hanging in the air and the dust I'd raised moving the coal. A bath was in order and that meant I had to strip to my underwear, bundle my clothes into my inside-out shirt and walk through the house into the bathroom – a trial that grew worse as I got older.

"Richard!" It was my mother, calling to the Old Man from the laundry room. "Dick, this has *got* to stop!"

The Old Man closed the *Ravenna Evening Record* with a snap and set his jaw. "What's the matter *now*, Pat?" He stood up from the La-Z-Boy he'd gotten for Christmas and strode toward the laundry room off the kitchen.

"My washer is filthy with coal again. I'll have to run an empty load and then re-wash Chuck's clothes, just to get the coal dust out. It's a lot of extra work."

The Old Man looked into the washer, where a layer of black was undeniably present. "That was the last winter load, Pat. It won't happen next year." For some reason, the Old Man turned toward me as he said that, and I knew immediately that it was not going to be the Old Man who fixed it.

That was mid-February of 1957. School was out in early June and the Old Man had not forgotten his promise. "Come with me, Charles." He led the way to the rear of the old farmhouse.

The Old Man took a spade and a pick, and proceeded to cut a three-sided rectangle about twelve feet by fourteen (the basement wall being the fourth side), with the coal window approximately centered. He turned to me and handed me the spade. "This," he indicated the space he'd marked, "is your job for the summer. You can do it any way you like, evenings and week-ends, all day every day until it's done, some of each I don't care, but it has to be done by Labor Day. Dig to the foundation, keep the sides vertical, and keep the dirt moved back from the edges. Come with me." He headed for the garage.

Inside the old wooden four-car garage, there was a hardware store's worth of tools. The Old Man pulled out a heavy-duty, steel-wheeled, construction grade wheelbarrow and tossed a square shovel, a mattock and a flat-bladed spud-bar into it. "You'll need all of those before you're done," he said. He was right in spades. I was on my third spade and second square shovel when I finished.

I took the wheelbarrow and tools up to the rear of the house and I began to dig. At first, I needed the pick to get through the compressed soil, gravel and cinder mix the first foot or so had become over the years. But by the end of the day, I could press the spade into the soil with one foot, and easily lift a full spade of earth out and toss it away. I worked from about nine that morning until five that evening, stopping only for lunch. I was proud of the work I'd done and I told myself the Old Man was sure gonna be surprised when I finished his hole by the end of the week.

Ri-i-i-ight!

The next morning, I could not move. I had my brother help roll me out of bed, where I struggled out of my pajamas and into jeans and a T-shirt while my brother stood by and snickered. Shoes and socks I carried downstairs. As I hobbled to the table, Mother looked up and saw me. She choked back the laughter I could see in her eyes and asked if I might better just rest today.

My back screamed protest at every shift in direction. My arms felt as if they'd been beaten. The quads and hamstrings in my thighs promised retribution at every step. Sitting down into a chair taught me instantly that back muscles have a lot to do with what your legs do. And my hands were so swollen I could barely close my fingers. But I just asked what was for breakfast. She smiled at me and turned to the stove. Two eggs (over easy), bacon, fried potatoes, rye toast, butter and coffee later, I tried the shoes again. I couldn't reach my feet, and I couldn't raise them above the first rung of the chair.

My brother began laughing again. Mother advised him that the day's chores were now all his, unless *he* wanted to dig the hole. "But, Mo-o-o-oom..." got him The Look. He went off to milk the cow and feed the other animals. "Stand up, Charles." She had her face under control.

With great care, I stood. "Reach slowly for your left toe with your right hand," she instructed and showed me, easily touching her toe. I reached down to my knee. "Pu-u-l-l-l yourself down, Charles," she said. But it was no use. I pulled. I pushed. I did all I could do, and that was the day I discovered I would *never* be flexible enough to touch my toes or even my shins (this became a huge issue in basic training a few years later). I'd had wrestling and football coaches try to get me lower, but they hadn't had the time to really work on it. Mother spent an hour that day and got my back and thighs stretched enough to allow me to walk, but I never in my life could reach below my knees.

I went to the rear of the house and took my tools down into the hole. Ten minutes of trying convinced me I would not be able to hold a spade handle that day, much less dig with one. I pulled myself back out of the hole and went inside. A pan of hot water and Epsom salts was the cure for my hands. I flexed them in the water and Epsom salts solution until the water cooled, and got another pan and did it again. After an hour, I could make a fist, but I decided tomorrow would do to dig again.

The next day, I decided that a half-day would be enough and recommenced the job. For the next few days I dug, shearing and straightening the sides with the mattock and square shovel, until I had dug about four feet into the ground. The Old Man came around to inspect, and pointed out that some of the dirt I was tossing out of the hole was falling back in because it was hitting the sides of the pile around the hole. "What," he asked conversationally, "did you think I gave you the wheelbarrow for?"

"Um," I said.

"Come out of there." He dropped a ladder into the hole. "And from now on, you always use a ladder. If you have to get out in a hurry, those vertical sides aren't gonna help you." Looking back, I can only imagine what the safety folks would say about a hole like that, with no shoring and no one outside it to help.

I climbed out. The Old Man pointed down the hill to a patch of burdock that grew in a low spot behind the house. "Take the dirt down there. Just dump it. I'll level it with the dozer when you're done. The Old Man had a small Caterpillar bulldozer he'd gotten in trade for some welding work. It was nearly impossible to start, but when he was determined, the Old Man could make it run. I just nodded and began filling the wheelbarrow.

When it was loaded, I pushed the wheelbarrow down the hill into the burdock where its narrow steel wheel promptly sank into the soft ground. This was obviously not gonna work. I turned to the Old Man.

"Back it outta there, and we'll get some boards." He turned away. I lifted the handles and hauled back on the wheelbarrow, which, overloaded to begin with, fell over on its side. The Old Man turned back, heaved a great sigh of over-extended patience and said, "Well, finish dumping it and bring it back up here. And let's get you those boards."

Dumping it was harder than it looked and the Old Man was obviously less than pleased when I finally got the old barrow back up to the driveway. He just turned and walked toward the garage. There was a stack of old lumber at the end of the garage and we pulled some planks and laid them end to end down the hill and across the low spot. For the next two days, I loaded the barrow, ran it down the hill, dumped it, shifted planks and repeated the process. Eventually, the dirt was moved, and I began digging again.

Each morning, I got up and went to the Aurora Country Club to caddy. A "round" (18 holes) of golf paid six dollars a bag, and I carried two. By two o'clock, I'd be home and digging. Three or four hours a day, I figured, and I'd be done by mid-July.

Then I hit blue dirt – Aurora Blue Clay, the Old Man called it. Aurora Blue is fine-grained, silty clay, with grains that compact into rock hardness when they dry and this was dry. Swinging a pick into it was barely less painful than swinging it into a boulder. New blisters formed and broke. Muscles I'd thought were inured to work developed new strains and aches. Progress became measured in inches and I began to fear that one summer would not be enough. Then came Thursday night, and it rained.

There were three inches of water in the hole Friday morning and I despaired of it being gone by the end of the day. But, when I returned from caddying, it was gone. I climbed the ladder the five feet into the hole and stepped off into a stiff mud from which I could barely extricate my foot. But what I *could* do was push a spade into it. So that's what I did. I pulled back on the handle – the spade didn't budge. I pulled it up – it didn't pull. I yanked it from side to side – it moved not a fraction of an inch.

Anger at inanimate objects is seldom fruitful. I stood between the spade and the wall, put my foot against the handle of the spade and *pushed*! There was a definitive "CRACK!"

The Old Man brought a new spade from Mantua Hardware on Saturday. The clay had stiffened, but was not yet as hard as it had been. I dug carefully, a half-spade at a time, and slowly worked my way down. Still, I broke the handle of that spade and one square shovel before I was done. It was the last week of August before I saw the top edge of the basement foundation eight feet below the surface where I'd started. I had moved about fifty cubic yards of dirt (not something I knew at the time).

I dug down another foot, and then dug a six-inch deep, two-foot wide trench around the wall, and the Old Man and I framed a foundation. He brought gravel and we filled the six-inch trench below the framing. A concrete truck showed up and we filled the frame, making a foundation a foot thick and two feet wide. When it had cured, the Old Man had a load of concrete block delivered and built walls up the sides of the hole, punching stones out of the basement wall every other row of block, and tying the block walls into the stone with mortar.

The block walls were only eight inches wide, leaving a foundation shelf of sixteen inches. A load of pea-stone was poured into the hole and leveled to the top of the foundation. The Old Man poured a floor four inches thick up to the walls, and rough-finished it (except for the last corner, where he left boot and ladder prints).

We cut a door into the stone wall below the window, filling spaces with brick where stones were removed too far into the wall, and built a heavy plank frame with two 2x2s nailed to each with a slot between them. We left an eight-inch space at the bottom. Short boards were cut and slipped into the slot from the bottom until the entire door was blanked. When the coal bin (for that's what I had dug) was filled, the bottom board was chivvied out of the slot (a truly aggravating process), and coal spilled out a short way into the basement. We kept taking out boards as the coal backed away from the door.

We roofed the bin with concrete, except for sky-lights through which the trucks poured the coal. Those we covered with sheet metal nailed to a wooden frame.

I didn't know it yet, but the little fat kid was growing up. By the time the job was done, I'd lost about twenty-five pounds of fat, but I only weighed about ten pounds less. The difference was muscle I didn't yet recognize.

CHAPTER 35

Berry Pickin' Day

I never seemed to see it coming, but every summer, toward the end of July, the easy days and afternoons of summer morphed into the dreaded hot-work days of canning season. There would come an evening when Mother would say, out of the blue and in relation to nothing else anybody had said all day, the dreaded words, "Charles, Giles, I want you to put on old clothes when you get up tomorrow, because we're going 'berrying.' "

Now, "berrying" meant blackberry picking – the worst of all summer harvests. Blackberries were not cultivated (that I ever heard of, anyway) in northeast Ohio during the '50s. You had to find your own. Finding them was easy. Things got hard after that. Blackberries grow on vines called brambles, thickets of thorn-infested brambles, in abandoned fields awash in waist-deep grass with blades fallen and tangled, ready to trip unsuspecting boys face-first *into* the brambles.

Once promising fields were found, Mother had to obtain permission from some of the owners of the lands before picking. With others, Mother had a standing invitation, but so did other folks. It was necessary to choose the right ripening day, which might, depending on hillside, shade and some quirk of nature, apply to only one field, or any number of fields.

The next morning, far too early for a summer day, we got up, dressed in old, ill-fitting clothes, piled baskets made of thin strips of wood stapled together into the car and headed for that year's chosen field. There we met "The Aunts," three of Mother's four sisters (Gertrude seldom joined in these ventures). Giles and I were usually the only family children, because the only others, two girls of almost our age, would, according to their mother, "Not be able to stand this awful heat for so much as an hour." Giles and I looked at each other and rolled our eyes. "Girls!" we said in unison.

And then the pain would begin – pain that was to last, with respites for 4-H camp, the County Fair and other work, into the beginning of school. But this first day was the worst. Carrying two quart baskets (small square baskets without handles) in each peck basket (an oblong basket with a wire handle or "bail"), and two peck baskets each, we approached the enemy. The first quart or two weren't so hard but then the outer berries were gone, and we had to *reach*. And reaching caused the pain.

When I say blackberry brambles are "thorn-infested," I do not speak in hyperbole. Blackberry thorns are many, everywhere, and sharp as the most finely pointed needle. For my mother and The Aunts, all tall women (though only my mother had reached the exalted height of five-feet-ten), reaching over and past, and down into, the first layer of the bramble brought few scratches. For Giles and me, the story was different. We had to reach within. In short order, our arms began to look as if we'd been referees at a catfight and lost.

But the agony was only beginning. As the day warmed, sweat began. It rolled saltily into the scratches left by the brambles, creating a day-long burning and itching that nothing could ease. Our hands grew sticky with berry juice, and blackberry juice is acidic, which adds to the burn. By noon, we were hot, scratched, itchy, burning, sticky and sick. Blackberries are the original SweeTart. Not one berry in a hundred is fully ripened, and not one in a thousand is fully sweet. So-o-o-o we ate berries. For every handful that went into a quart basket, a half dozen went into our mouths. There was no insect spray to worry about, so poisoning was not an issue but the insects were.

As we picked, and inevitably squeezed some of the berries, the odor of juice flavored the morning air. Bees, hornets, sweat-bees and leaf hoppers began to invade the picking area. Anything sweet was fair game including the berry juice on our hands, and the berries in them. I probably put more bees, yellow jackets and leafhoppers in my mouth than any other kid in America.

By three o'clock or so, the heat would be at maximum, exertion (and our constant complaining) would have exhausted Mother's sisters (Mother was made of sterner stuff), and they would prevail upon her to break off for the day. Baskets of berries would be loaded into the cars and we'd head for home, where the berries would be prepared for canning and/or freezing.

Mother half-filled a washtub with cold water and dumped into it all the berries it would hold while leaving some free water into it. She and her sisters swirled the berries around, and "stuff" floated to the top. Half-ripe berries, leaves, sticks, thorns and insects were scooped out with a strainer made of two layers of cheesecloth wrapped around the long handles of serving spoons. Finally, the water was poured off through a larger cheesecloth strainer and the berries were divvied up amongst the sisters. The process was repeated until all the three or four bushels of berries we had picked had been cleaned and sorted.

If five containers of berries were filled, four went into the basement for the next canning or freezing day. And the fifth container? Ah, yes that fifth container. That container was the best part of berry-pickin' day.

Mother pulled out flour, a can of lard, a large mixing bowl, a table-setting fork, a pint of cream, a bag of sugar and a three-inch deep, oblong Pyrex baking dish. It was cobbler-makin' time!

Pie-dough is mixed by "cutting" flour into lard (or Crisco, if you're a health-wimp), a little at a time, with just a few drops of water. It's important to make the least possible number of cuts. It's laborious and slow, and makes a dry, flakey crust that men have killed for. Unfortunately, Mother hadn't the patience for all that, so it fell to me. I made the best pie dough in six counties, mebbe all of Ohio. I may or may not have had patience, but I surely had a burning desire for blackberry cobbler, and a mother whose insistence that I exhibit patience created the illusion if not the reality of it.

Once mixed, the dough was rolled into a thin sheet, laid into the baking dish, fitted to the bottom and sides, and trimmed about a half-inch above the top of the dish. A layer of berries was laid in the bottom and covered with sugar. Dough was cut into one-inch strips and laid on the berry/sugar layer about an inch apart. Then she laid another berry/sugar layer, and a layer of strips was laid crossways. The process was completed for five or six layers, and the top layer of strips was extended a quarter-inch past the edges of the dish and brushed with a sugar and egg-white mix. The extra width of bottom crust was folded over the ends of the top strips and pressed together with the fork used to mix the dough.

Into the oven with the cobbler and on to preparation of the

topping – fresh cream mixed with a heavy load of sugar (but not whipped). It took about a half-hour to carefully mix the two until the sugar was dissolved.

Cobbler is best served hot. After dinner that night, of which we ate less than usual, the cobbler was served in small bowls. Four-inch squares for Giles and me, smaller squares for little sister and Mother, and a five- or six-inch square for the Old Man. The cream topping came 'round the table in a one-pint crockery pitcher (there was more in the fridge) and was lovingly poured over the cobbler.

Silence is essential when the first fresh-berry cobbler of the season is eaten. Eating cobbler requires intense concentration to savor each bite and portion. Each layer of piecrust strips has a slightly different texture, depending on the depth in the berry/syrup mixture, with the bottom being utterly saturated with syrup but still flaky, and the top tasting mostly like pie crust, with sugar and cream. Truly, it is a religious experience.

Later cobblers of peach and apple never measured up to that first fresh-berry cobbler of the summer. It was worth all the pain.

CHAPTER 36

The Deer Hunt

In 1957, the State of Ohio reinstituted deer hunting. Deer had been hunted to near extinction in Ohio and other Midwestern states decades earlier. At some later time, the State of Ohio Department of Natural Resources released captured Whitetail Deer in various wooded areas around the State. Now the herds had grown to a population that would again allow deer hunting and The Old Man entered the lottery for a license and *won!* The season began in early December and ran three days.

Few licenses were awarded those first few years and the Old Man was a bit of a celebrity. The little restaurant in Mantua was filled with locals on any Saturday morning, and they were all eager to talk about the hunt. The Old Man wore a black and red checked wool coat with a game pocket and a hat to match, and he stood out in a crowd of taller men every one of whom had advice on where to hunt, what to wear, the best sort of gun to use, and a host of other details about hunting an animal many of them had never seen in the wild, much less hunted.

A neighbor with whom the Old Man rode to work insisted that he had the perfect deer gun. The State of Ohio limited guns for deer hunting to shotguns firing slugs or buckshot. The Old Man had a twenty-gauge Winchester Model 12 pump-action shotgun with modified choke, but he had intended to borrow a twelve-gauge. The neighbor insisted his was better. When he brought it to the house, the Old Man laughed at first. The gun was a long-barreled 410-gauge slug-gun, designed specifically for deer hunting. It fired a .41-caliber slug, a relatively small round compared to a twelve-gauge or even a twenty-gauge (the 410 is the only shotgun whose gauge designation is also a rifle and pistol caliber).

This gun was similar to the Winchester Model 12 pump-action but was called a Model 42, with a barrel the length of a twelve-gauge. It had rifle sights fore and aft on a raised rib. It was chambered for three-inch magnum shells (standard shells are 2-3/4 inches long), and the barrel was floated above the forestock. The barrel wasn't rifled, but the slugs themselves were. The gun was essentially a short-range rifle and shot as true at fifty yards as a .30-30 rifle. Its only drawback was a supposed lack of "punch." The heavier slug of a twelve or sixteen-gauge, or even a twenty-gauge, would, it was believed, "knock a deer down." The truth was the muzzle speed of the 410 made up for most of the difference in mass. There was no essential difference, as attested by the ability of much smaller rifle rounds to successfully kill much larger animals than Whitetail Deer. The Old Man accepted the gun.

The first day of the hunt, the Old Man woke us early. My brother and I dressed for the cold we knew was coming. The Old Man wore his red-and-black coat (there was no "blaze orange" then) and insulated leather hunting boots from Baretta, water-proofed with "mink oil," a substance "guaranteed" to render any leather boot waterproof if applied "according to directions." The night before the hunt, the Old Man had spent a goodly amount of time scrubbing mink oil into every stitch line on each boot with a toothbrush, and wiping every surface over and over with a mink-oil covered sponge.

We drove about half an hour, to a patch of public land that

was mostly scrub, second-growth trees, brush and swamp. We parked off the road and crossed a rolling abandoned field of grass and scrub to the woods. Northeast Ohio was at the end of the glacier's advance twelve thousand years ago, and the land was flattened and then plowed into huge rolls and furrows as the glaciers advanced and retreated. Although the field looked flat, walking it was hard; the rolls and furrows were as much as man-high from top to bottom.

Once into the woods, the Old Man selected a heavily wooded patch that overlooked a game trail and parked my brother and me there. It was coming on nine o'clock, the official start of opening day. Later days would start at sunrise, but there was fear of too many men with too many guns, hunting in unfamiliar territory for an animal they might not recognize, so opening day started at nine.

"Stay here, boys." The Old Man kicked leaves aside and ground the butt of his unfiltered Camel cigarette into the dirt beneath the forest duff. "I'm going to make a circle and look for fresh tracks. I'll be about a half hour." He moved off to the right. The leaves were dry and the brush rattled whenever my brother or I moved, but the sounds of the Old Man's passage faded in seconds. I never learned to do that, although Giles did. I *did* learn to be better at it than anyone else I ever hunted with, but never as good as the Old Man or my "kid" brother.

After a few minutes, my brother pulled out a pack of the Old Man's Camels and offered me one. "The deer will smell it," I said.

"So? We don't have guns."

He had a point. I took one. "What about the Old Man?"

"He's half a mile away." My brother scratched a kitchen match on his jeans, lit his cigarette and offered the light to me.

I lit up. In for a penny

There was a shot not far away. The Old Man swore. My brother and I frantically buried our smokes.

A second shot, and then, "Come help me drag this deer, boys!"

We began fighting through the scrub. I almost tripped over the deer. We had only come about two hundred yards.

"Well, it's a good thing I shot this one, 'cause you two have made enough noise to move every other deer in this woods to Pennsylvania." The Old Man was happy. He was only ever sarcastic when he was *very* happy or *very* angry. He had no reason to be angry. The deer was a large corn-fattened doe.

He pulled a rope and small block and tackle from his game pocket and sent my brother up the nearest sizeable tree. My brother affixed the block to the largest low branch and lowered the tackle. The Old Man had roped the doe's rear legs together at the heel, and he hooked the tackle into the rope. My brother came down and we hauled the deer up.

The Old Man bled and gutted her, and we lowered her back to the ground. My brother clambered back up the tree and retrieved the block. The Old Man stuffed it back into his game pocket and retrieved from it the deer-haul halter I'd given him for Christmas the year before. He put it over the doe's head and attached it to both ends of the longer rope from the block and tackle, forming a loop.

"Grab on boys!" The Old Man stepped into the loop. We each took a side and began to pull forward. Unfortunately, the expected cold (and snow) had not materialized. We were pulling dry. The good news was, we were less than half a mile from the car. The bad news was two-fold. The rolling field was going to be a lot less fun crossing with a deer in tow over dry ground, and that deer was *heavy*.

We pulled and we hauled. We stopped and we blew. We traded the shotgun from one to another. We pulled and hauled and we stopped and blew again. We swapped the gun again. At the bottom of the highest roll, we looked up to see a small plane flying toward us. He dropped toward us and dipped his wings, turned sharply and did it again.

"DelFrate," the Old Man muttered, stopping, "what *are* you doing?"

"Who's DelFrate?" I asked.

"Game Warden... see the green and white colors? That's a DNR plane." He picked up the rope.

It took us a half hour to make the top of the rise, a horizontal distance of maybe a hundred feet, with an elevation change of ten. And I may have mentioned that doe was *heavy*. DelFrate and his airplane found other places to be.

Once we'd topped the rise and could see the car, things seemed to get easier. We pulled steadily and about a hundred yards from the car we ran across a small stretch of shadowed snow and learned why DelFrate had buzzed us. The buck's tracks were *huge*! He'd been trying to drive it to us, not knowing that our only license was filled.

The Old Man laughed. "I'll have to thank him for trying, but that old buck could have walked right up to us and we couldn't have done a thing."

We tied the doe onto the old '50 Studebaker and headed for home.

The Old Man hadn't successfully hunted deer in a good many years. He showed it off to everyone he could think of, even driving into Mantua on his way to the meat packing plant in Ravenna.

A few days later, we had venison stew. It was the best meal of the winter.

CHAPTER 37

A Day at Cat Rock

It was the summer of 1956 – hot, lazy and nearly over – almost the end of August. I had just turned fourteen and this summer's trek to Greenwood Lake, New York was going to be the last thing we did before school started.

My brother, Giles, and I had done just about everything a 14-year-old and 12-year-old could do for spending money. We had our 4-H projects, two each – a garden a-a-and, something else. After the first two years, it was expected that each project would earn a profit (after all, we were learning to be farmers, weren't we?) because farms that didn't make a profit were known as, "subdivisions."

Giles and I were golf caddies, farmers' assistants up and down Kent-Mantua Center Road (later shortened to Diagonal Road), celery farm muckers and stoop laborers in the potato fields. But for us, most of that was over. A week on vacation and back to school would limit most of our afternoon and weekend activities to home chores (of which none of our summer work had absolved us) and homework. But not this week – this week we were going to Nina's; always an adventure in so many ways.

Saturday morning at about four o'clock, Giles, Lyndella and I were awakened, told to dress and left to it. Ten minutes later, the process was repeated – with adult supervision. The Ohio Turnpike had been connected to the Pennsylvania

Turnpike not long before. Instead of a hundred-mile drive on two-lane blacktop all the way to PA, a good two-and-a-half to three-hour trip, it was a four-mile drive to the Ohio Pike, and an hour-and-a-half at seventy-five miles an hour to Pennsylvania. Of course, once we got to the PA Pike the trip was the same as always. We still had to drive the full length of the State of Pennsylvania and Pennsylvania is a *very long* state.

We kids were ensconced in the back seats. I say "seats" because the Old Man bought a second rear seat at a junk yard, and forced it between the rear seat and the front seatback. We crawled in and were asleep again before the car was out of the driveway. We started to come awake about seven o'clock and the traditional "eating our way across Pennsylvania" began. For breakfast, we didn't stop. Mother handed around bacon and fried egg sandwiches on toast. The Old Man and I had Beefsteak Rye – everyone else had Wonder Bread White. After breakfast, the Old Man rolled down his window and fired up a Camel. The aroma of coffee with cream fill the car as Mother poured a Thermos cap half-full and he drank it as he drove. The little bullet-nosed '50 Studebaker Champion had overdrive and even in the mountains she droned steadily along.

We hit the tunnels – seven of them – terrifying two-lane monsters with bad lighting and no separation from the oncoming lane and its bright headlights. Mother handed out fruit, candy, cookies, cake, and for me a special treat – cocktail onions. For reasons I never understood I had developed a taste for the little white spheres pickled in brine and vinegar, and she never failed to pick up a jar before our treks to Nina's.

About one o'clock, somewhere in the heart of the Appalachian Mountains, the Old Man would pull off at a scenic overlook with picnic tables and open the trunk. He and Mother would admonish us to stay away from the highway (they needn't have worried – the roaring diesels of the passing trucks terrified us) and cover one of the tables. Then the Old Man would pull a Dutch oven wrapped in blankets from the trunk. Mother had put a roasting chicken in it the night before, along with potatoes, carrots, celery and everything else that would make a one-pot meal. The chicken had spent about eight hours at two hundred fifty degrees, after which the pot was wrapped in quilts and allowed to continue to cook as we drove. It was a helluva meal as it always was.

Late that afternoon, we pulled into the driveway at Nina's and stampeded into the house. Well, we kids did. Not only had we not seen Nina for more than a year, but we hadn't seen a bathroom in three hours. Then we came out to see who else was there. I was beginning to learn the foibles of the Old Man's family, and I was looking for fire-starters. Most of Nina's family still lived fairly close, but we weren't the only ones who drove the whole damned day just to see a family that was sometimes more fun than a circus, and sometimes had all the charm of a mass cat-fight in driving rain.

The New Jersey sisters came up for the day a couple times, but their kids were less interested in us than we were in meeting them. Most of them were older than I and, as Easterners, simply couldn't be bothered with a pack of kids from the Midwest. But the Old Man's brother Oliver lived just up the road and his kids came down every day.

Then there was his sister Viola. She and Uncle Ross lived in Canada and drove over with their kids. We children didn't know it, but we were about to get schooled in the ways of religious insanity (and inanity), and I would be smack in the middle of it. Nina herself was a bit of a religious nut and we all tolerated her with varying degrees of bemusement. Her church was Anglican and she purely hated and reviled the Roman Catholic Church and anything associated with it. She made every effort to make people believe she had memorized the entire King James Version of the Bible. She could misapply the same verse three times in any half hour, and misquote it differently every time. All her daughters were able to do the same to some degree, simply in the interest of self-preservation, but Viola outshined them all.

Not only was Viola dingy as a truckload of school bells when religion entered the conversation (and she made sure it always did), she was also sex-obsessed; especially when it came to children. It was certain truth to her that Jewish (and Muslim) belief is that adulthood begins when boys are barely half-grown; and that from that day forward any woman or girl is unsafe from them. And, between Oliver and the Old Man, there were enough "of-age" male children to threaten every female cousin in sight.

I can hear you thinkin' it: "So what? You're gonna be around adults all day long."

Well, yes and no. Oliver's oldest daughter, Dorothy (known, much to her chagrin, as "Dottie Jean"), knew of a bobcat's den up in the middle of a boulder field on the side of one of the old mountains. She called the place Cat Rock and she wanted to show it off to her cousins, and even a couple of the Franklin boys (the Jersey cousins) deigned to come along.

So, we began asking parents. The Old Man admonished us to stay a ways back (bobcats not being partial to invasions by noisy teenagers) and Mother asked what kind of sandwiches we'd like. Oliver's kids had permission going in and the Franklin boys didn't bother to ask. All was good until Viola's daughters asked their parents. Ross thought it was a great idea. Viola thought that I had come up with the idea to lure my female cousins, especially her daughters, into the forest for immoral purposes. She began by announcing her belief that there was no bobcat, no lair and no expedition. Several biblical misquotes later, she declared that she would make a prophecy.

That was too much for Nina. Not only had her daughter begun her tirade before Nina could even get started, in Nina's own house, but she now proposed to prophesy before Nina had even gotten a word or biblical misapplication into the conversation. "No!" she declared. "You won't! You won't prophesy ahead of me in my own house. You have no sense of propriety. You are the child and I am the parent. The Bible says the child shall *never* prophesy before the parent; *nor* shall the child prophesy in the parent's own house without permission!"

Nina made it sound reasonable to everybody but Viola. As a self-proclaimed Bible expert, she simply declared her mother a liar, saying that no such statement existed, and anyway, if it did, there was another statement somewhere in the Bible that said that after a certain age, mothers were to defer to their daughters.

Say what? Just to be clear; I was a fair Bible scholar in my day and, so far as I was ever able to determine, none of that appears *anywhere* in the Bible.

Having declared Nina a liar, Viola prophesied that if we were allowed to undertake this trip without adult supervision, every girl in the family would be violated by dark. Nina tried to claim that she would have said that very thing, but it was a weak argument and she gave it up with pretty much zero defense.

But Viola had said too much. Hattie Larlham, wife to the

Old Man and mother to me, Giles and Lyndella, rose to the defense of her cubs. Daughter to a circuit-rider minister and child of West Virginia coal country, a world of devout believers and bible loving mothers, she brooked no nonsense from self-taught scholars and prophesiers. Besides, her oldest son had just been accused of planning the rape of his cousins.

She began by quoting (accurately) some verses on the matter of misuse of bible verses to accuse the innocent of crimes past or future and to justify abusive behavior. Then she attacked both women for accusing me (and some of the older male cousins) of planning the sexual assault of our cousins.

Her outburst was met with stony silence. Larlham her last name may have been, and her father a preacher, but the name was by marriage and the Church of the Brethren was no proper church. It had no royal history and it was in no way competition for the Anglican Church. Besides, Nina and Viola had self-righteousness and sanctimony, not to mention salacious fear, on their side.

The upshot was the worst of all possible worlds. We went on our expedition under adult supervision, although I tried to back out when it was announced that the adult would be Viola. Mother was having none of it. Children did not insult their adult relatives so. I had promoted the trip, along with Dottie Jean, and I was going. It wasn't a discussion.

Stopping frequently and for longer and longer periods, we trudged toward the boulder field. When we finally arrived, it was hot, the place smelled of cat (proving there was a lair somewhere in those rocks) and Viola had a plan. She sat herself upon a boulder and began reading, apparently randomly, from her pocket New Testament. Then she held a prayer meeting (with her doing all the praying). Dottie Jean, her brothers and sisters and the Franklins wandered away, but Giles and I were constrained by Mother's admonition to be respectful, and her own children were simply stuck... all-in-all, a truly bad day at Cat Rock.

Later in life, Viola would write letters to random nieces and nephews, including me, covering the envelopes and the margins of the pages of the letters inside with closely written biblical verse notations. The letters themselves, even without the scribbled verse citations, were incoherent religious diatribes – Chick Tracts without the badly drawn cartoons. I eventually was asked by my mail carrier to try to get her to stop, so I asked her to in a response to one of her missives. I never heard from her again.

Epilogue:

In the summer of 2011, I invited all the Larlhams I could contact to a reunion at the place where I grew up. The house is long gone, replaced by the campus of The Hattie Larlham Foundation, a facility for the care of developmentally disabled children that is the great legacy of Mother and the Old Man. The Foundation was celebrating its Golden Anniversary and I piggybacked the reunion to that.

But we are a small and widely scattered clan and not many Larlhams came. Gwen – a daughter of Viola who lives in Vancouver, on the west coast of Canada – was one who did and brought her daughter. It was she who, during a conversation with one of Jack Larlham's sons and me, asked whether the name *Cat Rock* evoked any memories. He had not been there, but the memories of that gruesome day flooded into my mind, and much of this story was written in my head during the ensuing sharing between Gwen and me of our memories of that day.

CHAPTER 38

'39 Dodge Pick-'em-up Truck

I was about 14, which makes this another 1956 story. The Old Man came home from a trip to the barbershop driving a beat up old red-'n-white '39 Dodge quarter-ton pick-up truck. The seats were cracked and torn, there was a diagonal crack across the passenger side windshield (back then, sheets of glass could not be bent, so windshields were made of two pieces of glass with a divider), the red was faded to a dusty pink, the white *and* red were covered in spots of rust and the front bumper was a six-foot piece of two by six channel iron welded directly to frame extensions. *Crumple zone? We don' need no crumple zone.* There would come a day when I would both rue and bless that utterly foolish repair.

I ran up to see what th' heck was goin' on.

My mother was working in the yard. "Dick," she said to the Old Man, "what on *earth* is that?"

"It's a pick-up truck," he said, not looking at her.

"I can see that," she said with exasperation, "but why is it here?"

The Old Man looked at her. I discovered an overwhelming fascination with the truck. "You know that real tall sign at Carl's Country Cars?" he asked. My mother nodded. "Well, he had a sale on it."

"Dick," she said, patience controlled evident in every syllable, "Carl *always* has a sale on that sign."

"Yeah," he said, "but this was different."

"Different?" she asked, with resignation. "What was different?"

"It said, ' '39 Dodge Pick-up – thirty-nine dollars,' " the Old Man said.

My mother gave up that line of argument. After all, thirty-nine dollars, even back in 1956 wasn't a horrendous amount of money. "We don't *need* a truck and we can't afford the insurance," she said, instead.

"We don't need to insure it," the Old Man said. "I got it to haul hay and stuff around the farm... and for Chuck to learn to drive," he finished in a rush. He looked at me and grinned.

Mother took the first part of his answer first. "Dick, we have fifteen tillable acres, and we rent those out," she said. "We don't have a reason to haul hay, or any other 'stuff' around this farm, so what's this really ab... Oh!" The second part of the Old Man's answer had penetrated. The light had dawned. The truck was for *me*. She looked at me and smiled.

"Well then," she said to the Old Man, "you'd better get to it." And she went back to pulling dandelions. "Charles," she called over her shoulder, "you'd better not get hurt."

I was stunned. I made motorboat noises "But, but, but I don't have a license."

The Old Man just said, "Get in."

I jumped and grabbed the passenger door handle, but...

"Not over there... Over here," he said, standing at the driver's door.

I walked around the truck in a daze and got in. The Old Man climbed in the other side.

As I struggled to make myself "comfortable" (hah – little chance of that) on the bench seat, I took in everything I could.

The dashboard was steel, with a patina of rubbed-out rust. The steering wheel was large and skinny, and almost too high for me (I was about five-feet-three at the time). There was a clutch with a button under it. Turned out that button was the starter button. You were supposed to press the clutch down onto the starter, thus precluding the possibility of starting the vehicle in gear. That meant you'd *better* have a functional emergency brake, or a third foot, if you wanted to start the vehicle on a hill. There was a gearshift that rose majestically from the floor to well above the level of the seat.

We spent about ten minutes getting the truck started, during which time it lurched and jerked itself forward nearly its own length. Finally, the Old Man, exasperated, said, "Throw it in neutral and set the brake." He explained how to press the clutch and feel the transmission go out of gear.

I made my first attempt. Pushing hard on the clutch, I grabbed the knob atop the shifter and shoved forward. I also shoved away from myself. The upshot was that I shot from first to second gear and slammed my knuckles into the steel dashboard in consequence!

"Ow!" I yelped, yanking my hand away and shaking it rapidly before sucking on the bleeding knuckle. My discomfort was not ameliorated by the Old Man laughing uncontrollably in the seat beside me. I looked at him accusingly. "You knew," I said, "and you didn't tell me."

His laughter reduced slowly to intermittent chuckles. "I forgot," he said. "I really did. The tranny is just a bit loose in this old bucket."

"Yeah," I said, turning back to the front, "it seems to be."

"Well," he said, "let's try again. This time pull it back but *easy!*" he admonished as I reached for the knob.

I pulled it into neutral and, after a couple more false starts, I got the engine going. The clutch was terrible and the tranny was worse. Slipping the clutch and feathering the accelerator were skills required to shift up. Downshifting required learning the skill of double-clutching along with all the other stuff. Nonetheless, in less than an hour I could start her, drive around the wagon path that circled the small fields, shift up and downshift, and bring her to a stop.

I spent the next two years driving Ol' Red all over the farm (and sneaking short trips up and down the dirt road on which we lived). After I got my license, we licensed her and gave her liability insurance, and I drove her to my first job as an orderly in the local hospital, but so long as I had her, I had a permanent bruise on the middle knuckle of my right hand.

Two other occurrences of note highlighted my ownership of Ol' Red. First, as I drove to work one day, a wasp flew into the cab and stung me in the corner of my left eye. I ducked away and swung the truck to the right as I did so. The truck left the road and started down an embankment toward a lake at speed. I yanked her left, double-clutched, shoved her into second, accelerated and slammed full bore into a maple tree. Remember the channel-iron bumper? Never moved! Neither did the steering wheel. The truck was fully drivable when I got her pulled out, and I was only a half hour late for work. But lordy, my chest hurt for the next week.

Seat belts? This was a 1939 pick-'em-up truck, not a race car.

Second, years later, Carl's Country Cars was identified as a chop shop for the Cleveland mob. The FBI dug twenty-seven cars (or what was left of 'em) out of the field behind Carl's before they decided they had enough and quit. Oh, he bought and sold cars (and red-'n'-white Dodge pick-'em-up trucks with knuckle-buster shifters) but mostly he dismantled cars for the mob.

I miss Ol' Red some days. I can still feel the bruise on my knuckle.

CHAPTER 39

Double-bitted Axe

A double-bitted axe is a vicious piece of equipment. Axes are made of steel – hard to sharpen and heavy to swing. Double-bitted axes have a cutting edge, or "bit," on each face, a straight handle and a mean streak. And, in inexperienced hands, they're downright dangerous to the axe-man, bystanders and target.

Came a day when the Old Man decided we needed to supplement our coal with some hardwood. We heated the old farmhouse with large-lump bituminous coal, which I had to bank off at night and get up at 4:30 am to re-fire. Sometimes it went out, and that made for a noisy morning, guaranteed to raise the Old Man's ire.

But this was a Saturday in late August of 1957 and firing the furnace was a once and future task for me. Today, the Old Man and I would cut wood. He handed me a two-man crosscut saw, clapped a gray corduroy fedora on his head, and picked up the double-bitted axe. "Careful," he said as we started out of the shed together, "this thing is sharp!" He had spent about two hours laying the bit onto a foot-pedaled grindstone (a wheel of sandstone) spraying sparks like a holiday sparkler. I stepped away and let him through the door first.

We got into the almost-new '55 Plymouth and drove down the hill, across the one-lane bridge and pulled into a flat graveled area at the side of our road.

On our twenty-five acre "farm," of which about ten acres

were marsh (soon to be swamp, courtesy of a family of beavers), a couple acres were a corner of second-growth woods. Some was cherry, maple and oak, but a lot of it was scrub. We were looking for older hardwood deadfalls. We walked about a hundred yards into the woods and we found a fallen silver maple.

Now, the thing about silver maple is that its branches grow upward at an angle. This means that any branch you try to cut will have another close enough to be in the way. Therefore, the trick is to strip away the smaller "in-th'-way" stuff. The Old Man decided that the quickest way to do that would be with the axe.

He took a couple swings, each a little fuller overhand stretch than the last, trimming a couple arm-sized branches away. Then he backed away, spit on his hands, regripped the axe and stepped back toward the tree. He took a short stroke to set his striking point. A little longer stroke popped a small wedge of wood out, and he swung the axe through in a wheel, bringing it over his head at speed and extending his arms. I heard the bit strike, and the Old Man squalled like a wounded bear.

He dropped the axe and grabbed me by the shoulder, spinning me toward the road. "C'mon!" he yelled, "I've gotta get home to your mother!" He was holding the top of his head and he looked scared. I'd never seen the Old Man scared, so I was scared, too.

"What did you do?" I yelled, nearly crying with fear.

"The axe hit me in the head," he barked. "Now let's *go!*" And he shoved me ahead of him and grabbed the axe with his unoccupied hand.

We stumbled through the woods at a half-run and I could

tell he was in a near panic. He held onto the axe and pushed me ahead of him, his breath coming in harsh gasps, and there was a sob in there somewhere, I was sure.

"Give me the keys," I said as we reached the car. "I can drive." I was only about two weeks into 15 years old, but the Old Man had given me the '39 Dodge pick-up and told me to practice in the fields. So I could drive, but...

"No," he whispered, "I'll drive. Get in."

I scrambled into the car and the Old Man threw it into gear. He slammed the accelerator down, popped the clutch and spun the wheel one-handed. We threw gravel into the woods and screamed out onto the road. He was in second as we crossed the bridge and never put it in third. We slid into the driveway at terrifying speed and he slammed on the brakes.

The Old Man flung the door open and raced for the house, calling, "Pat! Pat! Honey! You've got to take me to the hospital!"

As my mother came through the door, she called, "What on Earth are you hollering about, Dick?"

"I've split my head!" he answered.

"What? Let me see!"

"No! Just take me to the hospital!"

Mom didn't waste time arguing with him. The hospital was ten miles away. "Get out of the car, Charles," she yelled. "Dick, get in over there."

Mom was a nurse and she could've insisted, but she just took him.

I waited in an agony of fear for their return. About three hours later, the car pulled in and they both got out. The Old Man had a small bandage on his bald spot, he was carrying the corduroy fedora and he looked very sheepish.

"What happened?" I asked.

"Not much," the Old Man said, and he went inside.

"A one-inch cut," said Mom, with a wink. "The hat must've stopped the axe."

Later he told me that as he swung the axe over his head, the handle hit a branch above him (the sound I'd thought was the bit striking the tree) and rebounded. The corner of the blade just skimmed his head, cutting a slice in the center of the hat (and his bald spot) and the axe-handle bounced off the front of his head, but the hat protected it. The axe-handle didn't even leave a bruise, and the inch-long cut at the top of his head was closed with a butterfly bandage... not even a single suture... and covered with a gauze bandage.

CHAPTER 40

Gamblers' Pants and Underpants

"Why do we wear underwear?"
"In case we split our pants."

Well, that actually happened to me... big time.

For much of my young life I was the fat little kid in school. When I began my junior year of high school, having just turned 16, I stood five feet three inches tall, and I weighed a hundred and fifty pounds. During that year, I grew to five feet eleven, and I still weighed a hundred and fifty pounds. Unfortunately, most of that growth happened between the annual purchasing of school clothes (in August) and the replacement of school clothes (at Christmas).

That summer, when we went shopping, the Old Man had me try on some low-rise jeans. The husky size I'd been wearing always came all the way up to my navel, with a long narrow fly, making me look even fatter than I was. We found three low-rise jeans I could wear. One pair was made of light denim with gray and black vertical stripes. I called them "gamblers" pants. They fit perfectly and I wore them more than any others. But there was something going on that I didn't recognize. I was growing – up.

There came a late, chilly and windy November day when I was outside with a group at school. It was a biology class, I believe. I was wearing the gamblers' pants, and I bent over from the waist to pick up a damifino. There was a loud "Rr-r-r-r-i-i-i-i-ipp!" and a sudden feeling of freedom (not to mention *coldness*) in my nether regions. I had split 'em from the crossing of the seams just below the fly all the way up the back to my belt! What the changes I had not yet recognized had done included an increase in the distance from my groin to the top of my pelvis, and widened the pelvic collar. In short, my pants were too short in every dimension.

Too short, over-worn lightweight pants, unrecognized growth in several directions, and excessive stretch in too many dimensions at once, and suddenly I was extremely grateful for tidy whiteys without signs of excessive wear. Nonetheless, I grabbed for the point of exposure, stood up really fast, and tried to face the group. That didn't work out very well because they'd all been in a circle, looking at whatever it was that I was picking up. Every turn I made, someone was behind me. There was a good bit more laughter than I was comfortable with, and because I was teased a lot, my level of comfort with being laughed at pretty much started at zero and went down from there.

I was just beginning to get mad, when a very pretty girl, who hardly ever spoke to me, offered to loan me her car so I could go home and change. I accepted with silent and embarrassed gratitude. I lived only five miles away and even driving a car I wanted to be *very* careful with (it wasn't mine, and it was nearly new) over back country roads, some unpaved, it took me less than fifteen minutes each way. I was back to school in time for my next class, which erupted into laughter and applause as I entered. I decided to take the high road and walked quickly to the young lady who'd loaned me her car, presented her the keys with a flourish, and turned and waved to my "fans" which included Principal Converse, who had followed me into the room. He crooked his finger at me and walked out the door. There was absolute silence as I followed him.

"What exactly, Mr. Larlham, gives you the idea you can take somebody's car and drive off in the middle of the morning?" Mr. Converse was obviously not privy to my trials. "Don't you think it might have been a good idea to stop by and ask my permission? I like to think people will do that. Can you imagine everybody just taking whatever car they want to and taking off whenever they want to?" He took a breath.

"I split my pants," I yelped before he could start again. I turned around and bent over. "From here to here." I drew a line with my finger.

There was an explosion of laughter from behind me and the unlit cigar Mr. Converse kept clenched tightly in his teeth throughout the day (as it slowly shortened – and none of us wanted to think about how *that* happened) shot past my head, hitting the far wall of the hallway and dropping to the floor with a small wet splat. "Go," he gurgled, trying to hold back another explosion. He waved to the door through which I'd just followed him, "Go." He picked up his cigar, scrubbing the stain into the tile "Go."

I went. More applause. I bowed.

The clothing part of Christmas came early for me that year. Much to my chagrin, that did not mean that I got any more of the "good" stuff that Christmas. There were fewer packages but the Old Man was careful to remind me that we'd already bought my clothes for the year.

I've never even wanted to go Commando since my Gamblers' Pants Adventure.

CHAPTER 41

Cottontail Hunt

"Stupid, stupid, stupid; that's all I've got to say!" There was disgust in the Old Man's voice and a little wonder. As if he couldn't believe any son of his could do such a wel-l-l-l-l, *stupid* thing – even if that son *was* only sixteen years old. Heck, we'd been hunting together since I was nine and he'd bought me my first gun when I was twelve – a little Bay State .410 single shot. But I had outgrown that, and today I was carrying my new twenty-gauge, Winchester, raised-rib, Model 12 pump.

I stood there, the twenty-gauge hanging from my hand, and stared at the back half of a cottontail rabbit lying at my feet in the bloody snow. Blood on the muzzle of Meg, our little "too-fast-for-her-own-good" Beagle, straining in the Old Man's grip to get back to her meal, betrayed the fate of the front half. Nick, friend and traitor, snickered. My younger brother, now carrying my little .410, looked unsure. He wanted to laugh, but he knew the Old Man better than Nick did.

"Pick it up," the Old Man ordered, "and put it in your game pouch."

I reached down and picked up the remains of a pretty good-sized cottontail. As I fumbled with the side zipper of the plastic-lined game pouch that was part of my coat (and, therefore, behind me), the Old Man spoke again. "Clean it out, f'r Pete's sake!" he snapped. "D'you want a pool of blood and a pile of guts in th' bottom of your pouch when you get home?"

"Er," I said, my already overdeveloped penchant for witty repartee coming once again to my rescue, "no I guess not."

The Old Man just glared at me through the top half of his rimless octagonal bifocals. "I guess not too," he said.

I reached into the belly of the cottontail and brought out the remaining intestines. I hung them on the branches of a nearby understory shrub to keep Meg from eating any more.

"Scrub it out," the Old Man called over his shoulder as he headed back toward the brush pile from which this rabbit had erupted not five minutes earlier. I picked up a handful of snow and scrubbed out the inside of the rabbit. Nick unsnapped the game pouch flap and I stuffed the rabbit into it.

"Stupid, stupid, stupid; that's all I've got to say," Nick snickered. He sobered. "Your old man was pretty ticked off."

"Yeah," said younger brother, "and he was mad, too." He snickered.

"Nah," I said. "If he was really mad, we'd be going home." I looked over to where the Old Man was kicking another brush-pile and siccing Meg into it. "We'll keep hunting." I thought about the history of that brush-pile.

Years before, a tornado had ripped up woodlots and treed hills too steep to plant in the farming community in which we lived – on a 25-acre "farm" that had been bought mostly so we children could be brought up in the country. Owners of the land where trees had been downed banded together and hired a local sawyer to cut the trees into logs and haul them to his sawmill. Limbs down to four inches were cut into firewood lengths. Mixed hardwood loads of Maple, Oak, Cherry, Beech, and even some Elm, as well as loads of firewood, roared past our old farmhouse for weeks. Some of those logs remained in that lumberyard for more than a decade, unsawn.

Most of the landowners and their non-farming neighbors were hunters and we all hunted each other's land. Therefore, part of the deal was that branches and treetops too small to be firewood were to be piled into game shelters. This brush pile was one of those shelters.

Another cottontail erupted from the pile and Meg set out in pursuit, baying for all she was worth while she could still see the rabbit. But soon the rabbit made a turn, or dived into a thicket, or somehow disappeared from her sight, and Meg, now no longer able to see her quarry, began her "search bark," a series of short yelps and yips. While my brother, Nick and I spread out and waited for her to bring the rabbit around, I replayed the events of a few minutes earlier.

As they had just done, my father and Meg had flushed a rabbit out of a brush pile, and Meg had taken up the chase. Meg was a very fast beagle, and she had a couple bad habits. She would sight-trail and, if she had a straight shot at a rabbit that started close to her, or if we were hunting open woods and she could see the rabbit turn, she would occasionally catch one and eat it. Thus, the sobriquet: Meg, the too-fast-for-her-own-good-beagle. She also preferred the scent of fox to rabbit and would break off the hottest rabbit trail to run a fox, sometimes staying out for two or three days. This habit of Meg's was so unbreakable that eventually the Old Man sold her to a neighbor who hunted fox (a pastime my father considered less than sporting – the Old Man was not a trophy hunter).

This time there had been no fox and Meg had been on the far side of the brush pile when the rabbit lit out. The brush pile in question was almost at the top of a small hill, and Nick and I stood nearly at the top of another, across a swale through which ran a light trickle of water during a heavy rain. My brother was on the far side of the scrub for which the rabbit was tracking. It headed downhill toward the valley between the Old Man and me, angling somewhat away from us. I pulled up the little twenty-gauge and snapped off the safety, but the bunny darted and dodged from shrub to bump in the forest floor. I couldn't get a good look and, by the time he was close enough for a shot, I'd lost sight of him. I pulled the shotgun down, holding it at a very unmilitary "port arms," and began an eyes-unfocused search of the hillside upon which I stood, looking for motion.

And here came Meg. She had lost sight of the rabbit, but she had a good scent trail and was "bell-barking," a short yodel that ended in a bark, that told us she had the trail and was unlikely to overrun any turn the rabbit made.

I scanned ahead of her, looking unfocused for movement farther and farther out as Meg got closer to the last place I'd seen the bunny, on the assumption that it would maintain its general course.

As Meg crossed the bottom of the swale and headed away from us up the slope upon which we stood, and disappeared behind a shrub, Nick, who was not carrying a gun, whispered, "Look left! Quick! He's just sitting there under a bush."

I knew it would be just dumb luck if I could see him at all, so long as he sat still, but I swung my head to the left, scanning every shrub I could see as fast as I could see them. At the top of the elongated hill was a heavy copse of saplings ranging from finger-thick to an inch-and-a-half in thickness.

As my vision reached the saplings, my peripheral vision picked up movement down the hill from it and a bit to my right and all hell broke loose! The rabbit accelerated up the hill, throwing snow and leaves behind him. Meg saw him, gave a warble, and came charging up the hill at an overtaking angle! And my gunstock smacked into my cheek whereupon I discovered that I had changed the direction of where I was looking as soon as Meg opened up. I was now looking at *her* over the sights of my shotgun!

I swung to the left, and pulled the trigger as my front sight passed the bunny and tree bark, snow and leaves exploded in all directions and the rabbit disappeared behind the saplings, with Meg just steps behind.

"Get 'im?" called the Old Man as he jogged down the hill.

"Nah," I called back, "clean miss. I killed some little trees, though."

Nick thought that was pretty funny. "Killed some little trees," he snickered.

The Old Man was less amused. "You killed it," he called. "Go pick it up."

"No I didn't," I said. "I missed it."

"Meg quit barking," he yelled. "Now, get over there!"

"Aw, nutz!" I muttered. If Meg was silent, it could only mean one thing... she had the rabbit! I muttered other things a sixteen-year-old in the '50s didn't want his father to hear and took off at a trot along the side of the hill. My left foot hit the snow and wet leaves and instantly slid downhill, with me following immediately behind. My left hip hit the hillside, followed in rapid succession by my left arm and left ribcage. "Oog!" I announced, trying to get some air.

"Is that gun safetied?" the Old Man called as I slid to a stop. All sympathy was the Old Man. He trotted up the hill toward the place I'd last seen the rabbit, ignoring me.

My index finger slid guiltily to the safety and discovered, to my great relief, that I had, in fact, automatically safetied the

and help?" he asked her.

"Charles," my mother asked, "don't you have chores to do?"

If my mother thought I had chores, I had chores, whether I had chores or not. By the time the chores were done and I returned to the house, it had been decided that the Old Man and I would go. Nina was getting on and he hadn't seen her since the summer a year before. My mother was an RN and there was nothing the Old Man was likely to be *allowed* to do in the care of my brother and sister.

Early Wednesday morning, the Old Man and I loaded our suitcases, some sandwiches, a picnic jug of ice water and a thermos of coffee (with, unfortunately, cream already added) into the grass-green '55 Plymouth sedan, and headed north to the Ohio Turnpike. There had been a time, years before, when the trip took fourteen hours or more, but the Ohio Turnpike had shortened that considerably. Now, instead of leaving at three in the morning, we hadn't pulled out of the driveway until almost six. We expected an eight-hour trip... ten hours at the outside.

The Saturday before, the Old Man and I had taken the car into Ravenna for the obligatory twelve hundred-mile oil change and a set of tires. He had four "new" retreads with what he called a "strong" tread put on. We were going to be travelling through the Pennsylvania Appalachian Mountains on the Pennsylvania Turnpike in late November. Snow was not unlikely and the "old" retreads were about a year old. Retreads are made from a softer tread rubber than original treads so they grip well, but they wear out quickly.

He had the front wheels and bearings pulled and greased and the bearings replaced. While the car was being worked on, the Old Man and the mechanic talked about just about everything. I wondered how the mechanic could keep track of what he was doing. But then I figured he did it all the time. As it turned out, I probably should've said something.

Wednesday morning, just about six-fifteen, the Old Man swung through Gate Thirteen of the Ohio Turnpike off Ohio State Route 14, and we were on our way. It was about an hour to the Pennsylvania State Line and another hour to the first tunnel.

The Old Man drove, smoked his Camels and told stories. The Old Man's stories could be amazingly entertaining and, when we reached the Ohio-Pennsylvania line, it was a surprise. As we went through the Pennsylvania Turnpike gate, the Old Man pointed to a speed limit sign. The sign read "65 MPH – This Means You," and a Pennsylvania State Trooper glared out of it at us, his right forefinger pointing directly at us.

"Gotta be careful for a while," the Old Man said. "Troopers hang around this end of the Pike because folks coming off the Ohio Pike are used to goin' seventy-five. They just naturally drift up there and then the Troopers get 'em."

The Ohio Pike, finished in 1956 from somewhere north of Akron to the Pennsylvania connection, was still nearly brand spankin' new in 1958. Its central portion had only been completed months before. Its speed limit was seventy-five mph because the State was fairly flat and everybody thought the huge grass-covered lane separation between east-bound and west-bound traffic would protect them from the consequences of excessive speed. It even had its own Turnpike Police in brightly painted forest-green cars. All that would change with time but, in 1958, it was all new and wonderful. The first fully financed state-crossing turnpike in decades was finally open from Indiana to Pennsylvania.

But the Old Man was right. It was easy to get used to that speed and, because the last fifty or so miles of the west end of the Pennsylvania Turnpike had been newly completed to match the opening of the Ohio gate, it didn't look that much different when we were on it, which made the speed change even harder to deal with.

About fifty miles in, we came to the first of many fieldstone plazas that lined the length of the pike. Howard Johnson's (a restaurant and hotel chain) was the plaza manager, and the food was good. There was no "fast food" in the '50s so every stop was pretty much an hour out of the trip if you wanted more than coffee.

We went in and sat at the counter. The Old Man ordered two coffees and we sat a few minutes drinking the "trucker's coffee" they served on the pike. (Recipe, which I know, because I worked at one of the Howard Johnson's on the Ohio Pike one summer: Begin with hard-piped five-gallon coffee urn, three pounds coffee in the filter, let drip 'til done. Draw one gallon coffee into pitcher and pour through grounds. Repeat four more times. Serve; but not to children, most women or half the men you know).

He dropped a quarter on the counter (a cup of coffee was ten cents, which he still thought was outrageous) and we went to the car. He pulled into the gas station on the plaza, and got out. "C'mon Chuck," he said. So I got out while the attendant filled the tank, cleaned the windshield, and checked the oil and tires.

"Three bucks, fifty," he said to the Old Man. "Oil and tires are OK."

"Thanks," the Old Man said, handing the boy four dollars.

"Keep the change." He turned to me. "Here," he said, tossing the keys, "you drive a while."

The keys hit me in the shoulder and clanked on the concrete. I never took my eyes off the Old Man as I fumbled on the ground for them. "M-m-me?" I asked with all the aplomb I could muster (none, actually).

"Sure," he said. "You've got your license, and all the traffic's goin' one way."

We got in and I pulled out onto the highway. There was no speed control in 1958, so it was up to me to maintain sixty-five miles an hour for mile after mile and the road was climbing and turning. It got steeper and the turns got tighter as we climbed. In less than an hour, I was facing the first tunnel entrance, and I was *terrified*!

The tunnels through which the Pennsylvania Turnpike passed on the way to New Jersey were railroad tunnels! Back near the turn of the century, some railroad company (probably now, and in 1958, defunct) had laid a rail route through the Appalachian Mountains of Pennsylvania and had gone so far as to begin cutting the route and building the tunnels.

Somewhere in the future of that enterprise, the State of Pennsylvania came into ownership of the route including the now-completed tunnels. Along that railroad route (for the most part) and through those tunnels, Pennsylvania built its Turnpike. But there was a problem, as yet unaddressed in 1958. The tunnels were built for trains on tracks, not cars on roads. They were *very* narrow, one lane each way, with no separator between the lanes, and no breakdown lanes – just two lanes of traffic coming at each other at fifty-five miles an hour, a speed reduction that did little except add to the back-ups in times of heavy traffic.

I turned toward the Old Man and said, " " nothing – not a word. I just looked at him, and he looked back.

"You'll be fine," he said. "Turn on your lights and don't look at the lights coming at you."

I took a deep breath, shifted my butt firmly into the back of the bench seat and turned on the headlights. I entered the tunnel in a merging line of traffic that rapidly sorted itself out (there had been trips when we waited for what seemed like hours to get into a tunnel, but not today) and increased speed quickly to fifty-five miles an hour. The tunnel was a little more than a mile long, and it was, without question, the longest sixty seconds of my life.

After a few minutes out of the tunnel, the Old Man said, "You did fine. Mebbe you should turn off the headlights, though." The first thing we'd seen coming out of the tunnel was a billboard-sized sign at eye level that read, "TURN OFF HEADLIGHTS, PLEASE!" I had seen it, but it hadn't registered that it meant I had to *do* something (turn off my headlights). Sheepishly, I reached for the little knob and turned them off.

Later, as we approached the second tunnel, I discovered that I was much more confident. I relaxed as we entered the tunnel and easily maintained both speed and distance from the car ahead of me until the car started to shake – violently! There was a loud thumping coming from under the car and the wheel was live in my hands.

"What do I do?" I yelled.

"Just hang on," the Old Man said (much more quietly). "You can't pull over 'til we're out of here."

I couldn't help it – I dropped speed to about forty and gripped the wheel so hard I couldn't feel my fingers. Two minutes (hours, days) later, we exited the tunnel and I pulled off the road.

We got out and looked at the dented (from the inside) driver's-side front fender and the long strip of retread hanging off the tire. That was a problem with retreads (still is – you've seen the tire-treads along the road in summer?). As the friction and flexing heated both the tire carcass and the tread, the temperatures caused separation if the differential became too great and the heat-sealing of tread to carcass had been less than perfect. Apparently it had.

We changed the tire and headed east again. We pulled over at a roadside picnic table, and ate the sandwiches and drank coffee (I discovered I could stand cream in it if I had to). We were well up the side of a mountain, overlooking a bucolic valley. Farms were scattered the length of it and we could see tractors and vehicles moving on the roads.

"Time to go, Son," the Old Man said. "We need to stop at the next plaza and pick up a new spare and gas up. I'll drive then."

As we pulled into the plaza garage area, I was busy dodging trucks and pulled the wheel left. There was a metal-on-metal shriek from under the car. I touched the gas, and everything moved except the passenger-side front tire. "Uh-oh," I said. "That's funny."

"What's funny?" the Old Man asked.

"I think the right front wheel's locked up," I said.

"Let me see," he said, getting out of the car. I got out and he slid behind the wheel, put the car in gear and gave it some gas. It tried to spin on the right front wheel. He hauled the wheel left, gave it more gas and there was another grinding shriek.

A mechanic came out of the garage. "Sounds like a wheel

bearing," he said.

"I just had 'em replaced last Saturday," the Old Man said.

"You need to talk to that mechanic," the young man said. "I don't think he did a very good job. Let's get her in here and take a look."

The Old Man gave him the keys. The mechanic got in and put the car in reverse. The front wheel dragged for a second or two; there was a "pop," and it freed up. He put it in first and drove carefully into the garage and onto a lift. Once the car was in the air, he pulled the right front wheel, yanked the hub, and stuck a steel hook into the axle beside the spline.

As he pulled gobs of grease and chunks of metal out, the Old Man whistled. "How in the world did that happen?" he asked. The mechanic reached back in and pulled out an entire race of roller bearings, with a couple rollers missing.

"Left one in," was the laconic answer. "Must not've been paying attention, and shoved the new one in behind the old one."

I thought back to the visit to the garage. I definitely should've said something, I thought, but I couldn't imagine what I'd have said.

The Old Man's jaw muscles bunched until the corners of his lower jaw looked like he'd grown small fists below his ears. "How under the sun," I heard the low, patient voice of pure distilled fury, "did he get it far enough in there to put on the axle cap? How could he not *feel* it?"

The mechanic looked at the Old Man and took a breath, "I don't mean to excuse this, because fixing it is gonna cost you. But there is a great deal of space inside the sleeve this thing rides in. It's not really a hard mistake to make."

The Old Man was not mollified, but he couldn't see the

mechanic helping him as a target either. He told the mechanic to go ahead and fix it, and to come get us at the counter if we weren't back when it was done. But it took long enough that we were back in the garage before he finished.

It took the mechanic two hours to pull the spline, order one from a parts store or Plymouth garage in the nearest town and install it along with a new race of bearings once they brought it out. The bearing races had eaten chunks out of the one we'd come in with.

The remainder of the drive was uneventful. We ran into a little wet snow as we neared Greenwood Lake, but the roads stayed clear. It was snowing again as we pulled into Nina's driveway at about five in the evening. There were three tall iron pipes chained together and arranged as a tripod at the end of the driveway. A come-along hung from the chain, and suspended from the come-along was another chain. It disappeared into a four-inch diameter pipe that stuck up about eighteen inches out of the ground.

"O-o-o-oh," groaned the Old Man, "their well's quit on 'em." He looked at the snow falling and then at his watch. "C'mon, Son," he said, "it's gonna be a long wet evenin'."

CHAPTER 43

Replacing Nina's Well

The Old Man glared at the tripod through the increasing snowfall in the darkening evening. "Well," he said, "might as well go in."

We pulled our suitcases and some travel stuff out of the car and went inside where Nina pointed us to the bedroom we'd be sharing. We dropped our suitcases and headed for the kitchen. The Old Man went to the sink, got a tumbler from a cupboard and turned on the faucet. Nothing. Not a drop. Not a splash or a gurgle. Silence. He looked at Nina.

"I don't know, Dick," she said. "It quit this afternoon."

The Old Man heaved a sigh. "What was I thinkin'?" He put the tumbler down. "Who'd you call to fix it?" he asked. "And where did he go?"

"Oliver," Nina said.

"Where is he?"

"Dorothy called," Aunt Gwen chipped in. "He had to take her to the doctor."

"When?" The Old Man was sounding a tad testy.

Nina answered, "About noon. She had an appointment at one o'clock in Monroe."

The Old Man shifted gears. "I'll have to look at your pump. Where's the well-house?"

"Dick, Oliver installed a submersible pump for us last summer, don't you remember?" Aunt Gwen asked.

Aunt Gwen had been widowed decades earlier and she had lived with Nina for much of the time since, while working as an aide at a nursing home. As Nina aged, she became her caretaker as well. She was beginning to live that role even in the late '50s.

The Old Man's face began to get red, and I could see the muscles in the corners of his jaw bunch. He remembered. So did I. There'd been a heck of a row about that at the previous summer's get-together. A submersible pump is a watertight steel cylinder inside of which is an electric motor. The motor powers a pump impeller in a chamber below the motor into which water is pulled and then thrust upward into the pipe that carries it to the surface. The whole is a single combination cylinder that sits several feet into the water at the bottom of the well.

The advantage of a submersible is that it's easier to push water than to pull it, so much deeper wells with much smaller pumps are possible for residential use. The disadvantage is that, unlike a basement or pump house pump that lives above ground and can be accessed for repair, if the submersible pump itself fails, it must be pulled from the well along with all pipe and electric cord above it to work on it. The Old Man had fought the idea of a submersible pump on that alone. Now, he found himself on the short end of being right. He was not pleased.

"You mean we have to pull the pump?" he asked, "in this weather?" His voice was rising.

"Well," Nina said, "you and Charles could go up to Oliver's and get some jugs of water, I guess."

The Old Man ignored that. "Why isn't Oliver here?" he asked.

"Well," Nina said, "you were coming and I didn't see any reason to have both of you out in the cold, working on the well, so I didn't pester him." It was obvious that Nina had more confidence in her eldest son's well-repair abilities.

"Yeah, just the one who's been driving for ten hours," the Old Man muttered.

"C'mon, Chuck!" He opened the door and headed for the tripod. I followed reluctantly, but we needed water.

The Old Man inspected the tripod Oliver had erected and the come-along. The tripod was chained at the top and rings had been welded on legs, through which a chain had been run to keep the legs from over-spreading. The come-along was suspended by a chain from the top of the tripod, with another chain looped through the bottom hook.

A connection cap at the top of the four-inch diameter steel well casing married the electric cord in the well to an exterior electric cord in a conduit from the power supply and switch in the house. A special connector in the cap mated with a connector attached to the end of the cord from the pump. There was a similar connector mating for the well-pipe a little farther down the side of the well casing.

Oliver lived about a mile up the mountain road on which Nina and Gwen lived. "Chuck, you go up and ask Oliver to come down here," the Old Man said. "I'll get started."

So I got in the car and drove to my Uncle Oliver's house. There was more hugging and kissing mostly by my Aunt Dot (Dorothy). Finally, I broke free. I was surrounded by cousins, but not by an Uncle. "Where's Uncle Oliver," I asked Aunt Dot.

"He went back into Monroe," she said. "He starts a job in Pittsburgh on Monday and he needed some work clothes."

It figured. Oliver was a welder, worked for a major steel

erection company and got shipped all over the country. We show up, and he's on his way away. "Well," I said, "I guess he won't be able to help pull Nina's well."

"If he gets home in time, I'll send him down," she said.

I nodded and got back in the car. I was pretty sure he wouldn't "...get home in time." The Old Man was gonna need help and if Oliver wasn't available...

When I got back, the Old Man was standing by the tripod, glaring at it again.

"Oliver's in Monroe, getting ready for a trip to a new job-site." I said. "Looks like it's just you and me." I looked at a four-inch maple limb that stuck straight out from the tree it had grown from. It was about the same height as the top of the tripod. "Why didn't he just use the limb?" I asked, pointing at it.

"The pressure from the weight hanging off the chain-fall would crush the under-bark and kill it."

"Oh."

"Start the car and aim the headlights here. It's getting really dark."

I shivered. "And cold," I muttered as I opened the driver's side door to the Plymouth. It was still snowing, but it was colder and the flakes weren't as wet. The ground, however, was good and muddy.

I started the car, dimmed the lights and pulled it close to the tripod. The Old Man watched and raised his hand when I was close enough. I put the car in neutral, yanked up the parking brake and got out.

The Old Man had already removed the well cap and slipped the hook at the end of the chain through the steel ring at the top of the pipe connector. The first pull was easy. The chain fall pulled the pipe about three feet, at which point it was necessary to tie off the pipe and reset the chain lower down the pipe. The pipe was a one-inch diameter gray-iron pipe (inside diameter would be three-quarters of an inch). Running its length was what looked like a smooth black hose taped to the pipe at intervals, but left loose enough to hang an inch or two away from the pipe between tapings. The "hose" was actually an electric cord sealed in a sleek black plastic covering, and thus made for life under water. When we got to the pump, we would find it disappearing through a watertight sleeve into the top of the pump, where it would be connected to the electric motor in the pump.

The Old Man wrapped a length of chain around the well pipe, tucking it between the pipe and the electrical cord, and draped a link over the hook on the come-along, where it caught tightly. He took up slack, and then disconnected the well pipe from the tie-off. There was a small jerk as the well pipe dropped a partial inch and tightened the chain. Then the Old Man began jacking the handle of the come-along, slowly raising the well pipe. The submersible pump at the bottom would come up with it.

The come-along reached its shortest extension. The well pipe had come up another three feet above the top of the well. The Old Man took the length of clothesline he'd tied off with before, wrapped the well-pipe with it just below the chain and this time looped it over the tree limb beside the tripod.

He gave me the end of the clothesline and said, "When I tell you, take up the slack and then throw a couple loops around that limb. Then sling it behind your butt and sit back." He straddled the well, crouched down, wrapped his huge hands around the slippery well pipe and straightened. "Now," he grunted. The pipe rose a couple inches. I yanked up the slack and threw the rope over the limb, grabbed it, and tossed it over again. Then I slung it around my butt, and "sat." I held it in place using mostly the friction of two loops of rope against the rough bark of the limb (and the jeans I was wearing).

The Old Man bent slowly at the knees, until the well pipe was held entirely by the rope. He unwrapped the chain and released the chain-fall ratchet, extending the chain to its full length. Then he re-wrapped the chain around the well pipe and we repeated the process. But the next time we had the pipe lifted and re-wrapped, he just stood there for a minute. Then he went to the shed and returned with a pair of pipe wrenches.

He opened the jaws of each wrench and slipped them over the pipe; laying the handle over the side of the well pipe itself. He cut a couple short lengths of rope and tied each through the hole at the end of each wrench handle. The remainder of each piece was wrapped around the four-inch steel pipe that was the well casing and tied.

"So we don't lose 'em down the well," he said, before I could ask.

"Ah."

The Old Man tightened the jaws of each and placed them 180 degrees from each other, with the jaws overlapping. "Hold the heads, Chuck," he ordered, "and don't let 'em crush that electric cord." As he jacked the come-along, I kept the jaws sliding down the pipe. When he released the ratchet, the pipe dropped about a half inch, and the jaws grabbed and stopped it. He repeated the process and again we were successful. He tied the pipe off to the limb again with a short loop. Every two or three lifts, he retied the loop. Had the wrenches let the pipe drop or had we dropped one of them, we'd have lost no more than five or six feet of work.

Time went on. The work went on. I knelt in mud, shivering, and pressed down on cold iron. The Old Man jacked the come-along handle, swapped chain and swore at Oliver. I came to the conclusion that, one, his youngest brother could've found a way to get this done before we got there and, two, submersible pumps were born of the devil, specifically to destroy his visit with his mother.

Without warning, the devil's spawn was before us. The Old Man, filthy from the gunk that coated the pipe, wet, cold, shivering and angry, let out a sigh. "About damn time," he said. He released the wrenches and stood up. "C'mere, Chuck," he said, pulling the pump to the side. "Hold this."

I wrapped my arms around the pump and pipe.

"Back up as I release the ratchet," he said. "Lay the pump on the ground." He stepped to the come-along and released the ratchet. The pump and a hundred and twelve feet of iron pipe drove me backward until I sat abruptly in the mud, dropping the pump. It lay there, resting on my leg while I gasped for breath. The Old Man laughed. I glared at the Old Man. He laughed more. I glared harder but I couldn't help it. It *had* to be funny. In my mind's eye, I could see what he saw, and it *was* funny. I began to laugh. Freezing, shivering, wet, sitting in water, snow and mud, I laughed with the Old Man until my stomach hurt. Finally I ran down. My leg ached. "I've gotta get up," I said. "This thing is heavy."

"Just a sec," he said, and ran for the shed. He returned with a pad of canvas. "One of Oliver's tarps," he explained, laying it down by my leg. He straddled me and the pump, squatted down and slid his hands under the pump, lacing his fingers. Then he stood, turning sideways, and dropped the pump two inches to the tarp. "Heavy," he grunted.

The Old Man stood five feet, nine inches and he weighed a hundred and thirty pounds. But he was built like a wedge. His chest was fifty inches and his upper arms were as big as my thighs. His legs and hips were muscled but amazingly skinny for the body they supported. I had seen him lift two hundred pound billets of steel. Still, a hundred and twelve feet of one-inch iron pipe, plus the pump, was no easy lift.

He picked up a flashlight Nina had given him, and a rag. He wiped off the pump, and inspected it. Suddenly he swore. "Bimetal," he ground out. "Oliver, you're an idiot!"

"Huh?"

"Two kinds of metal," he said. "The pipe and the pump's fitting are iron. But your Uncle, who damn well knows better, put 'em together with a brass union."

"So?"

"It's a bimetal connection and the electrical properties are different for each metal. That sets up an electrical current when a liquid flows through them and *that* eventually makes a hole. Look here." The Old Man pointed to the thread just at the edge of the brass union. Water was seeping out of a small hole in the depth of the iron thread. "Bimetal," he said again. "Oliver, I oughta belt you one."

"I thought the pipe would be empty," I said.

"The pump has a one-way valve, so the pipe *can't* empty. If it didn't, you'd be pumping water the full length of the pipe every time you turned on the pump, before you got any to drink. On the other hand, this pipe wasn't full, either. It's been slowly leaking out through this little hole ever since Oliver turned it off. But the pump was about twenty-five feet under water, so the pipe stayed that full."

"Oh." The Old Man was the clearest teacher I ever had. There didn't seem to be anything useful to say.

He looked up, gauging the pipe. "This," he said, "isn't gonna be a lot of fun."

"Why not?" I just couldn't seem to say anything intelligent.

The Old Man laughed, and clapped me on the shoulder. "We have to do easy work the hard way," he said. "You'll see. First, we need to get to a hardware store. C'mon, get in the car."

I looked at the muddy mess the two of us were. "We'd better not," I said.

He looked at me and down at himself. "Maybe you're right. Wait here." He went to the house.

He came out with Aunt Gwen, handing her a piece of paper and talking fast. All I heard was, "...exactly that one."

"I will, Dick," she said, climbing into her 1950 Studebaker (for a little while the Larlham family had three or four of them).

The Old Man untied the wrenches and put them on the brass union. He began to turn the collar of the union counter-clockwise. "Hold onto the pipe, Chuck," he said. "When this pump comes off, I don't want that pipe to jump and damage the electrical connection. Lay over it." So I did and, when the pump came off, the pipe – did pretty much nothing. The upper end was lying against something well up in the maple tree, and it barely moved.

"That's good," he said, placing a pair of heavy pliers between the union base and the pump. "Hold these tight."

I squeezed the pliers and he turned the union base. It came off easily because the one advantage to brass is that it can't rust to iron. Then he turned to the pipe and we did the same. Then we went over by the house. Nina came out with coffee. "I saved a gallon of water before I called Oliver," she said. We just stood in the lee of the house, shivering, drinking coffee and waiting for Aunt Gwen.

A surprisingly short time later, the Studebaker pulled into the drive. "Uh-oh," the Old Man said, "I'll bet the store was closed."

But Aunt Gwen got out of the car, walked to the trunk and opened it. "This box is heavy," she said. "Charles, will you get it?"

I went to the trunk. The hardware store salesman had loaded tools and fittings into a wooden box – made of thick planks. I lifted it out. She was right – it was heavy.

"What the hell..." began the Old Man.

"Tom at the hardware store had some suggestions," she said. "He put in a vise, and a bigger threader and pipe cutter than you asked for. He said to turn the box over and bolt the vise to the bottom. He drilled some holes."

"How much?" The Old Man was stunned. Even I could tell. "How much is this gonna cost? I didn't bring a lot with us."

"Oh, he said you could bring it all back. He won't charge you except for the fittings." Gwen looked very pleased with herself. "Mother and I will pay, of course."

"No," the Old Man said quietly, "I think I can cover a new union." He took the box over by the pump, and emptied it. He set it on end. "Come over here, Chuck," he said. He held the vise against the bottom of the box. "Put the bolts through," he said, inclining his head toward four large bolts, and four washers and nuts lying with them, "and spin the washers and nuts up."

I jammed two bolts through the base of the vise and through the highest holes as he held the heavy plumber's vise over the holes. Quickly I slid the washers on and spun the nuts in. The Old Man released the vise, holding the box from falling over onto the vise with one hand. He picked up the other two bolts. "Grab that wrench," he said, pointing to a crescent wrench.

I grabbed the wrench and the last sets of washers and nuts. He slid the bolts through, and I ran up the washers and nuts. Then I set the crescent onto one nut, and the Old Man picked up a ratchet wrench and began to tighten the bolts. The crescent promptly spun out of my hand and landed in the mud. "Hold onto that," he growled. Saying nothing, I picked up the wrench, wiped it off, and reset it on the nut. Through the rest of the vise attachment, I didn't drop it again.

The Old Man set the box upright and pulled the pipe over, pushing it between the jaws of the vise – holding it down with his entire weight. "Spin 'er in," he commanded. I spun the vise as tight as I could. "Hold this down," he said, nodding at the pipe. I took his place, and he tried the vise handle. It didn't budge. "Good," he grunted. "Stand up slow."

I eased away from the pipe, and it began to lift the rear of the box. I knelt on the box. The Old Man pulled out his pocketknife and cut the tape holding the electrical cord to the pipe just above the end.

"Hold 'er steady," the Old Man said, picking up a pipe-cutter. He slid the cutter over the pipe to just above the threads, and tightened it against the pipe. The cutter consisted of a C-clamp shaped device with a roller on the adjustable "jaw" that lay against one side of the pipe, and an edged wheel "blade" in the opposite jaw that lay against the other side. Once the jaws were fitted, the Old Man spun the cutter around the pipe, turning a knob at the end of the handle periodically to tighten the blade against the side, slowly forcing the blade wheel to cut into the pipe. Every little bit, he put a drop of oil in the groove it was making and, in a remarkably short time, the threaded end fell off the pipe.

The Old Man put down the cutter and picked up a two-handled device with a flat piece between the handles, in the center of which a large hole was placed with what appeared to be three "teeth" set around it. Each "tooth" was about a half-inch thick, and had a half-dozen blades on the inner surface.

Time to show off my knowledge and intelligence. "What's that?" I asked.

"This, my lad, is a pipe-threader," said the Old Man, placing one face of the center hole against the cut end of the pipe and slowly turning and fitting it. I could hear the "teeth" bite. The Old Man said, "Sit heavy on that box, Chuck. This thing's gonna try to turn you over." He carefully moved his hands out to the handles, and, pressing inward, he began to turn them. After a quarter turn, he relaxed. "Get the oil can," he said, "and put a drop or two right against the threader."

I got up and retrieved the oil can, putting two drops on the pipe, right against the threader face. For the next several minutes, the Old Man did his best to dump the box over, and me in the mud. Before long, he no longer had to push against the pipe. The threader needed simply to be turned. But turning it took a lot of effort. Even with his hands at the ends of the handles, the Old Man was working hard and it took about fifteen minutes to finish re-threading the pipe. The Old Man straightened and spun the threader off. He took a wire brush and scrubbed the threads to remove burrs and bits of iron.

"Hand me that pot of plumber's putty," he said, pointing. A metal handle stuck up through the lid of the jar. The Old Man unscrewed the lid, and picked it up by the handle. A brush was attached to the end of the metal handle in the pot. "Keeps you from having to put a messy brush in your toolbox," he said. He scooped a dollop of greasy looking putty with the brush and spread it over the threads. He turned around and did the same for the threads on the pump connector. Then he replaced the lid and picked up an iron union, separating the halves.

Within what seemed like seconds, the Old Man had attached the two halves of the union to the pipe and the pump. "I'm gonna release the vise," he said, gripping the vise handle. I held the pipe and the vise let go. I managed to control the pipe and the Old Man pointed behind me. "Back up a couple steps," he said.

He bent and lifted the top of the pump. I moved the pipe forward until the two halves of the union met. The Old Man turned the collar of the union slowly, moving the pump around, until the threads caught. "Uh-oh," he said. "Don't let that move, Chuck." Carefully, he released the pump, while I held on for dear life. He grabbed the pot of putty and slid a brush-full around the threads of the union. "Woulda leaked for sure," he muttered.

Once the collar was spun tight, and wrenches had made sure of a firm seat, we retaped the last part of the electrical cord to the pipe. Then we carefully sidestepped the pump back to the well, dropping it through our hands carefully until the rope and chain caught it. Then we began the tedious job of lowering it three feet at a time.

Getting the pump fully returned took another hour, as the pipe described an arc above us, and each drop took one of us pushing a part of the arc toward straightness. But it was finally set, and we connected the electrical cord and well pipe to the connectors in the casing and house supply collar at the top of the well. I brought the well cap.

"Not yet," the Old Man said. He turned to the house. "Gwen," he called.

The kitchen window lifted. "Yes, Dick?" she asked.

"Did you get the bleach?"

"Four gallons, behind the driver's seat," she answered.

The Old Man inclined his head to their car. I went over and pulled four gallons of Clorox from the floor of the Studebaker and took it to him.

"We've contaminated the well," the Old Man said. "Germs from our hands and clothes, dirt, whatever was on that tarp – it's all dangerous." He proceeded to pour all four gallons of bleach into the well. Then he went over to a hose lying beside the house, hooked it up to a faucet near the foundation and turned on the faucet. "Switch on the pump, Gwen," he called.

In a moment, Gwen said she had. There was no sound or indication for a few moments. Then, after much coughing and spitting, a steady stream of chlorine-smelling water began to flow. He laid the hose in the driveway. "We can shower in about two hours," he said. He went back to the shed, returning with a couple old torn shirts.

"Rinse your hands," he said, "and wipe them on this. Get 'em good and dry before you touch *anything*." I did as he said, as did he.

We went into the entryway. The Old Man stuck his head through the door into the kitchen. "Gwen," he asked, "could you open our suitcases and get our robes?" I haven't worn one in decades but, back then, we all had bathrobes.

Gwen disappeared, appearing moments later with our robes. We stripped to underwear and put on our robes. Then we went inside.

Nina went to the fridge. "Want a beer, Dick?" she asked.

"Yeah," he said, "I think I will this one time."

I was stunned. The Old Man *never* drank. I found out, years later, the Old Man was an alcoholic. Once in a month of Sundays he'd have one beer but the thought usually terrified him. But he was wet, cold and exhausted – and thirsty. I guess the thought of going hours more with nothing at all to drink persuaded him.

Nina brought out two bottles of Guinness, handing one to the Old Man – and one to *me*.

"No, Mom," he said, "he doesn't get beer." He stretched out his hand and I gave him the beer.

"Give the boy a beer, Dick," she said.

"No beer, Mom. I mean it," he said

"C'mon, Dick," she said. "Give the boy a beer. "He's worked as hard as you have and he's just as thirsty."

Yeah – yeah, I was thinking, *Give the boy a beer.*

"No beer," the Old Man said, opening his.

"Dick..." Nina began.

"Give him a soda, Mom," he said. "No beer!"

"Dick, that's not fair!" It was Gwen's turn to try.

"No beer for children," said the Old Man.

"Give the boy a beer, Dick!" Nina, again.

Yeah – yeah – give the boy a beer. Me again – still silently.

"My kids don't drink," the Old Man said. His jaw muscles were bunching again.

I got a soda – a glass of Schweppes Bitter Orange. I was incredibly thirsty as I tipped my head back and poured it down my throat. I'm here to tell you, that's not a good introduction to Schweppes Bitter anything!

CHAPTER 44

Uncle Jack Comes to Stay

The summer of '59, we once again piled into the car and took off to visit the Old Man's family. We spent most of a week at Nina's, crowded into her two-bedroom "Sears house." The Sears & Roebuck Company was, at the time, a mail-order company as well as a retail company. Some years earlier, it had offered for a few years, pre-fabricated houses through its catalogue and Nina bought one. Her sons assembled it on the side of a mountain outside Greenwood Lake, New York, and there she lived until she died.

When it came time to leave, Dad had agreed to visit for a day or so with Uncle Jack (one of his younger brothers) who lived in a "twelve-wide" mobile home in Pennsylvania – a stopover on the way home. So we did. The five of us followed Uncle Jack and his family through the hills of southeastern New York and Eastern Pennsylvania to the mobile home park where they lived. There were five of us and, added to Jack's family of five children, his wife LaHoma and himself, the twelve-foot wide, fifty-foot long trailer was a bit crowded.

It came time for bed and four of us, my brother and I and Jack's boys Dewey and Jack Jr. slept in the back of Jack's station wagon. The seatbacks were dropped to make a flat "floor" for us to sleep on. The backs lay down to make a level surface, all right – but they were in no way "flat." They were sort of corrugated, with cross-corrugations at the top and bottom edges. The first attempt to make a bed out of that was an utter disaster. No one could've slept on that. So Uncle Jack's wife, my Aunt LaHoma, began hauling out quilts and blankets. The Old Man and Jack went over to a field next to the Mobile Home Park and, using a couple sickles, cut armloads of grass which they spread over the seatbacks and covered with a plastic sheet (Jack used Visqueen for storm windows, and bought it in large rolls). The quilts were laid atop the sheet and we were told to find a space between them.

It became immediately apparent that closing up the car wasn't about to work. There was not enough room between the back of the front seat, which didn't lie flat, and the rear door of the station wagon for us to stretch out. The rear door was left open and it didn't take long for us to fall asleep. Unfortunately, there were others who did *not* sleep. From whence they came, I knew not, but mosquitoes found us. None of us awoke until morning, but when the Old Man came banging on the car, it didn't take long for us to discover...

Mosquito bites! *Hundreds* of mosquito bites! Our ankles and feet (we'd slept in our clothes except for shoes and socks) were a mass of little red welts. Itch? Oh my, didn't they itch! The Old Man and Uncle Jack laughed as we realized the trouble we were in. We dove for our ankles, fingers clawed, eyes staring – and slammed into the car roof and each other. Scrabbling and scrambling, we struggled out the rear of the station wagon and reached again for those welted itching body parts.

"*Stop!*" The Old Man's voice cracked the morning chill. "*Do not scratch!*" He cuffed my brother who reached downward even as he listened. "Put your hands in your pockets and make fists!" Tears squeezing from the corners of our eyes, we did as he said. Without thinking at all, I found myself trying to pull my fists out of my pockets and reach down. We headed for Uncle Jack's mobile home.

Mother and Aunt LaHoma met us at the door. "Dick," Mother asked, "what was all the yelling about?"

The Old Man pointed to my feet. "Show your mother," he said. I pulled up my cuffs.

Mother turned to Aunt LaHoma. "Baking soda?" LaHoma nodded and headed for a cabinet. She grabbed a large metal basin on the way, reached into the cabinet and pulled out a large box of Arm & Hammer baking soda, much of which she dumped into the basin.

"Outside, boys." She pushed between us. "Jack, get me some cold water."

She took the water from Jack and sat us around the basin with all our feet in it. "Pour," she said to Jack. Freezing well water poured over our feet and ankles. Mother and LaHoma rubbed our feet with the thinning slurry of dissolving baking soda. Slowly, the itch subsided (for me it was fairly quickly because I don't react for long to bites or stings) and within a half hour we were all ready for breakfast.

So for the day, the Old Man, Jack, LaHoma and Mother were closeted in the mobile home, while the eight of us ran around the mobile home park, played and scrambled, and generally did what kids of diverse ages do – which is to say, not much. At dinner, the Old Man announced that in a couple weeks Uncle Jack and his family, trailer and all, would be coming to Ohio to stay with us. I couldn't imagine how that was going to work, but nobody invited my opinion. I figured we'd find out – and we did.

A couple weeks later, the Old Man put me in the passenger seat of a mobile home transport tractor, gave the man a marked-up map, and he and I took off for Pennsylvania. The idea was that I was to be spare hands to Jack and LaHoma, to help them pack. I didn't know that "pack" meant something different to Uncle Jack than it did to most folks.

We pulled into the mobile home park a bit later than we'd planned and found a beehive of activity around Jack and LaHoma's trailer. I found out what "pack" meant. It's not usually advised to leave everything you own in the trailer you're pulling, but Jack couldn't see renting a moving truck. Doors were wedged shut, drawers were taped shut, two-by-fours were cut to hold doors and cabinets shut where wedges and tape wouldn't work. The driver was not happy.

Jack and the driver headed under the trailer to check conditions of the suspension, brakes, tires, and such, to make sure they wouldn't fail during the trip. The driver kept arguing that the trailer was going to be overloaded and tires would blow. "OK, let's go get new ones." Jack was not the most patient of men. Patience, I was to learn, was not his best attribute, even in the best of times – much like the Old Man.

"No." The driver was looking at the soil. "Ground's too soft. I'd rather see how they do on the highway. We'll buy a couple extra spares. I'll pick 'em up tonight." So it was decided, and the driver took off for a motel.

Jack handed me a shovel. "C'mon! Roses to dig." I looked around. The little "yard" that surrounded the trailer had been carefully landscaped, and there were *many* roses and plants I didn't recognize. We were *taking* these?

I knew exactly what to say. "Huh?" I figured that covered just about anything.

"We're taking the roses." He began to dig. We dug roses until midnight, wrapped the roots in newspaper and loaded them into the kitchen. Roots, soil and all, a rose plant probably weighed three or four pounds. There were dozens of roses, flowering shrubs, and some tuberous flowers like Iris and Gladiolas. By the time we were done, we'd probably added another five hundred pounds to the trailer.

Morning came and the driver showed up while Jack and I were still disconnecting the services. We were going to breakfast, but the driver wanted to be on his way so we hooked the trailer up. "Let's go!" Jack was suddenly impatient. "We'll meet you for breakfast at the first plaza," he called to the driver. The driver and I climbed into the cab.

Before long, we hit the Pennsylvania Turnpike and headed west, toward Ohio. Jack's car was out of sight in minutes. The driver fought the rig and swore. "What in the *world* is *in* that thing?" he muttered.

"Roses," I volunteered. He looked at me. I nodded. "Roses. We dug up all the roses last night and put 'em in the kitchen."

He just drove for a little bit. Then, "Roses – they filled the doggone trailer up with *roses*!" He muttered for a while. Finally he said, "This is gonna be a long ride." We cruised past the plaza where I fancied I could see Uncle Jack, Aunt LaHoma and the boys (and Joyce) enjoying breakfast.

"We're not gonna eat?" I was hungry.

"I had breakfast. If we want to get there when they do, we need to keep moving." He downshifted as we pulled up a grade. "And we're gonna be really lucky to even do *that* at this rate." He downshifted again.

We eventually topped the short mountain we'd been hauling over and rolled toward the bottom. At the bottom there was an exit from the 'pike, and as we rolled past it I remembered my stomach. "Wish I'd eaten." I muttered.

"Well," growled the driver, "I'll bring you something back from town."

"Huh?"

"We just blew a tire." The driver was downshifting and braking, pulling over onto the berm.

"I thought you bought spares."

"Nah," disgust oozed from his lips, "I decided we'd be OK." He clambered out of the cab, walked around the front of it and scaled the fence, leaving me in the cab on a hot August afternoon. There was no air conditioning in vehicles in 1959.

About an hour later, as I lay in the grass on the slope of the cut we'd stopped in, a tow truck pulled up. The trucker and the tow driver got out and proceeded to change the tire. Then they inspected the others, and the tow truck driver bolted two ready-mounted wheels with tires to the back of the cab.

As we prepared to leave, Uncle Jack pulled up. He and the trucker spoke for a few minutes and Jack got in his car and pulled away. "Well," the trucker said as he shifted up and pulled onto the highway, "he's right. It would've been cheaper to buy tires and wheels and pre-mount 'em before we left; would've been even better to not overload the trailer."

There didn't seem to be a lot of room in there for me to talk, so I didn't.

A couple hours later we pulled into a plaza. "Lunch," the trucker said. "Your uncle's inside."

I went in. Sure enough, Jack and his family were there. After lunch, Jack said, "I'm just gonna roll on to your Dad's place and get folks settled. Wish I'd thought this out better, but the wagon's too loaded. You're gonna have to ride on in with the truck."

And so I did. We pulled into the driveway late and I went

into the house. The Old Man and Jack went to situate the trailer.

For a while, Jack and his family lived in the "apartment wing" that had its own little kitchen and bath, while we scrubbed and cleaned the concrete chicken coop. Hot water, stiff brushes, bleach and soap were in liberal supply for use by teenage boys. We washed and scrubbed and swept and – eventually it was clean. We put up insulation and inside walls and placed the trailer so the rear door led to the door of the coop. And that was their home for a year or two. Eventually, Jack bought a house down the road from us.

When he moved his family to the house, they took the trailer with them. The house sat at the top of a hill, a glacial kame made up mostly of gravel. The trailer was pulled around behind the hill and left unused. Eventually, Jack, the Old Man, Jack's sons and Giles and I dug through the side of the hill until we had cleared a basement under the house. Jack poured a foundation and floor. Then he laid up block walls and installed a walk-out door. Voila! Jack had a basement!

We spent a lot of time showing the boys how "country living" was done, and we all had a good time. We enjoyed each other's company. For the cousins, it was an adventure. For us, it was a change and it made life busier. When all was said and done, a good time was had by all.

CHAPTER 45

The Bonfire

I put the tip of my right forefinger on the button at the apex of the tiny-billed "Frosh Beanie" on my head, and "dinked." Ignoring the ignominy with a degree of difficulty the smirking sophomore in front of me could not imagine, I performed a knee-bend, or squat, while grinding out, "Yes, oh arbiter of my future, how may this humble Frosh serve you?"

It was the last day of this and I had been strictly instructed by the Old Man to endure. "Hiram College is like a little Harvard." The Old Man's pride in me for being accepted at this small but elite school was boundless – but when he saw what was happening during "Frosh Week," he was quick to head off trouble. "If you hurt one of these boys, you'll be lucky to get into Kent State." He was right. The scrawny son of a doctor or lawyer or Wall Street denizen looking back at me had one more day to humiliate me. I could endure.

"You live on a farm near here." It wasn't a question. Oddly enough, this boy had stopped smirking and there was an air of excitement about him

"Yes." I was less enthusiastic than he might have hoped.

"Come with me." The boy led me to a table outside one of the dorms, occupied by a half-dozen other upper-classmen. He waved me to a seat. "Take off that stupid hat."

I pulled off the beanie. "I'm told," the suppressed excitement was palpable, "that you've been bragging about splitting and cutting up logs for your furnace."

"No," I started to get up, "I don't brag. Some of the guys were asking me what it was like to live on a farm. That was just part of it." I pulled the beanie out of my pocket.

My erstwhile friend grabbed my arm. "Sit down," he was urgent. "Please; sit down. We need your help."

Now, that was interesting. I sat back down. I looked from face to face. Everybody nodded.

"We're going to have a Homecoming in October, and the Sophomore Class has to build the bonfire." A dim bulb began to glow. "Every year, the Sophs get a bunch of Frosh and go searching through the woods around here for deadwood. There's none left." The light was blinding.

"You want my logs." Rapid nodding all around.

"Okay." Every head stilled. "But (there's *always* a "but")," I was enjoying this, "they have to be split."

"Split?" The young man at the end of the table looked completely at sea. "How would we do that? We don't have any hammers or... or... uh splitting things."

"I have all the 'splitting things' you'll need. They're called wedges. And I can supply the 'hammers.' They're called sledges."

"Sledges and wedges," one of the boys snickered.

"Or you can bring your own." Snickering stopped.

And so it was agreed. One Saturday a couple weeks later, I piled a half-dozen young men into the green and white '49 DeSoto in which I took very little pride (damn thing steered like the steering column was only occasionally connected to the front wheels and it shook like a big wet dog between forty and fifty miles per hour). We took off for my home, twelve miles away. The constant chatter among my passengers was deafening. When the shaking began, the chatter stopped. But, we got up to fifty, the shaking stopped and the chatter picked up again.

Arriving at my home, we were met by my mother and the Old Man. I had arranged for more than hard work, but hard work would come first. All the boys were of good size (except for the little Soph who had kicked off this adventure), but I suspected the hard work side of their education had been rather lacking.

"I'll have dinner ready when you're done." Mother beamed at the boys and turned back into the house. The Old Man just said, "This way, boys," and headed off behind the garage.

I knew what we were going to find. There were a dozen oak, maple, cherry and other hardwood logs, ranging in size from ten to fifteen feet in length and from six to thirty inches in diameter. There were two axes stuck into logs, blades aligned with the grain, a sixteen-pound, a twelve-pound and two eight-pound sledges, along with several wedges and two three-pound "starter" hammers.

I'd figured we'd need about twenty "tall" logs for the fire, which would mean splitting about four of the longer logs into four to six "rails." Each rail would be ten to fifteen feet long, triangular, and four to six inches on a side. We would also need shorter pieces ranging from three to six feet in length. To that end, I had rigged our big Oliver tractor to a three-foot circular "buzz-saw" via a five-inch belt turned to be a Möbius strip.

The Old Man grabbed an eight-pound hammer and a wedge. He set the blade of the wedge at the top edge of the axe blade and, swinging the sledge like a framing hammer, he pounded the wedge about halfway in. The axe-handle dropped onto the log and there was a crackling series of pops as the split propagated along the log. At the end of the split, he repeated with another wedge. Each propagation was about four feet, and he'd begun with a fifteen-foot oak about twenty inches at the butt, tapering to ten.

One of the boys picked up an eight-pound hammer and a wedge. "Let me try," he said, setting the wedge. He flexed his wrist and swung the sledge twice. Unfortunately, only the first swing was effective. The second bounced off the wedge, skidded off the log and jumped past his leg, smacking his shin with the handle. The young man in question was a six-foot-two Scandinavian from Minnesota, built like a weight lifter and very impressed with himself. His vocabulary was impressive – there was no question about that, even if half of it was in Swedish.

The Old Man and I showed them how to swing the smaller hammers one-handed to "set" the wedges, how to stand to make sure no one else's shin met a hammer handle, or worse, an axe-blade, how to swing and set the axes to start the splits and how to swing the larger hammers to drive the wedges rapidly in so they would cause the grain to separate rather than burying themselves like over-sized weirdly-shaped nails. I soon took over the axe duties. Three near misses convinced me that these boys were never going to survive this experience if I didn't.

There was much laughter at first as hammers missed wedges, mighty overhand swings resulted in hammers flying forward into the garage wall and the sixteen-pound hammer was tried and abandoned by everyone. Two of the boys could use the twelve-pounder, as could I. Within three hours, we had our twenty long rails and another dozen or sixteen shorter rails.

I had the Oliver cranked up, and the boys laid one of the

short rails on the "rocker," a long shelf with a back, but no top or front. The log was laid on it with the amount to be cut off resting on a shorter shelf that extended beyond the other side of the circular blade. As the blade spun at high speed, the offset teeth made a buzzing sound, hence the name.

Once the first log was on the rocker, I pushed it forward into the blade. There was an extended *"zun-un-un-ung,"* and a two-foot piece dropped off the short rocker as I let the shelf drop back toward me. From that moment until all the short pieces were done, everybody wanted to play. Each of them insisted on a turn pushing the rocker. None of them wanted to pull the cut pieces away from the saw. But we soon had everything organized and, within an hour, all the short pieces were done.

I backed the Old Man's two-ton dump truck behind the garage and the long rails were loaded in, with the narrow ends extending over the top of the rear gate. Then the short pieces were tossed in. Time for dinner!

Mother had prepared a West Virginia dinner. There was coffee and milk to drink, the main course was butter-beans (white, fully ripe, lima beans) cooked with a ham-shank cut up and tossed into the pot, bone and all, and the side-courses were corn-on-the-cob and fresh peas. There was corn pone (yellow cornbread) as a base to the dinner, as well.

Mother had cooked the pone in "spiders" (large cast iron skillets) in her oven and she cut them into wedges, split them and laid them on the plates as each boy came by. She put a large dollop of butter on each split and ladled beans and ham over them. Each of us then took an ear of corn and a large spoon of peas and sat down. The Old Man said grace and we began to eat. There were a few minutes of silence and seven starving eighteen and nineteen-year-olds dug into a flavor-rich high calorie...

"Young man," Mother broke the silence. We all looked up (the name could apply to all of us after all). "Don't you like butter-beans?" We looked at each other. Rick, he of the first attempt at swinging an eight-pound hammer one-handed, was not eating.

"I can make you something else," Mother said. "It'll only take a few minutes." I knew it was true. There were always ready-to-cook food and sandwich makings in the fridge.

"No, Ma'am," Rick was obviously embarrassed, "it's just that I never saw anybody put beans and butter on cake before."

I looked at Mother. She looked at me. The poor boy had never eaten cornbread in his life. We could not believe the deprivation that some people endured.

Before the laughter could begin, Mother smiled. "Young man, I've had my cornbread called many things, but never cake. Please eat."

Rick took a tentative bite of bread and beans, chewed, slowly swallowed. We all watched, awaiting his verdict. "Ma'am," there was a note of wonder in his voice, "that was the most amazing bite of food I've *ever* eaten, and my mother is a *good* cook." He bent to his plate and said no more.

Mother blushed like a girl. The rest of us simply went back to eating. We were *hungry*!

When dinner was over, the Old Man drove the truck to Hiram, with me leading the way. Because the truck was even less road-worthy than the DeSoto, we did not experience the shaking on the way back. The boys and I unloaded the truck at the bonfire site, and the Old Man went home.

Everyone agreed, it was the tallest, hottest and best pre-homecoming pep-rally bonfire for a generation or more – and the fire the flying sparks started on the field-house roof was absolutely worth it.

CHAPTER 46

'59 Chevy: Part 1 – The Flying Car

There were times I was convinced the Old Man bought cars and instructed them to try to kill me. F'rinstance...

Sometime in 1961, the Old Man bought a used (no one said "pre-owned" in 1961) two-door '59 Chevy, otherwise known as a "coupé." Any model of the '59 Chevy was a truly strange-looking beast. But the coupé was a special case.

The '59s were wide and low, with horizontal "fins" functioning as the top of the rear fenders. These "fins" (or "wings," as they were quickly renamed) began as a vee down the length of the center of the trunk. From that vee, they curved gently up and out (mostly out) to slightly beyond the vertical sides of the fenders. There was a "scoop" taken out of the top of the fender and the bottom of the fin where they met, heightening the impression of "wings." The rear window sloped down to the top of the trunk (on the coupé, the very *long* trunk), and the whole effect was – this damned car can fly!

Well, that was the rumor, anyway. Our urban legend of the day was that the "wings" really worked. They didn't, of course, but everybody said they could and I had to prove it – didn't I? So, one day when my stupid side had control of my thinkin' side, I set out to do exactly that. It didn't start out that way, but...

Late one Friday night (I had come home from college, 12 miles away, for the weekend), the Old Man asked me to take the Chevy and go pick up my brother and a couple of his friends from some high-school event. On a country road, the traditional "two-lane blacktop" of story and legend, egged on by high-school kids I never should have listened to (I was a college sophomore, for th' luvva), but who wanted to know "Will this thing really fly?" I put my right foot as close to flat on the floor as it would go, shoe-leather and floor separated only by the accelerator. The big V-8 carried us effortlessly toward 80, then 90, 100, 110 and a left-hand curve came abruptly into view! I tried to back off.

It wasn't enough. I was too close. I could see that no headlights were approaching, so I drifted the car into the oncoming lane. I planned, as we passed the apex of the curve, to let her drift back to the proper lane, thus "straightening" the curve. But, as the apex approached, I could feel the rear tires losing contact with the blacktop. The too-skinny, hard plastic steering wheel felt like a live snake in my hands and I could see the world begin to move slowly to my right, directly in front of me. There was a light shimmy. We were going into a spin and every theory I'd ever heard on what to do ran through my mind like water through a fire-hose. None of it seemed to want to stay. But my passengers had thoughts on the matter.

"Slow down!" somebody yelled.

"Straighten 'er out!" from another expert.

Both of these were bad ideas and I could feel it. I lifted my foot ver-r-r-ry slightly, and held rock-steady to the wheel. I felt the rear end drop, *just* a little, and the drive-wheel catch – barely. The drive wheel on that car was the left rear, and the spongy shocks and leaf-springs let her lean *far* to the right in this left-hand bend, worsening the effects of the "wings" lift. There was a squeak and a wiggle but we were now fully into the curve. As much as I'd straightened that curve, I could still feel the back end coming out again. I eased the turn pressure on the steering wheel ever so slightly, and let the car begin to drift back out to its proper lane. The right front tire was squealing and I wasn't sure I could hold 'er when the time came to straighten out.

There was no more advice from the rear but I could hear everybody breathing. Somebody in the back was saying, "Oh jeez, oh jeez, oh jeez..." as rapidly as he could for as long as he had air. My brother, riding shotgun, had said nothing, but his right hand was braced against the steel dashboard and his left arm was stretched along the seat back – his left hand gripping it like a Nile Croc on a Wildebeest's leg.

We came closer and closer to the edge of the blacktop. If we dropped off the edge, we were on gravel, and I knew if the right rear wheel touched that, we were done. I kept a solid but light grip on the steering wheel, consciously relaxing my arm muscles as much as I could, moving the wheel in tiny increments with the changes in road and drift. Suddenly, it was over. The road was straight again ahead of us. I lifted my foot and felt the rear of the car settle. I slowed and pulled over. We sat. No one spoke for more than a minute.

"Damn," someone said softly, "they *do* work."

And so it seemed. Thanks to my brother and his friends, it became an article of faith in the little farming center town of Mantua, Ohio – the "wings" on a '59 Chevy worked!

But, of course, it wasn't so. Someone who actually understood terms like "lift" and "drag," and "coefficient" and "center of gravity" explained it to me one day in my distant future. You see, even though they were evocative of wings, those fins were no more functional than the wings on a Dodo.

But the '59 Chevy herself? Ah-h-h therein lay the true story.

To begin with, the V-8 in that long, flat, wide coupé made her front-heavy. The weight differential was about 53% front to 47% rear – a six percentage point difference. So-o-o-o when she started to lift, the car was already light in the bucket. Then there was the wing effect (Wai-ai-aitaminnit! You said the wings didn't work!) Yep. So I did. And so they didn't but the *car* did! And here's how.

The bluntly rounded front end, its effect accentuated by the rear-sloping front window, further reinforced by the fact that the roof itself sloped down from the front window to the top of the rear window, which itself sloped to the top of the trunk, which was essentially flat (and very long), all combined to make *the car* a wing! It's true. The '59 through '61 Chevys, especially the coupé models, were shaped in cross-section very like badly designed airfoils. And under the right circumstances, with the shape accentuated by the lack of weight in the rear, and with enough speed to provide lowered air pressure over that big flat trunk, the rear end would lift away from the road – as it had for me.

Had there not been two fairly large young men adding about three hundred and fifty pounds to the back seat, I'd have never held her. There were no seatbelts in '59 Chevys and no safety latches on the doors. The rear tires would've fully lost contact with the road, throwing us sideways in the turn. We'd have rolled like a log and all of us would likely have been ejected and have been seriously injured or dead by the time the car stopped. That car was probably the most dangerous car I've ever driven – bar none.

If you don't think the shape of a rear window is enough to change significantly the handling characteristics of a car at speed, just ask NASCAR. When it first arrived on the circuit, the Ford Taurus was so much the reverse of the '59 Chevy, that it won eight races in a row, until NASCAR figured it out and forced them to change the slope of that rear window.

CHAPTER 47

'59 Chevy: Part 2 – No Brakes!

That '59 Chevy was not only downright dangerous; she was ugly as sin when the Old Man bought her. The car was a dull brown with all the character of a barnyard hen. So he took it to a local body shop and had it re-painted. I drove him up to get it, and he pointed to a two-tone – robin's-egg blue and copper! I'm *still* not sure that combination worked. But the Old Man was proud of it. Brown or two-tone, that car was the forerunner of Steven King's "Christine." That Chevy tried to kill me twice more before the Old Man got rid of it.

I topped a hill on Mennonite Rd., coming into Mantua one October Saturday afternoon in 1961. From that vantage, I could see SR 44, Mantua's Main Street and the Mennonite Rd., SR 44 intersection with the red/green traffic light (no yellow – both colors lit up a few seconds before it changed to red) hanging over the center of it, a third of a mile down the hill. I could also see the gravel trucks and semis rumbling north and south on SR 44.

As the Chevy started down the hill, I touched the brakes. I didn't want to have to brake at the last second. Besides which, the speed limit was twenty-five and I was pretty much still a teen-ager, so far as Jerry, the Mantua Chief of Police was concerned. Cops *loved* to ticket teenagers (still do, I reckon). So-o-o-o I touched the brakes. There was a momentary resistance, and my foot slammed to the floor, taking the brake pedal with it. The car began to pick up speed.

I began my life-saving countermeasures by reciting a list of all the curses and Anglo-Saxon words for bodily functions and excreta I could think of. Fortunately, at that age, the list was short. When I finished it, I still had time to *do something* before we wound up trying to occupy the same space as one of those trucks, an attempt I had been assured by my high-school physics teacher would be unsuccessful – more so for the Chevy than for the semi or gravel truck.

The Chevy was a stick shift, so I shoved in the clutch and slammed 'er into second gear and took my foot entirely off the gas. The big V-8 began to whine about holding back all that weight, and the tranny joined in. Unfortunately, it quickly became apparent that, although the tooth-vibrating double whine was becoming rapidly unendurable, the car was not slowing enough. I looked for a place to "park." I looked right. The town armory – *cum* VFW Hall, *cum* DAR hall, *cum* whatever – sat well back from SR44, with a huge manicured lawn filled with maples and a very large cannon on a caisson. That was *definitely not* gonna work. I looked left. Nothing but houses and driveways, each of which had a block or stone wall along the uphill side of the driveway – not likely to be welcoming.

I threw in the clutch and went for first gear. The transmission crashed and gnashed like a "car-eater" in a junk yard. I double clutched and played with the gas. Still noth... "CLANK!" First gear was engaged, and the car stood on its nose. *My* nose was bloodied by the steering wheel. I fell back and breathed a sigh of rel... *we were still moving*! Bucking and grinding, to be sure, but moving. The light was red – trucks were crisscrossing in front of me at *incredible* speeds I was gonna *die!*

I reached for the "emergency" brake and yanked it back. It wouldn't budge, and then, it was suddenly free – and obviously not working. The trucks were still moving and I was getting very close to that intersection. I turned off the key and re-bloodied my nose. The stupid car kept trying to *start!* One way to start a stick-shift car is to get it up to speed (maybe only three or four miles an hour) and, with the key on, throw it into second gear. With the key off, the car in first gear and a hill that kept us rolling, the bucking, spitting, back-firing and stop-starting were incredible. But *we weren't stopping!*

I gave up. I decided to spin the steering wheel right and crash into a tree. As I braced myself, I took a last look forward, looked right again, and reached to spin the steering wheel, and a memory, a picture blazed in front of my eyes – the traffic light was *green!*

I reached down, turned on the key and, as the engine caught, I floored the accelerator. The Chevy shot across the intersection just as the light changed to red-and-green and went airborne as the road dropped away again on the far side of the intersection. I realized that the whole drive-train would disintegrate when we hit if it was still in first gear, so I threw her into neutral and let 'er run out below the intersection. Eventually, the road flattened and we stopped.

I got out and began the trudge back up the hill to call for a tow. But I had passed a gas station at the intersection and one of the pump-jockeys was already on his way down the hill with the old Studebaker pick-up with a hook mounted in the bed that they used for towing.

I called the Old Man from the garage. "Well," he said as I finished my story, "you've probably ruined the transmission or the rear end."

"Oh," I said.

"It'll be a while 'til I get there," he said. "Have 'em fix the brake-line and look at the tranny and the rear end."

The Chevy was up on the lift and the mechanics were already working on it. "C'mere," one of them said. "Look at this." He pointed to the side of a shock absorber. The brake line was nestled up to it and a hole had been worn into the line as the shock moved up and down against it. Hydraulic fluid covered the rear underside of the car. He pointed to a small steel cable running next to the brake line. It had frayed and broken against the same shock absorber.

"Emergency brake line," he said. Then he growled, "There's lotsa room under here. They coulda kept 'em from rubbin'. But you've got another problem. Emergency brake's froze up. That's why the cable broke. You couldn'ta moved 'er without tools."

The emergency brake was a device that mechanically pulled the brake shoes against the brake drum if the hydraulic system failed or if you wanted to keep your car parked on a hill. Most of us just put the car in reverse with the engine off and the car parked, to do that. But there was a reason we called it the "emergency" brake, as well as "parking" brake, and I'd just experienced that reason. In this case, through lack of use, plus a generous application of road salt for a couple winters, the pivot for the lever that was pulled by the hand-brake cable had rusted solid. I couldn't have moved it had the cable been brand new.

Three hours later, I had smoked half a pack of Camels, the mechanics had replaced the broken cable and brake line, freed the "emergency" brake pivot and taken the back off the "punkin' " (the rear end differential case). The Old Man showed up in a borrowed car. "Show me," he said.

I pointed to the car, still on the lift – the mechanics working on the access port to the transmission.

"No," he said. "Show me what happened."

I walked with him to the intersection and pointed up the hill he had just come down. I began in a rush pointing to places on the hill where I'd been when I did various things. As I got to the intersection and my realization that I didn't have to crash the car, it came to me that I had done all that in less than a minute. It had seemed to take forever. When I was done, the Old Man didn't say anything for a few seconds. "Good thing you didn't wreck it," he said, finally. "You could've been hurt."

"Yeah," I said, unable to think of anything else to say.

The Old Man turned and walked to the garage. He and the mechanics engaged in a conversation I couldn't even begin to follow. After a bit, he came over to me. "It'll take 'em about two more hours," he said. "You wait for it and bring it home." He pulled out a checkbook, wrote out a check, signed it and handed it to me. I looked down. The name of the garage was there, but there were no numbers on it. I looked up at him.

The Old Man grinned. "They'll tell you how much," he said. "You write it in there," he pointed to the spaces for amounts, "and tell me how much when you get home."

I nodded. "What do they have to fix?" I asked.

"Nuthin' that matters, Son," the Old Man said. "Nuthin' that matters." He turned and looked up the hill. Then he turned back to me. "Helluva job, Son," he said. "Yessir, a helluva job." He clapped me on the shoulder, got into his borrowed car and drove away.

As I watched him go, I thought of another time, not so

many years earlier. I'd shot a rabbit and let one of the dogs get to it and eat part of it. "Stupid!" he'd said that day. "Stupid, stupid, stupid! That's all I've got to say."

It took me years to realize that having me bring the Chevy home was a "get back on the horse" kind of thing. It was a funny thing – as I got older, he got smarter by the year.

CHAPTER 48

We're in the Army Now

Dinner at the Larlham household, second week of August 1962, on a hot, sticky afternoon. Giles had graduated from high school, but he was having trouble finding a job and didn't want to go to college. I'd finished my sophomore year at Hiram College, a small, elite liberal arts college in northeast Ohio, but I was failing and I knew why – I didn't want to go to college either.

Giles lifted his head, sat back, laid down his silverware and took a breath. Something was up. Had he found a job? Had he gotten married? Was his girlfriend pregnant? Had he... "I'm joining the Army." It was not a request, not a demand, and most definitely not an invitation to debate. It was just information. Mother put one hand to her mouth and took a fast breath. Larry-bird, one of the higher-functioning of the children we were caring for was eating with us. He copied her and giggled.

The Old Man missed all that and went directly into command mode. "No," he said flatly, "you're doing no such thing."

Giles took a breath. "Dad –"

"No." The Old Man was full bore, head down to the wind, determined to put a stop to this foolishness and remind Giles who was boss in this house. "You need my permission, and I'm not givin' it. Now, finish your dinner."

Giles pushed his chair back and stood up. "I turned 18 two days after you turned 51, back in April, Dad – remember? You don't get to give me permission; not now – not ever again." He turned and walked out the door.

The Old Man was stunned, but I wasn't sure he should be. He and Giles had been having their mini-wars every few months since Giles became a teenager. He would shout. Giles would yell. Things would escalate. Giles would storm out of the house, usually to return in the wee hours of the morning, and everyone would pretend he'd never left. Occasionally he'd stay with Uncle Jack for a day or two. This time was different. No yelling, no escalation, no threats. Giles just walked out, closing the kitchen door quietly.

The Old Man didn't move, didn't speak, didn't anything. After a bit he picked up his fork and absently put food in his mouth.

"Giles go out," Larry-bird said brightly into the silence.

"Yeah, me too, Larry-bird." I stood up and turned to the Old Man. "I'll talk to him. We'll see what he says tomorrow."

I gathered my dishes and put them in the sink and went outside. No Giles. I lit a smoke and headed for the Hooch. The Hooch was a converted concrete chicken coop. When Uncle Jack brought his trailer and hooked up the back door to the coop, we had renovated it into a couple bedrooms and a sitting room with a carpet and a fuel-oil fired space heater. When he bought a house down the road and took his family and trailer there, Giles and I moved into the coop. Somewhere I had picked up the term "hooch" as GI slang for house, at least in Korea, and that's what we called it. I had no idea how real that term was soon to become to me.

I opened the door to the Hooch and the odor of fuel oil

mixed with cigarette smoke hit me as it always did. I ignored the odor, which faded rapidly, and looked into the sitting room. Giles was sprawled on the beat up old sofa we'd scrounged from who-knew-where, reading a comic book. He looked up at me and grinned.

"You supposed to talk me out of it?"

"I guess."

"You gonna?"

"Nope."

He nodded and went back to his comic.

I grabbed an ashtray, walked past him, filching a couple comics on the way by, and dropped into the broken-down easy chair that went with the sofa.

Giles looked up. "Those're mine."

I raised a hand in acknowledgment.

A couple hours later, I went to bed. He woke me some time after that, trying to get into his own bed without turning on a light and waking me. Ah, well...

I awoke in the dark to the smell of smoke. I lay very still, willing my brain to tell me what was wrong with the picture it was giving me. I focused on a red dot that abruptly brightened. I saw the shadows of a face. What th'... Brain finally caught up with itself. The red dot was the lit end of a cigarette and the smoke was cigarette smoke. My concrete chicken coop *cum* Hooch wasn't burning down around my ears.

I rolled upright and swung my legs over the side of the old Army bunk that served me as a bed.

"Smoke?" the Old Man was holding a pack of Camels toward me. He gave them a quick shake and a couple popped above the top edge of the pack. I took one and tamped it a couple times. He fired a lighter. In the flare, he looked haggard.

I lit up and said, "Watch your eyes."

The Old Man looked away as I reached over and switched on the ancient (and probably dangerous) floor lamp. Behind him, I saw Giles come awake. The Old Man turned the chair a little while Giles lit a smoke, so he could see both of us. We all smoked in silence for a couple minutes. Finally...

"You can go," he said to Giles. To my amazement, Giles said nothing. He just nodded. The Old Man turned to me. "You go with him," he said. "Don't let him hurt anybody and don't let him go to jail."

I said, "Okay." There didn't seem to be a lot of room for discussion. This was perfect. I'd just arrange for readmission to Hiram College three years hence and worry about whether I was actually going to do it or not when I got back. At the very least, I would put off flunking out for at least three years. Yep – this was absolutely perfect.

I went to the campus that morning and collected letters from the head of the Biology Department, the Dean of the School of Science and the College President, all assuring me that I could return upon completion of my commitment to the Army. On my way back home, I stopped in Mantua and rented a safety deposit box for three years, into which I deposited those letters. Three years later, only one of the three signatories remained at Hiram, and those letters were all that stood between me and refusal of readmission.

Giles and I went into Ravenna and met the recruiting sergeant. All enlistments were for seven years, but not an active seven years. We had three choices: 1) Regular Army (RA), a three-year enlistment with only inactive reserve thereafter – three and out; 2) Volunteer for Draft (VD – yeah, I know), a two-year enlistment, with a couple years of active reserve responsibility, followed by inactive reserve for the remainder of the seven-years, and 3) Reserve or National Guard (weekend warrior), a six-month training and active duty enlistment, followed by seven years of weekends on an army base and two weeks of active duty every year. We chose RA; three years and done.

The recruiting sergeant arranged for our enlistment day in Cleveland a few days away, told us to bring razor, toothpaste, toothbrush, comb and brush, two changes of underwear and clothes and no more than twenty dollars in smaller bills. If we smoked, he recommended a half-carton each. Late in the day a few days later, the Old Man dropped us off at a run-down hotel in Cleveland, shook our hands and headed home. We went into the lobby.

The clerk looked up. "Recruits? What branch?"

"Army."

"Good enough. Papers?"

We each had an envelope with several papers. We handed them over. The clerk sorted through them and took a couple papers from each. He held them up. "Ah-ha! We get paid," he said.

He gave us keys with room numbers, told us when the bus would show and promised to wake us. He handed us each meal tickets for half a dozen places in the vicinity of the hotel. We went up to our room, dumped our suitcases on the beds and went looking for a deli.

The clerk roused us at five o'clock the next morning and the bus came at six-thirty. The recruitment center for all services was somewhere in the old train terminal. When we got there, the bus pulled into an underground garage and Giles and I, along with a dozen other guys, exited. An Army sergeant stood on a raised platform with a microphone and, once the buses had pulled out, he began to call names.

He called Giles first and pointed him toward a door. I was called a couple names later and sent to a different door. Inside I was stopped under a sign that said, "Station 1," and questioned almost faster than I could answer, my temperature was taken and I was told to strip. Carrying clothing over one arm and shoes in the opposite hand, I was sent through a curtain, where I found Giles stepping on and off a step-stool about eight inches high – the height of a standard tread and riser on a stairway.

"Giles, what in..."

"Come over here, young man! I'll tell you when to speak." The voice came from my right so I turned that way. A doctor was standing there pointing to a chair by a table. "Sit down!" He reached out and I handed him a folder I'd been given at the first station and sat down. While he flipped through the folder, a young soldier strapped a blood pressure cuff around my arm and pumped it until I couldn't feel my fingers.

"I don't need –"

"Did I ask what you need?" The soldier looked almost bored, despite the tone of great anger. He looked at the readings he'd written down. He pointed to Giles. "See what he's doing?"

"Yes."

"Go over there and do that until I tell you to stop, understand?"

"Yes."

He looked at Giles. "You," he barked, "on the step stool. Stop and come over here."

Giles stopped. We passed each other. "Go get 'em, Chuck."

"Did I tell you to talk?" from the soldier.

"Nah, I've been able to talk without being told to since I was two," from Giles.

It was gonna be a long two months of Basic Training. I began stepping on and off the step stool. After a little while, the soldier called me over and retook my blood pressure. "Well, you didn't pass out, and you're up to almost 100 over 50. I guess you can enlist."

He handed the information to a doctor who looked it over and raised an eyebrow. "Two of... oh, brothers." He scribbled his name at the bottom of the sheet.

"Go through there." The soldier was already taking another blood pressure. He nodded toward another curtain.

Through there turned out to be a room with about two dozen young men in it. Two doctors were performing rapid physical examinations, including the infamous "turn your head and cough" maneuver. Each examination took less than two minutes. In twenty minutes we were all told to finish getting dressed and go through the next door. The next door led to a room with a small podium, an American flag and little else. We all stood around and looked at each other.

An officer appeared and introduced himself, told us we were about to take an oath of fealty to the USA and, if we wanted out, this was our last chance. Nobody moved. Two minutes later, Giles and I were soldiers.

We were ushered out of the room into a room with a bank of cameras. It took no more than another two minutes to create a photo ID, get it signed and laminated and send us on our way. In the next room, a sergeant explained that the buses would carry us back to the hotel and tomorrow they'd pick us up and bring us back to the terminal where we'd board a train for Fort Knox, Kentucky. "But," he said with some relish, "you just got a free pass to every major league sporting event in America. So long as you're active duty, they're free and the Indians are playing tonight."

Now, that wasn't the greatest news I'd ever heard. The Cleveland Indians in the '60s were hardly a first tier Major League Baseball team. A consortium was just trying to keep the team's head above water and in Cleveland until somebody with real money bought it and kept it here on his own hook. To that end, they functioned as a minor league team to several other teams, sending their best players regularly to play for rivals in turn for cash infusions and the infamous "player-to-be-named-later."

There had even been recent controversy over the team's name and "Chief Wahoo," the team's mascot. That was squelched by the local newspapers reminding everyone that the Indians were originally the "Spiders," and were renamed the Indians in honor of their best player at the time, a full-blooded Native American named Frank LaJoi. The Chief Wahoo character was retired from animated advertising war dances but remains to this day as a basic symbol of the team.

I was about to tell Giles we'd skip it when the Sergeant said, "Early Wynn's pitching for his three-hundredth win."

Early Wynn's career was about over, but he desperately wanted that three-hundredth win, and he wanted it as a Cleveland Indian starting pitcher. He knew full well he'd be relegated to the bullpen as soon as the milestone was reached but he feared that demotion might happen whether he won or not. In those days, most relief pitchers were starters who could no longer throw more than three innings. In fact, in later years, one of the premier relievers in all of Major League Baseball, one

Dennis Eckersley, was a starter for the Cleveland Indians and pitched a perfect game for them. That, however, was not Early Wynn's destiny this night.

I persuaded Giles to go and, early in the game, the Indians built a lead of several runs to the opposing team's single run. Then came the eighth inning and Wynn began to struggle, letting in a couple runs and nearly opening up the game to the enemy. But a double play bailed him out and he sat to await the ninth inning. The manager spoke with him, as did several players, but he shook his head and sat.

Before long, the Cleveland players had been cleared from the batting lineup and Wynn was back on the mound to start the ninth inning. The score was something like ten to three in the Indians' favor. By the end of the top of the ninth, the score was eleven to ten and the Indians were unable to make up the two runs they needed in the bottom of the ninth inning, or even one to tie the game. We headed back to the buses.

The next morning, we returned to Cleveland Terminal where we were sent to wait with half a hundred other new soldiers in a room filled with old furniture and last year's Look and Life magazines until nearly noon. A couple soldiers came in and told us the train was running late. They collected us and took us to a diner in the terminal where we were allowed to buy a soup and sandwich with a coffee or milk. One of the soldiers handed a voucher to the clerk and we ate in enforced silence. We returned to the room of broken furniture and old magazines for another hour or two before we finally boarded a troop train about two o'clock in the afternoon.

We didn't make Elizabeth, Kentucky, home of Fort Knox, until about eight o'clock the following morning. We got off the train and came face-to-face with one Sergeant Wetzler, a short angry little man in whose hide Giles and I were to be thorns for the next eight weeks.

"Stand still and shut up!" Had that giant bellow come from that little...

"Face front that's ME, you idiot... everybody face front!" Yep, it was his voi...

"Ten-HUT!" There was ragged shuffling and muttering as people tried to create some sort of ranks.

The sawed-off little sergeant looked skyward. "Lord," he prayed, "I ain't been all that bad a guy. And I only killed people I was s'posed to. Why," he looked out at us and extended his arms toward us, "why did you do this to me?" He took a breath and looked directly at us. "Just follow me. Don't try to march. You'll learn that tomorrow."

Somebody behind me said something and, without even looking, the sergeant said, "I didn't ask you to talk, and until I do, you don't talk understand? Yer in the Army now!" He took off at a brisk walk and Giles and I followed. Minutes later, we clambered aboard olive-drab school buses for our trip from the terminal to Fort Knox.

Later, after a morning of continuous insults and casual disrespect, we stood in line for uniforms. As we were handed ill-fitting green fatigues (the Army's name for ugly green work clothes) I said to Giles, "You can't touch 'im, Giles. You'll piss off the whole damned Army – and the Old Man will never forgive me if you wind up in a military prison."

"Yeah," he said, "I know – but dreaming about it will keep me sane for the next eight weeks."

Yeah, we were in the Army now – in spades.

CHAPTER 49

'59 Chevy

Part 3 – Gimme Back My Wheel!

I came home for Christmas, the winter of 1962. I was on my way to Korea, having just finished US Army Basic Training and Field Medic Training. While I was there, I borrowed the Old Man's '59 Chevy coupé. I went into Ravenna on some errand and then I headed for Hiram College where I had spent the last two years. I was in uniform and, for some reason, I thought that walking around a liberal arts college in a military uniform would be a fine thing to do. Mebbe then – not three years later, as I found out, much to my chagrin, three years later.

Coming out of Ravenna, I picked up a hitchhiker with a lot of bags and stuff, who turned out to be a freshman returning early to Hiram. I never did find out why. I told him he'd lucked out as I was, in fact, going to exactly the same destination. I helped him pitch his bags into the trunk, noticing that he was about half my size. I was, at the time, five feet eleven inches tall and I weighed a hundred sixty pounds. The young man stood about five feet six and weighed maybe a hundred twenty-five. I did the heavy lifting.

We had driven about six miles, my passenger filling me in on changes at the college (not all that many, but then again, I'd only been gone one semester). It turned out we were both biology majors and we talked a bit about that. We'd been listening to a steady thump coming from the right front. I looked at him. "Tire bubble," I said. "I'll have to change it when we get into Hiram." We weren't travelling fast (the daytime speed limit on a State Road in Ohio at the time was sixty-five mph – nighttime was fifty) so I figured that even if it blew, we'd be OK. As we climbed a hill between two cut walls of earth about twenty or twenty-five feet high, a wheel and tire appeared, rolling diagonally down the cut side of the hill, above and ahead of us.

"Some idiot," I said, looking over at my passenger, "has let a tire get away from him. He could hurt somebody down here doin' that."

"Urgk," he said, pointing forward. The tire was bounding forward and down the hill. My passenger had realized that the wheel and I were going to reach the same spot in the road at the same moment.

"I see it," I said. "We'll miss it. I'll just slow down and it'll cross ahead of us." I touched the brake.

The right front corner of the car dropped with a crash and tried to stop! F'r th' luvva... that was *my* wheel!

I was able to fight the car straight and keep it moving (ignoring the screeching and scraping of the wheel-drum on pavement and the mumblings I assumed were prayers, or possibly curses, coming from the passenger seat) until we had crested the hill. Once we were up there, I let the car pull right until we were off the road (luckily, the verge was about ten feet wide at that point for some reason).

I turned to my passenger and pointed over my shoulder to a large farmhouse across the road. "I'm going to call for a tow," I said to him. "You can wait here and ride with me and the tow-truck into Mantua, or you can try your luck at hitching out here in the middle of nowhere." He just looked at me.

I got out of the car and walked over to the wheel, now lying in the middle of Ohio's State Route 44. I tipped it upright and gave it a light shove toward the car. It wobbled up to the bumper, struck it lightly and fell over into the ditch. "Good enough," I grunted.

On the farmhouse porch, I was met by the lady of the house – the wife of a distant cousin of my mother's. I explained and she invited me in to use the phone. I called a local Sinclair gas station (it was owned by the son of our next-door neighbor) and he said he'd be there as soon as he could. First, he was going to stop by a junkyard and pick up a new hub and wheel. I rang off and accepted a glass of water. While I was drinking it, there was a loud banging on the door from the front porch.

The lady opened the door, started to speak and stopped. We both just stood and stared at the sight in front of us. Filling the door was the largest deputy on the Portage County Sheriff's staff. He stood at least six feet six and he weighed at least three hundred pounds. From a right hand the size of small backhoe bucket dangled the slight form of my passenger. From the other hand dangled pretty much all his bags and belongings.

Raising his left hand and looking directly at me, the deputy rumbled, "Is this stuff yours, soldier? I found this kid cleaning out your car."

I was startled for a moment, having forgotten I was in uniform. Recovering, I said, "No, it's all his. I was giving him a ride to Hiram."

The deputy looked disappointed. "You're sure?" he asked.

" 'Fraid so," I said. Then I had a brainstorm. "Put him down," I said. The deputy looked uncertain. "It's OK," I said. "He's not a thief. He's just a student and his ride back to school just ended. He needs another one."

The deputy looked at me with undisguised suspicion. "I don't..." he began uncertainly.

"Sure," I said, "you take him. It's not that far. Besides, you owe him. You scared 'im half to death." We both looked at my passenger. He had stopped shaking, but he still looked ready to run.

The deputy stared off into space. Finally, "OK," he said, "but we'll have to wait until your tow gets here."

So that's what we did. The deputy and I sat on the porch and smoked and swapped stories. The young man stayed in the kitchen with the farmwife, despite our request that he join us. Eventually my tow showed up.

I called the Old Man from the garage. "What'd you take it there for?" was the first thing he said.

"Because I know Charlie," I answered.

"So do I," he barked. "He'll cheat you, and I'll get stuck with the bill."

"If you do," I said, "I'll cover you."

The Old Man calmed down. "How much could it be?" I heard him mutter. Then to me, "Do you need a ride?"

But Charlie had the new wheel balanced and on the car. "Five bucks," he said. "Don't tell your old man." He winked. I never did.

I paid and left, finally making it to Hiram. But it was, after all, a school holiday and no one I knew was around. I wandered around a bit, and finally went home.

Epilogue:

Three years later, I returned to Hiram as a junior (much to the dismay of some of the faculty) and I made friends with most of the juniors and seniors in the Biology Department. One afternoon, in a basement Café booth, I heard one of the seniors with whom I was friends talking on the other side of the booth-back. The story he was telling was this one. In the better part of a year, I hadn't recognized him – nor had he recognized me.

"I've been waiting for him to show up," said the storyteller. "I wanted to thank him for a most interesting day but I guess he reenlisted or something, 'cause I haven't seen him."

I got up and walked around to his booth. "Sure you have, Denny," I said. "You've been tutoring him in lab this whole semester."

CHAPTER 50

Long Trip Home

August 13, 1965, was a day of days. I walked into the Captain's office in the Training Support Company of the Medical Training Command at Ft. Sam Houston, San Antonio, Texas, threw him a snap perfect salute and handed him the papers. He looked at them, looked up and returned my salute. "One last chance," he said. "You can reenlist right here."

"Cap'n," I said, "the answer won't change if you ask me a thousand times. I've been a soldier long enough. Time t' go home."

He looked down and signed the discharge. Somewhere, in a parallel universe within this multiverse in which our universe lives, another me said, "Okay," signed up for the heart surgery team training, got his Master Sergeant or Specialist 8 stripes, and spent the next thirty years touring the world (with two or three tours of Viet Nam and a tour in Desert Storm) as a Medical Specialist on an elite Army heart surgery team. I hope his life was long and good, but this is not his story.

When I'd returned from South Korea, I'd had my choice of bases for the next phase of my service. I'd chosen Fort Sam Houston, an Army hospital and training base in San Antonio, Texas, where I'd trained as a medic. About halfway through my last sixteen months as a soldier, a friend asked me to double date with his girl's friend and I agreed. By the time I mustered out, we had been dating steadily for at least half a year. I had said from the beginning that when it came time to leave, I was leaving.

Came the day, I had intended to have my brother Giles come down from Fort Hood in Killeen, Texas, and pick me up, but the girl insisted she would drive me as far as Indianapolis. She had relatives in Wisconsin and she would leave me with Giles and head north from Indianapolis. I threw my duffel in the trunk of her '64 Pontiac GTO and climbed behind the wheel. My girlfriend had brought her best friend (the girl who'd introduced us via my Army buddy) to help her drive to Wisconsin and back to Texas. Her friend got into the back seat, she got into the front passenger seat and we headed north toward Killeen to connect with my brother.

In Killeen, we pulled into the driveway of the house my brother and his wife were renting. In very little time, Giles' '59 Ford Galaxie was loaded front, top and trunk. Giles was married and his wife's cousin had come to visit them a while earlier, so there were packages, duffel and suitcases for a permanent move filling every available space. But soon enough, the Galaxie was ready to go, and he and his wife, their infant son Michael and his wife's cousin piled in and we all headed north. Somewhere between Killeen and Dallas, he stopped, I didn't, and my girlfriend's little GTO had a bent nose. Pontiacs of the day had a split grill with a wedge of body material between the two ends. When Giles stopped, I hit his bumper with that wedge of body metal, bending it.

We took turns driving (each car had three licensed drivers) and got to Indianapolis at about five o'clock the next morning. We were all so tired we were groggy and it was not unlikely that we'd run into trouble. And there it was. My brother suddenly decided to dive down an off-ramp, and I was too close to him to follow him down. Any such attempt would have rolled the little GTO.

I kept driving east until I found a State Troopers' barracks. We stopped and I explained the situation, describing Giles' car, including a badly distorted left front fender and, sure enough, about a half hour later, one of the troopers showed up with little brother's '59 Galaxie in tow. "I just flat f'rgot you were following me," he said. "We needed gas, and I saw a station down there."

I suddenly realized where we were. We were on the eastern outskirts of Indianapolis, headed for Akron, Ohio, and this was where my girlfriend and her friend were supposed to leave us to visit a cousin in Wisconsin. "Time for me to head north," she said. "You take care of yourself."

I grabbed my duffel and kissed her. "S'long, Darlin'," I said. "Get some sleep and drive carefully."

She smiled a little weepily. "I won't write," she said. "I couldn't deal with that."

I felt bad, but I'd known. She was a fun person but I was leaving and she'd held onto the hope I was staying. It's always hard when only one of a couple is in love. "I understand," I said.

I got one letter about a year later. I fear my answer was not what she'd hoped to get. It was not a successful exchange and I never heard from her again.

I slung my duffel into the Galaxie and crowded into the back seat next to my sister-in-law's cousin. There wasn't really room for me, the Galaxie wasn't air conditioned (the GTO had been) and we were rocking down a brand new expressway. The girl went to sleep on my shoulder and it wasn't long before my arm followed her into slumber land. Unfortunately, I could not sleep. I sat there, crammed against the door, my right arm a dead mass, my eyes open and gritty as a sand beach. We faced at least an eight-hour drive yet and I was exhausted, but unable to sleep. I feared...

The car rumbling onto the left breakdown lane woke me. "What th'..." I bellowed.

"Flat tire," my brother answered, "and those bastards wouldn't let me into the right lane." He brought the car to a shuddering stop.

I got out and looked. "Just as well," I told him. "The flat's on the driver's rear tire. We'll be away from the traffic."

He looked out at the traffic howling by at six-thirty in the morning of a soon-to-be sunny day. "Bastards," he said again. He began hauling stuff out of the trunk.

We found the tire and bumper jack, loosened the lugs and raised the car. He had a speed wrench and some WD-40 and the lug nuts came off with only a slap or two at the X-bar of the wrench. The entire change took less time than it took to re-pack the trunk, which we were unable to do completely. We had to jam some small pieces of luggage into the car, making an already crowded situation even worse.

"Are we in Ohio, yet?" I asked.

"Just over the line, about five hours from home," he answered.

"I'll drive," I said.

"Nope," he said, "we're gonna sleep. That flat tire woke me up, and you too, I could tell. Get in."

He pulled off the highway at the next exit and we slept for four hours in a motel that would be out of business in a year. There was a Holiday Inn, a new phenomenon that followed the new freeways, under construction just down the road. The sign advertised king-sized beds, but the old man at the desk wouldn't rent us just one room. "You kids ain't usin' MY place for no orgy!" he sneered. I looked at the Holiday Inn. He'd be letting anyone use it for anything they wanted it for before long and he'd lose it anyway. I paid for the extra room.

"Call us at noon, please," I said.

"Yeah," he said, "noon." And he did.

We stumbled out of bed, piled into the car and headed home.

About five hours later, my brother pulled into our parents' driveway. He and his wife had an apartment arranged in Kent but I was staying with the folks until school started in late September. We all got out and went into the old farmhouse. Much kissing, hugging and hand-shaking ensued.

We had stopped for gas about two hours earlier and I'd called home to let them know when to expect us. Mother had prepared a meal of epic proportions and West Virginia ingredients in the two hours they'd been waiting for us. My father had read the paper twice. He had no idea what it said.

After dinner, I went outside. After the August evenings in San Antonio, the air felt cool and slightly damp. I looked around at the old farm. The barn was gone. The children's hospital we'd been building when I left was nestled into the hillside and the concrete block chicken house I'd been living in when we'd joined the Army three years earlier was being converted into an actual house. Things had changed mightily. But I could hear the trill of red-wing blackbirds in the marsh at the foot of the hill and crickets and grasshoppers sang in the dusk. I was home.

CHAPTER 51

Little MGA

I came back inside. The farm was different, but the blackbirds still sang and the night was still quiet. I'd just come home from three years in the Army and all I really wanted to do was go to bed.

We'd made it to our folks' place (mine too, until college started) and they'd fed us way too much. We'd talked late and I'd finally gone outside to see whether the night felt the same as it had one August night three years earlier. I'd decided it did.

My brother and his wife were headed for her parents' home near Kent and then to an apartment they had rented. I was headed for bed as soon as they'd gone. But...

"Chuck," the Old Man said when the door had closed behind them, "I bought you a sports car." He was the absolute picture of suppressed excitement.

So much for bed. I looked at him. I had no idea how to respond, but I was sure my ever-ready savoir-faire would come to my rescue. But remember, this was August, 1965. There was a new Ford out there that was different from anything else on the road. It was the first thing that came to mind when the Old Man said "sports car." "You bought me a Mustang!"

The Old Man's face fell. "No," he said. "It's just an MG."

I was stunned. I had no idea what to do or say next. This was way beyond my wildest dreams. All thoughts of a Mustang went out of my head. But how was I going to make him believe it? I had to say something.

"Holy Judas Priest!" I said (the Old Man didn't hold with taking the Lord's name in vain, but Judas made an acceptable stand-in), "you really meant it when you said 'sports car.' I don't believe it. A real MG? You bought me a real MG? Where is it?" I headed for the door.

"It's in New Jersey," the Old Man laughed. "I bought it from your Aunt Jean. You'll have to go get it."

I breathed a mental sigh of relief. He'd accepted that I wanted the MG more than a Mustang. The fact that it was true probably helped. My skill at witty repartee came once again to my rescue. "New Jersey?" I said. "Aunt Jean? How am I gonna get there? I don't have a car. Besides, if I drive, I can't drive two cars back."

The Old Man laughed again. "Bus," he said, "you'll take the Greyhound – tomorrow."

It was Sunday night. We'd driven 1,500 miles in two days, with four hours real sleep and I was gonna get on a bus tomorrow and head for New Jersey? "Tuesday," I said. "I'll go Tuesday. Tomorrow I'm sleepin' in 'til noon."

"All right," he said, "Tuesday." And so it was.

The only bus going east on Tuesday was a late evening bus. We stopped in every town, village and crossroads in Ohio and Pennsylvania between Akron, Ohio and East Rutherford, New Jersey. We rolled into the terminal nearly 24 hours later and I was exhausted. Between the stops and the noise, I hadn't really slept since Tuesday morning.

The bus terminal in East Rutherford was at the bottom of a hill so I couldn't see much of the town. I looked around and found a taxi, gave him Aunt Jean's address and tossed my duffel into the back seat. Thirty minutes later, after twisting and turning through what seemed to be every precinct or borough in the city, he pulled up in front of a two-story house at the top of a hill. "Here y'go, soldier," he said. "That'll be seventeen dollars."

I got out of the cab and looked down the hill at the bus terminal. "I'll give you five," I said. "And before you open your mouth, let me say that you're welcome to call the cops. I'd like to show them what a seventeen dollar ride looks like."

"What about my tip?" he asked.

"OK," I said, "here's a tip. I just spent three years learning to kill people. You should stop arguing with me. That's a two-dollar ride."

My Aunt Jean came outside to see what was taking so long. I pointed to the terminal. "Took us half an hour to get here from there," I told her. "He wants seventeen dollars."

She looked at him. "You get nothing," she said. "I have your hack number so I'd just go if I were you."

"But he said he'd give me five," the cabbie said.

"He lied," she said. "Come on, Charles." She headed toward the house. I grabbed my duffel and followed her.

"Hey..." the cabbie said. I ignored him and heard the cab start up and go.

"Won't he complain?" I asked.

"No," she said, "he knows better. Seventeen dollars, indeed! I wish he would complain."

We went into the house. She showed me to a bedroom and then ordered take-out from a deli. While we waited for the food, we went out to look at the MG.

She pulled back the door of a detached garage and flipped a light switch. "There," she said, pointing to a low-slung, drop-nosed, black two-seater. "That was Danny's car. Now it's yours."

I was vaguely disappointed. It was an MG all right. But I'd been expecting a classic roadster, a TC or TD convertible. But the car that had been backed into this garage was a 1957 MGA. This car, it turned out, was what was known as a "solid-body coupé." It wasn't even a convertible. The top didn't detach at all. Most MGAs came with two tops – one soft and one hard. This one came with only the hard top, which was permanently attached.

But it took me only a moment to realize that nobody I knew had any kind of sports car. I promptly fell in love, as only a guy can fall in love with a car. "Wow!" I said, "she's gorgeous. Why is Danny selling her?"

"He's not," Aunt Jean said, "I am. I've already sold her to your Father."

"Why?" I asked.

"He didn't take care of it," she said. "The engine didn't get an oil change for I don't know how long and it had to be repaired."

I looked at her.

"Busted a wrist-pin and threw a rod," she said, "and warped the cylinders. But she runs now." She handed me a set of keys. "Start her up," she said.

I opened the door and discovered that the first thing I had to learn about this car was how to get into it. After some twisting and contorting, I had both feet on the pedals, and I was ready to go. To my astonishment, Aunt Jean walked around to the passenger side and slid gracefully into the seat. She looked over at me and grinned. "Let me show you how she works," she said.

"Uh..." I said – my well-known gift for witty repartee

coming to my rescue.

Fortunately, I could already drive a stick (my '39 Dodge truck had seen to that) but she showed me the starter button on the dash, where the four forward gears were (I'd have started in second, or thought I was maxed in third) and how to find reverse. MGs came with a pattern on the plastic shifter knob but someone had replaced this one with an oak knob with a metalwork MG emblem in it – no pattern. Then I put 'er in first, pressed the starter button, gave her a little gas, let out the clutch and "hic blurt splug..." she died without ever leaving the garage.

Aunt Jean laughed. "She likes a little rough treatment," she said. "More gas and faster clutch."

I tried again. The floor of the garage was gravel and I heard it hit the back wall as we shot out into the driveway. Aunt Jean laughed again as I slammed the brake and clutch pedals to the floor. I carefully put the little car in neutral and set the emergency brake. "Maybe not quite so rough, Charles," said my smart-aleck aunt. "I'll get out now and let you go around the block a few times."

And so I did. I discovered that the little shifter moved like butter, going from gear to gear in bare inches with a little click when the trans locked in. The steering was so tight it felt as if I were wishing her around corners.

When I decided I could actually drive her, I pulled back into Aunt Jean's drive and got out to look her over. She was sleek and black, and polished to a high shine. Her wire-spoke, knockoff wheels were chromed and gleaming. There was an oddly shaped hole at the bottom of her grill and a little investigation revealed its purpose I found the crank in the trunk (a device I actually used more than once).

The next day, I drove her to Greenwood Lake, New York, where my father and his eight brothers and sisters grew up, to visit my Grandmother and Aunt Gwen. It was a bittersweet day, and I never went back.

Early the next morning, I headed home to northeast Ohio. First, I checked the oil, which showed full but came out sludgy and black. "I told you he didn't take care of it," Aunt Jean grumped. On the way to the Jersey Pike, I stopped for an oil change, putting in 10W-30 detergent oil, the standard oil of the day.

I headed for home. It wasn't long before my first understanding of how differently these little cars handled came to me. I passed a semi on the Jersey Pike and, as I reached the tractor's rear wheels, I was suddenly fighting the wheel for my life. There was a bow-shock of air that nearly forced me under the trailer. I slammed the little car into third, pulled left toward the verge and accelerated away from that deadly semi.

Sports cars, it seemed, behaved just a tad differently than full-sized sedans and pick-'em-up trucks when encountering highway conditions. From then on, I swung wide and maintained a firm grip on the leather-wrapped steering wheel as I passed any large vehicle.

Only one other adventure came my way on that long trip. Somewhere in the steepest mountains on the Pennsylvania Turnpike, a station wagon full of kids began to harass me. Pointing behind me and shouting, they nearly forced me off the road. The road was nothing but curves and I was beginning to think that they were intent on forcing me down the side of the mountain.

As we rounded a curve, a service plaza came into view. I aimed for the entrance drive, and the station wagon swung in behind me. I slid to a halt as we got to the parking area and scrambled out of the little car. The wagon pulled up and the teens piled out. I dropped into a fighting stance, hoping someone would see and come bail me out.

"You've blown your engine," the lead boy said.

I straightened up. "What?" I asked, calling up my last reserves of conversational banter.

"We've been trying to stop you for the past five miles," he said.

"I could tell," I answered. "I thought you were trying to push me off the side of the mountain."

The boys looked at me. "What?" the driver said. "No, you've been trailing a big blue plume that nearly choked us to death."

I clambered back into the car and turned her over. Sure enough, a huge puff of blue smoke erupted from her tailpipe and I shut her down.

"We'd better push her," the driver said. I just nodded.

The service plaza had a garage attached to a Howard Johnson's restaurant. The mechanic listened to the story and told me to start her up. As soon as I did, he told me to shut down.

As we all coughed our way out of the garage, he said, "Son, you have a problem. What did you do to this car?"

I told him the story and he laughed. "Your cousin probably put in oversized rings and knurled the pistons after he threw that rod," he said. "It's cheaper than rebuilding the engine. Then he put in non-detergent oil because it would gunk up and he wouldn't be burning oil all the time. When you changed the oil..."

"I cleaned the rings," I said.

He changed the oil and filter, filling the sump with non-detergent oil and sold me six cans and a spout to carry with me. Every seventy-five miles or so, I would pull over and add a quart of oil. After a while, the oil began to stay and I finally made it home with two quarts to spare.

My folks came out to see it and I proudly showed it off, giving them each a ride for a couple miles. My father enjoyed it, but my mother loved it. After all, this was the girl who owned the '27 Indian motorcycle. I didn't tell them that night that my brand new used MG needed an overhaul – *right now*. That's another story.

CHAPTER 52

A Visit from Uncle Oliver

Not long after I retrieved the MG from New Jersey, the Old Man and I were busily finishing the job of turning the old concrete chicken coop that had been the "Hooch" Giles and I shared as our own apartment (sans kitchen) into a house while I attended Hiram College, about 12 miles away. I was working for food and found (food and a place to sleep, work clothes and necessaries like razors, toothbrush and toothpaste, and so forth), but I was learning how to wire a house (the Old Man wasn't an electrician, but when it came to construction, he was the original Renaissance Man) and that came in handy later in life.

We were outside, taking a break and having a smoke in the late September afternoon, when a car we didn't know pulled into the driveway. Two men, one of them vaguely familiar, clambered out.

"I'll be damned!" the The Old Man almost never swore. "I will be damned. It's Oliver. What on Earth is he doing here?"

"S'pose we go ask," I said. The Old Man just looked at me and headed for the car.

Turned out my Uncle Oliver and his daughter Shirley's husband, Larry, were travelling between jobs, that summer day back in the mid '60s. They worked for an international tank (water and oil – not the Army kind) and bridge building company, one that the Old Man and all his brothers had worked for before the War. Their route took them through northeast Ohio and Oliver decided to stop and see the Old Man. They hadn't seen each other for several years and it was only about four miles off the Ohio Turnpike to our house.

Once the back pounding and hugging were over and Larry was introduced to the Old Man and me, he and I showed Oliver and Larry around the little farm. Conversation was mostly a matter of the Old Man and Oliver catching up on each other's families. Before long, though, it turned to "Do you remember..." and "Did you know..." vignettes. One of them started out with Oliver asking, "Did you know that the Company still has 'The Rule?'"

"What's 'The Rule'"? I asked and the three of them burst into laughter.

Oliver looked at the Old Man and said, "You should tell him." He turned to me and said, "Charles, I wasn't even there. I was the last of the brothers to go to work for the Company and, by the time I did, I discovered I couldn't work any job your Dad, your Uncle Bill or Uncle Jack were working."

The Old Man lit a Camel and offered them around. When everybody had lit up, he laughed and told his story.

The Old Man was the eldest of the four sons of William C. Larlham and he had been the first to go to work for the Company. It was the first job he'd gotten that paid well enough to fully support his mother and his brothers (all of whom were younger) and sisters (most of whom were older) still living at home. The Old Man's father had died when the Old Man was only sixteen, leaving him, as the eldest son, to provide for the family. While his mother turned the family home into a "hotel" (we'd call it a bed-and-breakfast), the Old Man went out to work.

The Old Man insisted everyone else stay in school and graduate, even though his father's early death had meant he couldn't. He hired in as a member of the "bull gang," the laborers who worked at ground level, lifting and hauling steel, paint, tools and whatever the ironworkers, welders, riveters and anyone who worked the high steel needed done. The real money was up in the air, working the high steel, so he worked at learning to weld and got out of the bull gang as rapidly as he could, working his way through high steel jobs with only one goal – to become a high-steel welder. He had a knack for welding and he was soon in demand. It wasn't difficult for him to persuade the Company to hire each of his brothers as they graduated high school and decided they wanted to join him.

All the brothers, it seemed, had a knack for high steel work and for welding. Usually they were spread around the country, but occasionally a couple of them would wind up on the same job – but almost never three. They were all rowdy and all of them together made for the occasional "interesting" evening, much to the chagrin of foremen and job superintendents. However, it did, once in a while, happen that all of them were assigned to the same job – usually a tank farm or refinery turn-around where they would be working apart from each other. This time was different.

Bill, Jack and the Old Man were working a "ball-on-a-stick" water tower together. Water tanks at the time were built either sitting on the ground or sitting on steel beams raised on a framework. The sides of the tanks were vertical, riveted and often cable-wrapped, and covered by a pitched roof, if they were covered at all.

The ball-on-a-stick design, reminiscent of a golf ball on a tee and since then the standard for water towers, was new and controversial at the time. It was feared the seams on the bottom of the tank would split. In fact, the design was only possible because of the strength of welds on the seams at the bottom of the "ball," as opposed to rivets which could not have held the weight of thousands of gallons of water. The "stick" was simply a hollow tube that housed water lines, stairs or elevators to the tank, controls at the base, and so forth and served to hold the tank in the air.

The "stick" on this tank was finished, and the "ball" was half done. In order to keep it round while the bottom bowl of the tank remained open at the rim, twenty-four eyebolts were welded near the top edges of each course of steel plates and twelve three-quarter-inch steel cables were strung across the cup of the ball and tensioned like piano wires. Unfortunately, there was only one access from the rim to the ground and, on the day in question, all three of the brothers were on the far side of the ball when the lunch whistle blew.

A trip around the catwalk would take several minutes and it rapidly filled with men. Jack, ever the daredevil, grinned at his brothers and said, "Bet I get to eat before you do!" With that, he grabbed the cable that lead directly to the ladder way, swung his feet up and hooked his ankles over the cable and, from there, he proceeded to "monkey-walk" his way across the cup of the tank.

When he reached the other side, he laughed and waved. "See you at lunch!" he yelled across.

"Hang on!" called the Old Man, and he promptly grabbed the cable and started across. The sharp ends of the little wires that made up the cable dug into his legs, and even through his leather welding gloves into his hands. This was a lot tougher than he'd thought and it was a lot scarier. Hanging over a bowl that deepened to nearly fifty feet at the center and supported only by your own strength was the most frightening thing he'd ever done. But if Jack could do it, he could. Besides, going back would mean "monkey walking" toward his feet – even harder, if it was possible at all. He kept going. Things could be worse, and soon they were to be.

As he neared the mid-point, he heard Jack call to Bill and, almost immediately, he felt the cable move. It moved down and back up. He stopped. It moved again and again. He craned his neck and looked behind him. Jack knelt behind him with both hands gripping the cable. As he watched, Jack pulled up on the cable. As it moved upward, carrying him with it, the Old Man looked beyond his feet. Bill knelt there, gripping the other end of the cable, and he too was pulling the cable upward. As the Old Man watched, Bill's hands plunged downward.

The Old Man gripped the cable and yelled at his brothers to stop. Instead, they began to include a side-to-side motion. In short order, the Old Man found himself being spun around the cable. Truly terrified, because the energy involved threatened to tear his grip from the cable, and the cable was shredding his gloves and even his heavy canvas welder's pants, the Old Man screamed at them to stop. But Jack and Bill were ahead of him. One or both of them had realized the trouble their brother was in as soon as he completed the first spin and they damped the cable as rapidly as they could.

As soon as it stopped, the Old Man began a rapid shinny and finished his trip in half the time the first part had taken. No one spoke as he clambered onto the catwalk and glared at Jack. Then he looked to where Bill was, but Bill was shoving his way along the catwalk and men were moving aside, bracing against the wall of the tank, to let him by. "My God," he yelled as soon as he reached his two brothers, "we nearly killed you!" Jack and Bill both towered six feet two or better and the Old Man stood only five feet nine, but men watching said his anger made him seem larger than either of them. He glared at both of them for a few seconds, turned and started down the ladder way.

When all three brothers had reached the ground, they discovered the job superintendent and the welding foreman waiting for them. "My office!" the super growled. When the five of them were inside, he wheeled on the brothers. He opened his mouth, and couldn't find words. Finally, "You three..." he said. He closed his mouth. He looked at them. No one spoke. He opened it again. "You're fired!" he said.

The three brothers turned and left the office. They left the job amidst an eerie silence. No one spoke to them, nor did anyone speak at all. Because they were travelling together, they had to ride to the campground together. No one spoke. When they reached the little airstream, the Old Man said, "I'll call the home office. You two start straightening up the trailer so we can travel." Jack and Bill didn't say a word. They just went into the trailer and the Old Man drove into town to find a telephone. When he returned, he had kept them employed, but

"There's a condition," he said. His brothers looked at him. "We can never work together again. Ever!"

The Company, from that day forward had an unbreakable rule. It even applied in the shipyards during wartime when the Company built warships faster than they could be sunk.

The Old Man looked up at Oliver and said, " 'No two of us shall ever work the same job at the same time.' They still use that?"

Oliver laughed. "Like I said," he chuckled, "it's still there."

It turned out to be why Larry and Oliver were travelling. The foreman found out Larry was Oliver's son-in-Law, and one of them had to go. He wouldn't ignore it and he wouldn't ask the Company to waive it. As far as the Company was concerned, they were both subject to the rule. So Oliver took a few days vacation to drive Larry to another job and then drive back to his. Sharing the driving and taking turns sleeping in the car, they had made excellent time. But it posed a problem. They'd been sharing travel and expenses ever since Larry had started with the Company and they couldn't do that any longer.

Oliver laughed again, "You three are still screwin' up my life!" And he laughed some more.

He looked at me. "Be glad you're the oldest," he said. "Being the youngest of four brothers is a bitch."

Epilogue:

I work as an Environmental Engineer for a large electric utility and it's up to me to prevent large oil spills into bodies of water. One way to do that, a few years ago, was to replace a failing six-million gallon oil tank at a power plant. It turned out the tank was built by the Old Man's former employer, so I called them. A man answered on the third ring.

"Dave Smith," he said. I knew it had to be a different Dave Smith. The Old Man was nearly 90. I gave him my name.

"Really?" he asked. "My grandfather used to tell this story about these three brothers..."

CHAPTER 53

The Old Man and Me and the CCC

Early spring, 1932, a not particularly tall but powerfully built young man wrangles horses and nails up barracks in a Civilian Conservation Corps (CCC) Camp built on the side of a small alluvial flow in the Uinta Mountains in northern Utah, not far west of Wyoming. It's still cold and the camp is an orderly establishment of tents, roads and a lumbering operation and sawmill. Wood has been cut and sawn into boards for curing for the past two summers. Now it was time to build; to turn Logan Canyon into a recreational ground.

***

June 1967, a Greyhound bus pulls up to a restaurant on the south end of Logan, Utah. I get off and take my duffel from the driver. He shoves my shipping box (most of my possessions nailed into a pine quadrangle) against the restaurant wall. No one else gets off and no one gets on. The bus pulls away.

After the better part of three days and two nights sitting up in that bus, I was grateful to get down. A June bus ride through the plains states (we covered parts of Iowa, Missouri, Kansas and Nebraska) is a lot less interesting than you might think. I saw wheat. After a while, I got bored with wheat. So I watched the mountains come to us. I watched those mountains come for the better part of two days. When I got bored with that, I watched wheat go by again. Then I'd watch the mountains come at us again. When we got there, we were there for half a day before I realized it. Foothills can fool ya.

I had come to Logan for Graduate School at Utah State University (USU). I was enrolled for a Master of Science in Wildlife Biology. The professor for whom I'd be working as a Graduate Assistant (read "flunky") had told me he'd pick me up at the restaurant in front of which I'd been unceremoniously "dropped." I looked around. The town was less "Western" than several I'd been through in the past few days, but its "Westernness" was undeniable if a tad indefinable.

I leaned against the wall next to my box and watched people for a time while I waited for the ride I'd been promised. I decided I wasn't too out of place. I did not have the requisite cowboy hat, but then again, most of the males I saw didn't. About half of the males did have cowboy boots but I was wearing a pair of "heeled Wellingtons," so that seemed to be all right. My jeans and shirt were farm-worn, and so were lots of those I saw. I figured I'd fit in OK. Besides, this was a university town, wasn't it? How badly could I stick out? I decided to get out of the sun and wait in the restaurant.

Nobody was likely to be able to walk off with an eighty-pound box without me noticing, so I left it there and stepped into the restaurant. As I walked over to the counter, I was looking out the window. I got to the counter next to the cash register and looked around for a waitress or hostess and looked squarely into a fifty-gallon fish tank that contained about two dozen rainbow trout.

"Table for one?" asked a pleasant female voice to my right.

I looked around. The woman who obviously owned the voice was smiling at me. "Pets?" I gestured toward the tank.

"Lunch," she answered. "Pick one." She picked up a smallish net on a handle and made to hand it to me.

"Just coffee," I laughed. "I'm meeting somebody. I'll just sit at the counter."

I was about half through my coffee (Good coffee, I was to learn, was hard to come by in Utah. People who think drinking coffee is sinful have trouble caring what it tastes like.) when the door banged shut and the skinny guy in ragged denim jacket and beat up jeans and boots who stood there said, "Lar-ham? Anybody here named Lar-ham?"

"No," I said, standing up, "but I'm as close as you're gonna get."

"That your stuff?" He gestured over his shoulder in the general direction of the street.

"If it's a wood box and a duffel bag, it is."

"You gonna help me load it?" He turned to the door.

"Sure." I dropped a quarter on the counter and followed him out.

A grayish-blue, sway-backed, crew-cab International Harvester pick-up truck chugged quietly at the curb. My ride.

The skinny guy walked to the end of my box. "Grab on," he said, bending and taking hold of one end of my box, "let's get 'er in th' truck."

I grabbed my end and we lifted, slinging the box easily into the bed of the truck. "Toss your duffel in here," he said, clambering up into the bed, "I'll tie it all down."

I slung my duffel up into the bed and he grabbed it, shoving it between the box and the bed-wall. He grabbed a rope and tied it all firmly against the bed-walls of the truck.

"Get in." He jumped down and opened the driver's side door, motioning to the other door with his free hand and I climbed in.

Grabbing the knuckle-buster shifter and releasing the hand

brake, he rammed the truck into first gear, let out the clutch in a series of stuttering jerks, and we headed up what turned out to be Main Street. In the center of Logan, we passed the Coyote Bar and Grill and turned right. He downshifted, grinding the poor little truck's gears, to make the turn and shifted back up too soon, lugging the engine. Once we had straightened out and headed up the hill toward the eastern mountains, he turned to me. Disdaining to watch the road, he stuck out his hand, "Dave Balph," he said. "Sorry I'm late, but this old bitch doesn't like me."

Don't much blame 'er, I thought, but aloud I said, "Chuck Larlham – thanks for picking me up. Where are we headed?"

He turned to face the mountains, thereby unintentionally putting his attention back on the road and avoiding the on-coming traffic into whose lane he had been drifting. "Up there!" He pointed to a gap in the mountains. "Summer Camp's about twenty miles up the road." The truck's nose disappeared down a steep, short grade, and popped back up in front of me as we crossed a bridge. My new boss, David Balph, Ph.D., Biology, rammed the accelerator down and we began to climb.

The road from Logan, Utah, to Pickleville, Wyoming, was forty climbing miles of twists, sheer drops, blasted-out ledges, rockslides and people driving way too fast. About twenty miles in, there was an old CCC Camp that was used by the Utah State University School of Forestry for field study for incipient Foresters and by the Wildlife Biology Department for Dr. Balph's study of Uinta Ground Squirrels. Hence, the presence of one R. C. (Chuck) Larlham in a beat up old pick-up truck heading twenty miles up that mountain, and driven by an obviously insane college professor. I was terrified in the first two miles.

***

The Army surplus deuce-and-a-half, carrying a dozen or more young men up a winding mountain road, came upon a truck heavily laden with summer watermelons. As the young men in the truck bed held on to the slats and yelled, the driver of the deuce-and-a-half swung out to pass the farm truck. They came even and a slender fellow in his early twenties swung over into the watermelon truck. He began tossing watermelons to his fellows in the old Army truck, clambering forward over the melons to keep up with the passing truck. As he reached the front of the old farm truck's bed, he swung down onto the running board, handed a five-dollar bill through the driver's window and, reaching out, was grabbed and hauled back into the other truck with his fellows.

***

Slowly, I relaxed. Despite the rough start and the narrow two-lane road filled with switchbacks upon which we travelled, I began to take in the scenery. Logan Canyon is a "green" canyon. Vertical faces of rock appear every so often, carved directly down through softer rock as the Logan River wended its way west or by men using dynamite to build a road. But most of the canyon had gentler slopes running back from the road, or the other side of the river (which we crossed several times). Those slopes were covered in sage (yes, in spring it's purple) with a strong line where the cover changed to subalpine fir. Higher in elevation, the subalpine fir gave way to pinion pine. Throughout the sage-covered slopes were colonies of quaking aspen (cloned trees rising from the roots of a "mother" tree), which invaded the edge of the subalpine fir.

Colors were muted (a condition that would change

dramatically, come autumn), but the general ambience of the ever-changing scenery was nearly hypnotic. I had never seen western mountain ecology, and I was soon fascinated.

"Deer," announced Dr. Balph, "across the river. There." He pointed.

I couldn't see them at first, but they abruptly appeared, browsing on the sage and grazing on the tough sparse grass scattered among it. There were no antlers (it was, after all, June) so I could not identify sexes, but I gathered we were looking at a small herd made up almost entirely of does and fawns or young-of-the-year. "Wow," I said, "that was weird."

"Couldn't see 'em, could ya?" He was chuckling. "I'll bet you didn't see them at all until one of them moved."

I thought about it for a second. "You're right," I laughed, "motion caught my attention."

"Mule deer," he said, "they blend into that brown soil and sage pattern like nobody's business. Bet you'll be able to spot 'em by the end of summer." He pointed ahead and across the road, "Rick's spring."

I looked and saw a small hole in the rock wall to our left, about man-high and wide. I saw a trickle of water running out the base of the hole into the roadside ditch. "Who was Rick, and why is a spring named after him?"

"Don't know, but it's a pretty famous spring. There's a fountain inside when the snowmelt starts. Reaches to the ceiling. Apparently, melt water gets to here and hits something less porous because it shoots out of the floor of that little cave pretty hard. Slows down later and it's pretty much gone by mid-August."

We rode in silence for a while. Abruptly, "You should call me Dave."

"Huh?" I was startled out of my sightseeing.

"Everybody does, so you should too."

"OK." I was all right with it, but the whole thing was so out-of-the-blue I was a little nonplussed. "Dave it is," I said, "but it's gonna feel awkward for a while."

"Nah. Not with everyone else doin' it too." Turned out, he was right.

We swung right onto a dirt drive. Dave hooked a thumb over his shoulder. "Tony's Grove," he said, "swimming lake up there after the Fourth."

"Of July?"

"Yeah, it's at eighty-five hundred feet. Snowed in 'til then. Once the snow's gone the Park Service opens the road."

"So, they open the road..."

"End of June – First of July."

"And people go swimming on the Fourth?"

"Oh sure, the sun's been on the open water for weeks by then."

I let it be, but it seemed unlikely.

***

"Haw!" he yelled, hauling on the reins. The two-horse team swung left along the rock pile and he straightened them out. They pulled the sledge hauling the boulders under the counter-weighted crane and men began criss-crossing chains around the rock, finally looping them into the hook of the crane. From across the ridge of rock came a loud "G'up!" and the crack of a whip. There was a sharp whinny and the crane began to lift the boulder from his sledge. He snapped the reins and the team moved out. He drove them around the end of the ridge and up to the team that was pulling the counterweight down and

around, swinging the boulder to the top of the man-made ridge. As the boulder was set and men began removing the chain slings, he ground-hitched his team and walked over to the other drover. "Don't do that again," he said. It was an unmistakable command. "Don't ever hit a horse with that thing again." He gestured to the nine-foot bullwhip in the drover's right hand.

"You gonna stop me?" The other drover was larger, a little older, and well muscled.

"Do I have to?" the smaller drover asked.

By way of answer, the bigger man dropped the whip and swung a right-hand roundhouse. Ducking the punch easily, the smaller man fell naturally into a boxer's stance, stepped close to the bigger man and threw powerful punches into his stomach until two large arms suddenly appeared, wrapping the big man's stomach and protecting it. The smaller man took a half step back and threw two punches, breaking the bigger man's nose in both directions.

He picked up the whip and coiled it. Then, spinning like a discus thrower, he slung the coil out into the center of the lake for which they were building a base for a diving board and a small dock for canoes, and other "recreational improvements." He unhitched his team by picking up the reins. "Gee," he said softly, and they drifted right, pulling the sledge back toward the CCC Camp.

***

We crossed the Logan River one last time on a rusting steel bridge and drove about a quarter mile up to a cluster of what looked like old Army barracks. Toward the rear, there were two smaller structures that looked like chicken coops. Dave saw me looking at them. "Turkey coops," he said, "your sleeping quarters."

I laughed and Dave looked over at me and grinned. He pulled the old IH club-cab over in front of the coops and three young men came out of them. I got out of the truck and Dave made introductions. It seemed that about a dozen graduate students were doing various studies on the ground squirrels and four of us were staying at the camp for the summer in the turkey coops. The barracks were, in fact, built to pre-WWII Army barracks design, as was the mess hall and cook shack. The USU Forestry Department used the old CCC Camp as a summer field-study camp for the Forestry School undergrads and they claimed the barracks. We ate together in the mess hall.

We unpacked my stuff and Dave handed over two cans of white gas for the little Coleman stoves and lanterns that heated and lit our sleeping quarters. The barracks and mess hall had electricity but no one was willing to hire an electrician to string power to two "turkey coops." That made us the turkeys, as one of my new friends put it later that evening.

We toured the grounds. A grid of white-painted lath was established in all the open areas of the camp. Some of the areas with fairly dense sage were also gridded. Each lath was driven into the ground, with the tops having letters or numerals painted on them. The grid was set up on the cardinal points of the compass. Laths were 40 feet apart. The basic study of the ground squirrels consisted of establishing and maintaining a "book" of all home ranges, territories and home burrows, and, of course, each animal.

The animals themselves were marked with a fairly simple code, based on bars, dots and "Vs." Each animal was captured in a live trap and hydrogen peroxide was used to mark the fur. Live traps were maintained constantly and markings were renewed each time an animal was caught. The first capture of an animal also involved removing one or more toes from each foot, making permanent identification possible if it stayed out of the traps long enough to lose all its markings.

Lifeguard-style towers were set out at regular intervals and we sat on those with binoculars. Every fifteen minutes, each of us would sweep the portion of the study area assigned. There was full overlap to account for positional offset caused by our point of view from the chairs – either parallel to the lath rows across the ground squirrels to the laths, or perpendicular to the laths. We would mark the approximate location of each above-ground animal by estimating how many tenths of a grid-length it was from each of the four stakes that made up the "cell" in which it was found. The animals ignored us so long as we stayed at least ten feet away from them.

For much of the summer, I took my shifts watching the animals, exploring the Uinta Mountains close by, learning to fish for trout and generally enjoying the hell out of my life. I wrote letters to the woman I would marry the next Christmas season and complained bitterly about the food (which, to be fair, was terrible!). My fellow ground squirrel study grad students and I became something I was unused to; a tightly knit band of people with a shared purpose, and a shared interest. We became a dozen good friends.

I didn't visit Tony's Grove Lake that summer and did not see it, in fact, until deer season that fall. But I was fascinated by the descriptions I heard from foresters and others who had. There was apparently a diving board and platform, a canoe dock (only canoes and kayaks were allowed on the lake), a few old cabins that could be rented and several "dry" camping sites for trailers or tents. There was also a shower *cum* locker room for swimmers, and the world's most noxious privy.

***

The first snows were coming and the CCC Camp had to break for winter. They'd built campsites, improved Tony's Grove as a "recreational attraction" and it was time to go. The Logan Canyon Road would close for the winter soon and there was no place for men in the mountain winters of northern Utah. The Army workhorses were well cared-for and looked it as they clattered up the ramps into the trailers that would take them back to New Mexico.

He looked around at the barracks, the mess hall and even the turkey sheds. When the Sar'nt Major had told him he was responsible for the horses, he'd been pleased enough but turkeys? "Animals is animals," said the Sar'nt Major, and brooked no discussion. So, the cook wanted turkeys and turkey eggs? Turkeys and turkey eggs he'd get and he did. By end of fall, the last egg had been scrambled and the last turkey had been roasted and eaten.

As the last trailer loaded, he wandered into the stables. He'd built them in the spring, tethering the horses to a strong rail until it was done. He'd cared for them, fed them, bedded them and cleaned up after them. And he'd never see them again. He shrugged. He wasn't a horseman, anyway, and he'd seen all the back ends of horses and what they produced he ever wanted to see. He turned and walked to the bus that would take him to the railroad in Salt Lake. The plan was for a short leave back home in New York and then a temporary assignment to a North Carolina CCC Camp with a return to the Utah camp the next spring.

He never saw Utah again.

***

Came late summer, and the ground squirrels began to hibernate. It seemed early to me but, by mid-August, there wasn't a ground squirrel to be found. In a story to be told another day, three of us headed east to see family before classes began. The owner of the car we rode in dropped me at home, where I borrowed the Old Man's new Plymouth and drove to northern Virginia to visit my intended. As I was leaving the home of her parents to head back to Ohio, I totaled the Plymouth. Things were a little out of balance between us for a while.

Once back in Utah, three of the "Squirrel Club" and I rented a third story walk-up in town and I began my fall classes. We bought hunting and fishing licenses and drove up the mountain to hunt grouse, snowshoe hare and deer. We even had an elk-hunt, but that's a whole other story.

Came December, and finals. I took a couple of finals a day or so early and high-tailed it for Salt Lake City, where I caught a train to my future. I was married December 23 in Falls Church, Virginia, and our honeymoon was a cross-country trip back to Utah. But there was a stop-off in Ohio to spend a day or two with my folks. A little rebalancing was needed.

This time, I had a chance to tell the Old Man about the wonders of northern Utah. As I described the trip to the camp, and the camp itself, he suddenly asked, "Did you ever swim in the lake across from the camp?"

"No," I said, "never got around to it. I had oth... wait – what lake?"

The Old Man chuckled, "Tony's Grove Lake, Son, the lake I helped to build."

I goggled. Never before or since have I goggled, but that day I did.

He laughed again. "I built that camp," he said. "I don't believe it. You're staying in the CCC camp I built!" Then he told me about the life he'd lived in Utah, a generation earlier. His grandfather had purchased his contract when jobs opened up in the steel construction industry and he'd never been back. When he was nearly talked out, he asked again, "Did you ever swim in Tony's Grove Lake?"

"No," I had to tell him, "never did."

"You have to," he said, "you absolutely have to. There's a surprise in that lake that you'll remember forever." And he would say no more about it.

The next summer, I found his name where he'd said it would be in the mess hall and at Tony's Grove Lake. The stables were gone, along with his name there, but it was enough.

And I swam in Tony's Grove Lake. I climbed out on the low board and dived. As I slid into the water, I discovered the surprise. A thin wire of ice encircled me about twelve inches into the water. It slid down my body like a circular knife of ice, feeling for all the world as if it were skinning me alive. I made for the surface as powerfully as I could. My wife, my beloved Laura, whom I privately thought of only and ever as "The Luvly Laura" from nearly our first date, told me I came out of the water like a porpoise and let out a scream that would have made her fear for my life had she not been looking at me.

There was no help for it I slammed back into the water, sinking partially below that thermocline, and splashed as rapidly as I could possibly swim toward shore. I swore, loudly and fervently, that I would kill the Old Man the next minute we were in a room together. The Luvly Laura reassured me that I would do no such thing.

She was right, of course.

© Black Rose Writing

CPSIA information can be obtained
at www.ICGtesting.com
Printed in the USA
FSOW03n0507221116
27557FS